W9-AAJ-078

Marmalade Days: Fall

Carol Taylor Bond

Includes Day by Day Activities in all
Subjects, Bulletin Board, Songs,
Fingerplays, Games, Poems,
Flannel Board Activities, Recipes,
Worksheets, Patterns, and More.

Copyright © 1987.   Carol Taylor Bond

Published by ₱ PARTNER PRESS
Box 124
Livonia, MI   48152

ISBN O-933212-35-6

Distributed by:

Gryphon House
3706 Otis Street
Mt. Rainier, Maryland   20822

Acknowledgements

I wish to thank the following people for their help, encouragement, and support: Charlotte Murchison for her endless assistance, Susan Myrick for her motivational nagging, my husband, Brantley, and my children, Amy, Scott, and Destin.

I gratefully acknowledge the authors, publishers, and friends listed below, for granting permission to reprint materials in this book. Every effort has been made to trace the ownership and to acknowledge the use of materials not written by the author. If any error inadvertently occurred, please notify the publisher for corrections in future editions.

> Boy Scouts of America, National Office, Irving, Texas, for the "Indian Sign Language" and "Indian Picture Language" charts from the Wolf Cub Scout Book.
>
> Charlotte Murchison for the "Aunt Charlotte's Spice Cake" and "Caramel Icing" recipes.
>
> Educational Service, Inc., Stevensville, Michigan, for the ideas, "Egg Carton Witch," "Witches" (game), and "Hunter" (game), from the Spice Series books, Holiday, and Action.
>
> Janette Woolsey and Elizabeth Hough Sechrist for the game "Dance with the Indian" from It's Time for Thanksgiving by Elizabeth Hough Sechrist and Janette Woolsey, published by Macrae Smith, Philadelphia, 1957.
>
> Jeanette Childress and Mary Lou Maples for ideas shared including the "Big Eye," "Big Ear," "Hungry Squirrel," "Acorn Sets," "Indian Cooking Scene," "Hard & Soft" sheet.
>
> Liz Cromwell and Dixie Hibner for fingerplays from Finger Frolics, published by Partner Press, Box 124, Livonia, Michigan 48152.
>
> "I'm A Nut" action song, reprinted by permission of Sterling Publishing Co., Inc., Two Park Avenue, New York, New York 10016 from HOLIDAY SINGING AND DANCING GAMES by Esther L. Nelson, © 1980 by Esther L. Nelson.

In Memory Of My Father,

Richard P. Taylor,

"The Magician Of My Childhood"

Table of Contents

Table of Contents

Table of Contents

Introduction - The Unit Approach

The units in Marmalade Days were developed in my classroom over a period of six years. When I began teaching, I had books of the skills and concepts to be taught, a collection of ideas and methods, and a roomful of eager and very active five year olds. I needed a program--one which included these skills and concepts, used a variety of methods and materials, and "fit" the young child with his natural enthusiasm and short attention span. I found my answer in the unit approach.

The unit approach is the correlation of learning activities around a central theme. One benefit of using this approach is that high interest is maintained in all subject areas. Learning basic math skills by making a Halloween Counting Booklet or counting flannel board clowns is much more stimulating to a child than rote counting or flash cards. Another "super plus" of this program is that many skills can be integrated into one activity, making for effective use of time and an enriched program. Thus in presenting the Shadow Play in the Pilgrim unit, the children not only learn about the Pilgrims but also develop speaking and listening skills, learn appropriate audience conduct, and experience enjoyment in learning.

Units are not meant to totally replace the class curriculum. Other programs such as alphabet study or sequential math skills can be taught in addition to the unit study. In addition, activities may also be altered to reflect the unit theme. For example, a math lesson during the Halloween unit becomes adding pumpkins or ghosts.

The units need not be used as arranged in the book. In fact, a perfect unit to begin the year is "Mother Goose" which was omitted due to its excellent presentation in Let Loose On Mother Goose by Terry Graham.

About the Book

Purpose

The purpose of <u>Marmalade Days</u> is to provide the teacher with <u>complete</u> learning units. Included are activities for each subject, step-by-step directions, ready-made worksheets, patterns, and pictures of finished projects, words and actions of fingerplays and action songs, tunes or music for songs, recipes, and letters to parents. The teacher, therefore, is free to plan, gather and process materials, and concentrate on the actual teaching and evaluation processes. Due to copyright restrictions, the words to some songs and stories could not be included. In most cases, the titles of the books or records containing these are listed.

Format and Methods Suggestions

<u>Introductory Page</u> - Each unit begins with an introductory page which includes the proposed time of the unit, the unit objectives, and the room environment.

<u>Proposed Time</u> - The time indicated will be extended if the unit is being used in a supplementary manner.

<u>Objectives</u> - The objectives state the purpose of each unit.

<u>Room Environment</u> - The room environment includes bulletin boards, door, table and wall displays, and centers. Most of these are made by the children or they are constructed using the children's art projects.

<u>Daily Topics</u> - Each unit is divided into daily topics. For example, the daily topics of the unit "My Five Senses" are Sight, Sound, Touch, Smell, and Taste.

<u>Subject Headings</u> - Each daily topic includes the following subject headings: Concept Information, the Language Arts - Social Studies - Science block, Art, Math, Music - Movement - Games, Story Time, and Extras.

<u>Concept Information</u> - The concept information provides the teacher with background information on the daily topic. From this, the teacher extracts points of interest to be shared with the children during the discussion. Sample vocabulary words are underlined.

<u>Discussion</u> - Discussions are used to establish and introduce the daily topic. Using the concept information, a foundation is established for the daily activities.

Discussions should be more than just lectures. A variety of methods can be used to present the simple discussions in each unit. Have the children role play or close their eyes and "visualize" the information. Place items relating to the information in a sack and take them out at the appropriate time. Dress up as a character described in the discussion and let the children interview you. Before or after the discussion, hold a brain-storming session on the daily topic. Read a book or show a film which covers the subject matter. Use questions to check for understanding. Preceding the discussion, hold up pictures or "real" objects. Call on the children to tell what they know about the picture or object. Use the pictures and "real" objects to strengthen understanding as you relate the information. Use your imagination and vary discussion methods. The children will respond with their interest and excitement.

<u>Vocabulary Words</u> - Vocabulary words may be written on the blackboard and defined before the discussion or defined during the discussion. During

the discussion, define a word by offering an alternative word or brief description. Be sure to pick up the discussion at the point before the defined word so that the thought may be completed.

Language Arts - Social Studies - Science Block - In the Language Arts - Social Studies - Science block, a variety of activities are offered which further develop the unit concept. You may substitute appropriate books and films which are available in your area. Reproducible sheets and patterns are found in the Patterns, Pictures, Etc. section following each unit.

Art - On most days, several art activities are offered. This allows you to choose the art activity based on skill levels, time allotment, and the availability of materials. Even when patterns are used in the unit art activities, encourage creativity by offering choices of colors, materials, and design methods. It is also a good idea to set up an art station for small groups at activity time. Include easels and paints, clay, crayons, scrap paper, scissors, glue, and so forth. This practice allows the children to create artwork with few restrictions. Patterns and pictures of projects are found in the Patterns, Pictures, Etc. section following each unit.

Math - The Math section offers nonsequential activities which teach basic skills such as counting, one-to-one correspondence, number values, spatial concepts, and sets. Ready-made sheets are found in the Patterns, Pictures, Etc. section following each unit.

Music - Movement - Games - Music - Movement - Games contains songs just for singing, action songs, movement activities, and games. Many of the songs are sung to the tune of other popular songs as indicated. When necessary, the music is supplied in the Patterns, Pictures, Etc. section.

Story Time - Story Time is a time set aside each day, preferably before nap time or after lunch, for the children to relax and enjoy a story. You may substitute any books or stories pertaining to the topic theme.

Extras - Extra activities include the Kindergarten Kitchen, field trips, presentations, parties, concept reviews, and the evaluation process.

Kindergarten Kitchen - For cooking activities, assemble ingredients and tools. Write the recipe on an experience chart illustrating each ingredient. At the bottom of the page, draw and label the tools used to prepare the recipe. Spread the ingredients and tools on a covered table. Read the recipe to the class, passing around samples of the ingredients. Encourage the children to describe the appearance, feel, taste, and smell of each ingredient. Present each tool and discuss the appearance, use, and operation of each. Allow the children to do as much of the measuring, mixing, and pouring as possible. A food fund can be set up for expenses.

Field Trips - The most successful field trips are those which are well planned. Make arrangements well in advance with the proper authorities. Explain the points of interest appropriate for the age of your class. Several days before the trip, confirm the arrangements.

Send home letters explaining the trip and requesting chaperons. Permission slips should be included. A chaperon will be needed for every three to six children depending on age. Do not forget name tags.

When you return from the trip, have the children send pictures of "what they liked best" along with a dictated and signed thank you note.

Culmination Activity and Concept Review - Both of these activities serve to "wrap up" the unit of study.

Evaluation Process - Along with daily observations, checking of work, and observation during culmination activities and concept reviews, the children may be tested individually for concept understanding. Use a check list based on the unit objectives and concept information of each daily topic. A space is provided for this.

Patterns, Pictures, Etc. - This section follows each unit and contains pictures of bulletin boards and displays, patterns, project pictures, ready-made worksheets, and letters to parents. It also contains words and music to some of the songs in the units.

Valuable Junk

Below is a list of valuable junk you will be using with each unit.   The corresponding activity title is in parentheses.   You may wish to send this list to parents at the beginning of the year or each unit.

Circus

large appliance box, refrigerator-size   (Popcorn Booth)

six-foot board   (Simple Machines demonstration)

cement blocks   (Simple Machines demonstration)

large jars   (Popcorn activity)

old oversized clothes   (Clown discussion)

medium appliance box   (Clown for Beanbag Toss)

rings from plastic milk jugs   (Performing Elephant)

small cereal boxes   (Animal Wagons)

empty film or thread spools   (Animal Wagons)

tongue depressors   (We're Animal Crackers)

Family

old magazines   (Sets of Family Members)

large appliance or furniture box   (Box House)

tongue depressors   (Counting Houses)

Senses

old magazines   (Things We Like To Taste)

old sheet   (Blindfolds for Art in the Dark)

paper towel rolls   (Rhythm Instruments)

orange juice cans and tops   (Rhythm Instruments)

cold drink caps   (Rhythm Instruments)

Valuable Junk

corrugated cardboard   (Rhythm Instruments)

frosting containers or margarine tubs   (Feely Boxes)

scraps of nylon net, carpet, lace, packing "squiggles,"

paper doilies   (Hands Are for Feeling)

egg cartons   (Haunted House)

baby food jars   (Sniff Jars)

baby food jars   (Tasting Jars)

old magazines   (My Favorite Tastes)

medicine cups   (Raisin Count)

Fall

fabric scraps   (Harvest Time bulletin board)

old clothes   (Seasons discussion)

milk or bleach jugs   (Super Stuff Bucket)

Columbus Day

walnut shell halves   (Ships Upon The Sea)

Halloween

old newspapers   (Paper Bag Pumpkins)

medium or large grocery sacks   (Trick or Treat Bags)

baby food jar lids   (Halloween Snapper)

egg cartons   (Egg Carton Owl)

old pantyhose   (Stretchy Owl)

coat hangers   (Stretchy Owl)

egg cartons   (Egg Carton Witch)

coat hangers   (Coat Hanger Ghost)

Valuable Junk

cereal boxes, coffee cans or

    large ice cream cartons   (Tepee door display)

Indians

large grocery sack   (Paper Animal Skins - rugs)

empty roll-on deodorant bottles   (Paper Animal Skins)

cardboard toilet tissue rolls   (Indian Puppets)

large table-sized shallow corrugated cardboard box   (Table Display)

adding machine tape   (Picture Messages)

oatmeal box or coffee can   (Tom-Toms)

egg cartons   (Egg Carton Totem Poles)

old sheet or scraps of unbleached muslin   (Dyed Indian Headbands)

large grocery sacks   (Indian Vests)

cardboard pieces   (Work surfaces for Clay Coil or Pinch Pots)

large grocery sack   (Indian Headdresses)

leftover crepe paper or crepe paper streamers   (Paper Plate Shields)

Pilgrims

old sheet   (Shadow Play)

Circus

Proposed Time: 5 days

Unit Objectives

To develop understanding of the circus

To help the children understand circus occupations

To develop understanding of circus animals

To encourage enjoyment of the circus

Room Environment - Bulletin Boards

"Under the Big Top"

To make a "big top" which is three feet wide, cut a strip of stiff cardboard six feet long and three inches wide. Several pieces may be stapled together. Twelve inches from each end, fold the strip and press on the fold. These two sections will be stapled to the bulletin board close enough together to cause the remaining portion to curve outward as shown. (If the middle of the curve sags, tie a thin piece of string around the strip and tack to the bulletin board.) Cut multicolored crepe paper streamers approximately twenty-eight inches long. Place all streamers together at one end. Fan streamers out and staple together to form roof. Staple roof on bulletin board at the center and eighteen inches above the curved strip. Drape the streamers over the curved strip and secure with a dot of glue. Trim edges. Cut two streamers for the outer walls of the tent. Staple. Cut a triangular pennant (4" x 10") from felt or paper and place on the top of the roof. Draw circus figures or enlarge and cut out the "Circus Family" figures. From these trace and cut out tagboard patterns. At Activity Time, each child can trace, color and cut out one circus family member. Staple beneath the "Big Top."

Note: Coloring books or Duplicating Master Books feature circus figures.

1

"Clowns, Clowns, Clowns!"

Take pictures (close-ups) of the class, two or three children at a time. Cut out the heads only. Glue onto the children's "I'm a Clown!" clowns. (See Art - Day 2.) Mount a picture of a jalopy, a trampoline, a cannon, a donkey, a tiny bicycle, a tall unicycle, and other "clown props" on the bulletin board. Staple clowns in different positions all over the bulletin board.

Room Environment - Displays

"Popcorn Booth"

Cut and decorate a large appliance box to resemble a circus concession booth. Use to sell popcorn at recess. (See Popping Corn - Day 1.)

Day 1 - Introduction

Concept Information

A circus is a show of <u>acrobats</u>, <u>clowns</u>, <u>wild animals</u>, and other exciting <u>acts</u>. The name circus comes from the word circle. A circus is usually in a tent with rings or circles in the center for the different acts. In one ring, you may see elephants dance; in another, the <u>lion tamer</u> <u>commands</u> the lions; and in another ring, the dogs do tricks. High overhead, the <u>trapeze artists</u> and <u>tightrope walkers</u> perform. The <u>audience</u> sits in the seats enjoying the show.

Some circuses <u>travel</u> from town to town in trains, and some travel in trucks. One large tent is put up for the circus <u>performers</u>, <u>workers</u>, and animals to live in. The wild animals are kept in large cages.

The circus is like a small town. Many times the children in circus families learn their acts at a very young age. When they have learned well enough, they join the family on the trapeze, walking a tightrope, or training animals. Besides the performers there are other kinds of workers in the circus. There are cooks, teachers, <u>ticket sellers</u>, <u>money clerks</u>, <u>animal caretakers</u>, and people who sell popcorn, cotton candy and <u>souvenirs</u>.

The circus is different from anything else. There are so many wonderful things at the circus to enjoy.

Discussion

Use the World Book Encyclopedia, The Circus by Brian Wildsmith, or similar reference to show circus pictures as you present the concept information and define vocabulary words.

Circus Rhymes

Read the following statements to the children. Call on those who volunteer responses.

1. I wear a funny face and jump up and down.

    I do back flips; I'm a circus _____. (clown)

2. I'm a circus elephant; I eat hay.

    I'm very big, and my color is _____. (gray)

3. I'm a circus performer; I work hard, of course,

    To balance on the back of a prancing _____. (horse)

4. I announce the show, this act and that.

    I'm the Ringmaster in the center with the tall black _____. (hat)

5. I'm a circus animal with fuzzy black hair.

    I do many tricks; I'm a dancing _____. (bear)

6. I'm pink and fluffy and a special treat.

    I'm cotton candy that you love to _____. (eat)

7. I'm big and round, and I'll give you a hint.

    I'm also called the "Big Top." I'm the circus _____. (tent)

8. We're the people who watch the circus, and when it's done

    We laugh and clap; it's so much _____! (fun)

Film

Show the film "The Circus Comes To Town." Choose a child to pantomime one of the circus acts while the others guess what it is. Encourage everyone to participate.

Circus Alphabet Booklet

At the top of each page, write an alphabet letter and what it represents, such as "A is for Animal Acts," "B is for Big Top," and so on. For a class booklet, give each child a page to illustrate. For individual booklets, duplicate all pages for each child. (To conserve paper, one sheet can be cut in half to form two pages.) Make covers from construction paper. Staple together.

Word suggestions:

A - Animals

B - Big Top, Band

C - Clowns, Circus, Cages

D - Dancing Dogs

E - Elephants

F - Flying Trapeze

G - Gray Seal, Gray Elephant

H - Horses

I - Ice Cream

J - Jugglers

K - King of Beasts,
     Keeper of Animals

L - Lemonade

M - Monkeys

N - Net

O - Orangeade

P - Peanuts, Popcorn

Q - Quarters

R - Ringmaster

S - Seals

T - Ticket Booth, Trapeze

U - Unicycle

V - Velvet Costume

W - Whip

X - Xylophone

Y - You at the Circus, Yo-Yo

Z - Zebra

Simple Machines

Discussion - Define a machine (something built to do some kind of work). Ask the children to name some machines (such as lawn mowers, power saws, tractors and so on). What work do they do? Show simple machines such as an egg beater, ice tongs, pencil sharpener, can opener, pizza cutter, etc. Discuss how they work and their uses.

Demonstrations - Define an inclined plane. Lift a wagon full of toys and place on table. Put one end of a six foot board on the table and rest the other end on the floor. Roll the wagon up the inclined plane. Compare the two tasks. Define the wheel. Move a box of stones across the floor. Now place wooden dowels under the box and roll. Compare. Define a lever. Place the six foot board on cement blocks. Lift different things with and without the lever. Compare.

Show a circus film or circus illustrations. Instruct the children to look for machines used in the circus. (Examples: wheels - trucks, pulleys, unicycle; levers - spring boards, whips, hammers; inclined planes - ladders, ramps).

Art

Circus Mobile

Preparation - Provide a paper plate which has been cut from one edge to the center, scissors, and crayons for each child. Cut five 10" pieces of yarn in different colors for each child. Duplicate circus mobile sheets on heavy paper.

Procedure - Direct the children to draw lines on the back of the paper plate dividing it into eight wedges. (First draw a "+", then an "x".) Use crayons to color the sections. At the slit, overlap both edges and staple to form a peak. Pass out circus mobile sheets for the children to color and cut out. Punch holes in each and attach yarn. Staple other ends of yarn to paper plates (or cut "L" slits in paper plates, knot yarn and insert in slit). In the last piece of yarn, tie a knot at one end, thread through the point of the paper plate, and tie other end to a paper clip for hanging.

Cotton Candy

Preparation - Cut out cotton candy shape and trace on tagboard to make patterns. Provide thin tagboard or heavy paper, scissors, and crayons. Shake red and white powdered tempera together in a paper bag. Add cotton balls and shake. You will need about twenty-five to thirty cotton balls per child.

Procedure - Trace and cut out cotton candy shape. Glue pink cotton balls to top portion. (You may be able to purchase pink cotton balls.)

Math

"Big Top Dot-to-Dot"

Duplicate and pass out sheets. Direct the children to complete and color.

Poem Activity

Read "Eight Balloons" by Shel Silverstein from A Light in the Attic. Draw eight balloons on the board. Direct the children to number them one to eight. Reread the poem having the children "pop" (erase) the balloons one at a time. Stop and count the remainder after "popping" each balloon.

Music - Movement - Games

Song - "The Circus Comes to Town Today"
Tune - "Mary Had a Little Lamb"

The circus comes to town today,

Town today, town today.

The train rolls in and the tent goes up;

I just can't wait to go!

    The clowns do tricks as the elephants dance,

    Elephants dance, elephants dance.

    The pretty lady swings and the big lions roar;

    I'd like to watch forever!

The circus left our town today,

Town today, town today.

The tent went down and the train rolled out.

Goodbye, goodbye 'til next year!

Story Time

Book - International Circus - Viking Press

Book - Clifford at the Circus - Norman Bridwell

Kindergarten Kitchen

Popping Corn for the Class

Materials - Hot plate, one large and one small skillet or frying pan, popcorn popper, oil, popcorn, salt, one spoon, napkins, large sheet.

Procedure - Heat a tablespoon of oil in the large skillet. Drop a few kernels of corn into the oil. When they pop, show the class the unpopped corn and the popped corn. Explain that inside each kernel of corn there is moisture (a small amount of water which causes slight dampness). Heat a small amount of water in the small skillet. Explain that when heated, the water inside the kernel changes to vapor or steam just like the water in the skillet. The vapor which is trapped inside causes the kernel to swell and the outside coat to split.

Spread a large sheet on the floor and place the popcorn popper in the middle. Seat the children around the sheet at a safe distance from the popper and the electrical cord. Heat oil and add popcorn. Do not cover. Watch the popcorn pop. No one is to eat any until all of the popcorn has popped and the popper is moved to a table.

While the children are enjoying the popcorn, pop a "supplementary batch" at the table.

Popping Popcorn to Sell

Before You Begin - Obtain permission to sell popcorn as a money-making project. Obtain a list of things which can be purchased for the school with future profits. Enlist parental aid.

Planning - Discuss the activity with the class. Brainstorm for ideas, and list materials you will need on the board or experience chart. Pop popcorn for the class at Snack Time. From this, figure prices, amounts, etc., and share with the class. Decide the location of the activity, considering space and electrical outlets. Send notes home asking for volunteer cooks, popcorn poppers, and food warmers. Also ask the parents to send large grocery sacks and a scarf, shower cap, or hairnet for their child. (Some hamburger chains will donate hats like their employees wear.)

Several days before the event, duplicate and send home notes with all the students. (Four or five notes can be typed on one master.) Explain the project, the cost of the popcorn, and the date it will be sold. Arrange for an adequate supply of litter receptacles.

Materials - Purchase popcorn, oil, salt, disposable plastic gloves or baggies, and small paper bags. (Some merchants, paper plants, etc., will donate these things. Be sure to write a thank you note and include the children's art work.) Collect flat boxes like those used to hold canned cold drinks, potholders, rubber bands, measuring cups, plastic scoops, change box and change. Write the total supply cost on the board for future reference.

The Day Before - Send home note to Parent Helpers explaining their duties. Cut off tops of large grocery sacks to serve as "bowls." Open small bags and stand in flat boxes. Make price signs for booth. Cut out construction paper tags of different colors to designate groups. Explain group rotation, jobs, safety rules, hygiene, and acceptable behavior.

The Day - Pin on group tags and put on head apparel. Set up one table for each popcorn popper, one for baggers, and one or two for food warmers. If only one Popcorn Booth was constructed, an extra "Selling Table" should be set up. The time to begin popping the corn will depend on the size of your school and recess schedules. Station one or two Parent Helpers at each table to supervise.

The Stations -

> Cooking Tables - Supplies: oil, popcorn, popcorn poppers, measuring cups, grocery bag bowls, potholders, salt.
> Student jobs - Pouring oil, holding measuring cups, pouring popcorn into measuring cups, delivering popcorn to "Baggers."

Parent jobs - Pouring popcorn in and out of the popcorn popper, salting popcorn, supervising.

Bagging Tables - Supplies: small bags (opened) in flat boxes, plastic gloves or baggies and rubber bands to put on hands, scoops.

Student jobs - Hold open bags, scoop popcorn to fill bags, deliver to "warmers."

Parent jobs - Supervise.

Warming Tables - Supplies: warmers, plastic gloves or baggies.

Student jobs - Unload bags, place in warmers, remove bags, load in flat boxes, deliver to "Sellers."

Parent jobs - Supervise.

Selling Booth and Table - Supplies: money box, change, poster with price of popcorn.

Student jobs - Hand out bags, accept money.

Parent jobs - Instruct on accepting and issuing change, supervise.

Begin the Activity. Be sure all children have the opportunity to participate at every table, if only for a short time. Your rotation methods also depend on the number of "customers" and recess times. During the whole process the teacher should be free to move among the stations, supervise, signal rotation, and encourage cooperation.

Clean Up - Assign groups to sweep, wash and move tables, collect trash and put up supplies.

The Next Day - On each of seven large jars, scotch tape a penny, a nickel, a dime, a quarter, a half dollar, a dollar bill, and a five dollar bill. Review identification of denominations. Pass out money to each child.

Call on the children to identify the money they have. Ask the children to "deposit" the money in the proper jar. Once all money is deposited, empty each jar and count the number of coins or bills. List on the board: 100 pennies, 50 nickels, 20 quarters, and so forth. Now go back and put the monetary value beside each: 100 pennies = $1.00; 50 nickels = $2.50; 20 quarters = $5.00, etc.

Add the amounts and announce the total. Point out the total amount previously posted. Explain that this was school or personal money already spent which must be paid back. Therefore, it must be taken out of, or subtracted from, the money made on the popcorn. Subtract on the board and explain the profit made. List the things for which the money can be spent. Take a vote and present the money to the Principal. Give all children a "Super Salesman" badge.

Day 2 - Clown

Concept Information

One very special member of the circus family is the clown. Everyone loves clowns because they do tricks to make us laugh. Clowns must learn how to put <u>makeup</u> on their faces, how to dress up in funny <u>costumes</u>, and how to do <u>tricks</u> and <u>stunts</u> to make people laugh. Every clown's face is different. Some are white and red; some are pink and blue. Some have bushy hair; some have no hair. Some clown faces are happy, and some are sad. Clowns' costumes and <u>acts</u> are different also.

Language Arts - Social Studies

Discussion

Set a large bag in the center of the group. Ask the class to watch quietly until you are finished with this "activity." Take out a pair of oversized pants with suspenders and a colorful shirt. Put these on. Next take out a pair of huge shoes, a funny hat and, if possible, a clown wig. Put these on, add a stuck-on nose or clown mask, and ask, "What am I?"

After the children guess and enjoy this, share the concept information and define vocabulary words. Show a poster of different clowns. (You may obtain one for $2.00 from Ringling Brothers and Barnum and Bailey Circus, 3201 New Mexico Avenue, N.W., Washington, D.C. 20016.) Encourage the children to notice similarities and differences. Let them choose their favorite clown face and explain why.

Variation: Invite a parent to dress up as a clown and walk in on cue.

Greasepaint For All!

Preparation - You may order official makeup kits from Ringling Brothers and Barnum and Bailey Circus at the above address for $4.50 per kit or you may use the following:

Clown White - Purchase white cover up makeup.

Colored Greasepaint - 2 teaspoons white shortening

5 teaspoons cornstarch

1 teaspoon white flour.

Blend to form a paste. Add a few drops of glycerin to make mixture creamy and food coloring for desired color.

Brown Formula - 1 teaspoon white shortening

2 1/2 teaspoons unsugared cocoa

Mix as for colored greasepaint.

You will also need an eyebrow pencil, lipstick, cold cream, and tissues. Since the children enjoy keeping their clown faces on as long as possible, it is more practical to schedule this activity late in the day. The children wear their "faces" home. Send the explanatory letter home which also enlists parental help.

Procedure - For a base, coat face with cold cream, removing excess with a tissue. Only a light film will remain. Mark off areas on the face for different colors with an eyebrow pencil. Using two fingers, fill in the areas with greasepaint. The brown mixture and lipstick are good for details. Remove with cold cream, shortening, or baby oil.

Book - You Think It's Fun to Be a Clown! by David Adler
Read and discuss the book.

Fingerplay - "Circus Clown"

I'd like to be a circus clown,

And make a funny face. (Make a funny face.)

And have all the people laugh at me,

As I jump around the place. (Act silly, make a face.)

Seatwork - "Clown Sequence Sheet"

When we tell a story we say what happened first, next, and last. Use the blackboard or sequence cards to demonstrate putting stories in sequential order. Pass out the Clown Sequence Sheet and read the directions. Provide crayons, scissors, and glue.

Art

"I'm a Clown"

Preparation - Enlarge "I'm a Clown" sheet and take pictures of the children as explained in Room Environment - Bulletin Boards, "Clowns! Clowns! Clowns!" Provide scissors, glue, crayons, and one clown for each child.

Procedure - Cut out and decorate the clowns. Glue precut photographs (faces) on the heads. Mount on bulletin board.

Paper Plate Clowns

Preparation - Supply the children with paper plates (one per child), scissors, glue, yarn, and the Scrap Paper Box.

Procedure - Review basic shapes on the board. Demonstrate using these shapes to make facial features. Pass out materials. Direct the children to make a clown face with shapes.

Personalized Clowns

Preparation - For each child staple together a large sheet of black and a sheet of white construction paper. Set up a stool and lamp near a wall. Make a silhouette of each child by tracing the profile shadow on the white paper. Cut out both "copies" at one time. Put the names on the backs. Supply the children with crayons or markers, scissors, glue, and scrap paper.

Procedure - Hand out the white "silhouettes." Ask the children to make themselves into clowns by decorating their "faces" with crayons or markers and/or scrap paper. Side by side, display the black and white faces on the wall or bulletin board. Share the results.

Clown for Beanbag Toss

Preparation - Obtain a large appliance box. Draw a large clown on one side. Mix tempera in different colors. Provide brushes.

Procedure - During Activity Time, assign small groups to paint the clown. When it is dry, cut out a hole above each hand, in the stomach, and mouth. Number for points. In teams or at Activity Time, the children take turns tossing beanbags for points. The teacher keeps score.

Note: Holes can be cut in the other sides and labeled with alphabet letters or numerals. The child tosses the beanbag and names the letter or numeral for team points.

Math

Flannel Board Activity - "Silly Clowns"
Five silly clowns tumbling through the door
One ran away, then there were four.

Four silly clowns doing tricks for me

One fell down, then there were three.

Three silly clowns, waving at you

One went to sleep, then there were two.

Two silly clowns playing in the sun

One went swimming, then there was one.

One silly clown looking for fun

He caught the circus train, now there are none!

Make flannel board clowns using pattern sheet. Put all clowns on the flannel board and remove one at a time as you recite the poem. Repeat letting the children manipulate the clown figures.

What's Missing?

Color the "What's Missing?" picture cards. Cut out and glue on tagboard. Laminate, if desired. Hold up one card. Explain that the same clown is shown twice but something is missing in one of the pictures. The children take turns guessing.

Music - Movement - Games

Song - "Oh, I Wish I Were"

Tune - "If You're Happy and You Know It"

Oh, I wish I were a funny circus clown.

Oh, I wish I were a funny circus clown.

Oh, I would flip and I would flop

And, oh, I'd never want to stop

Cause I'd rather leave a smile than leave a frown.

Game - Pass the Hat

Make simple cone-shaped hats for the children. All but one of the children put on the clown hats and stand in a circle with their left hands behind their backs. The teacher beats a drum or two rhythm sticks to signal the pace.

Tell the children, "Reach to your neighbor (on the right), remove his or her hat and put it on your head. Each time I signal, you will do this again." Begin the beat, speed up, and then stop. The player without a clown hat drops out. Remove one more hat and start again. The last clown left wins.

Story Time

Book - Joey the Clown - Kabalevsky, D.

Book - The Clown Arounds - Joanna Cole

Kindergarten Kitchen

Clown Cake

Ingredients:

    cake mix of your choice (2 layers) and needed ingredients

    2 cups white frosting

    food coloring

    gumdrops

    lifesavers - assorted colors or flavors

    black licorice (rope kind)

Equipment:

mixing bowls

rubber spatula

mixer

1 9" round cake pan

1 8" x 8" square pan

measuring cups and spoons

hard cardboard

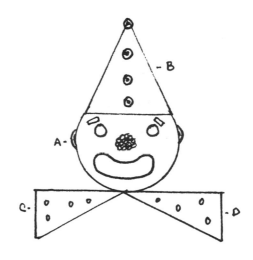

Mix and bake cakes. Remove four tablespoons of frosting and set aside in small bowl. Divide the remainder in half and put each portion in a bowl. Leave one batch white. Use food coloring to color one batch blue, and the smaller portion red. Cut the cakes, as shown. Put pieces on a cookie sheet and freeze for an hour. Assemble, as shown, using icing to stick pieces together.

Frost A white, B, C, D, blue, and the mouth red. Use green gumdrops for eyes, red gumdrops for nose, and assorted colors for tie. Use licorice for eyebrows and ears. For pom-poms, place lifesavers on the hat.

Open-Clown-Face Sandwiches

(Peanut Butter)

Ingredients:

Buy or make peanut butter (recipe on next page)

1 slice of bread per child

grated carrots

raisins

coconut

sliced radishes

cauliflower flowerettes

Spread the peanut butter on the bread and make a clown face, using any of the ingredients. Share the creations and then enjoy for snack time.

Peanut Butter

Ingredients:

1 pound roasted peanuts

salt

peanut oil

Equipment:

blender

rubber spatula

Shell the peanuts. Place in blender, along with a small amount of oil, and grind. Salt to taste. Refrigerate, if desired. Yield - 1 cup.

Note: Save the Shells!!! (See Day 3 - Science and Math.)

Day 3 - Elephant

Concept Information

One of the most <u>interesting</u> of all the circus animals is the elephant. People seem to never get tired of watching them. There are many reasons why the elephant is so <u>special</u>. The elephant is the biggest animal that walks on four legs. "Jumbo," <u>P. T. Barnum's</u> famous circus elephant, weighed 12,000 pounds and measured almost eleven feet at the shoulder. Perhaps the most <u>extraordinary</u> part of the elephant is the trunk. It is about six feet long and weighs 300 pounds. Elephants use their trunks to pick up heavy objects like logs, to pick up hay or peanuts to eat, to "hug" their babies, or to shoot a stream of water.

All elephants have large ears, but not all elephants have tusks. Tusks are long, white, pointed teeth on either side of the trunk. The elephant's tusks are used for grinding food, fighting, and carrying things.

An elephant can stand for a long time without tiring because of its great straight legs. Some elephants sleep standing up while others prefer to lie down. The elephant's feet are round with huge nails. Its skin is <u>baggy</u> and wrinkled. It is thought that elephants cannot see well, but they can smell and hear very well.

The first place elephants were found was in <u>Africa</u>, but now they live in many different places including America. Elephants usually live to be sixty or seventy years old.

The elephant <u>trainers</u> of the circus are called "bullhands." Circus elephants are called "bulls" even though they are usually female. A bullhand must be <u>patient</u> and kind. Circus elephants are trained when they are still young. <u>Voice commands</u> are used to get them to do their tricks. Elephants like to make their trainers happy. But sometimes the elephants fight among themselves and have to be separated. The "bossiest" elephant in the herd is the leader.

<u>Language Arts</u> - <u>Social Studies</u> - <u>Science</u>

<u>Discussion</u>

Enlarge and display the picture of an elephant. Indicate the various parts. Relate the concept information and define the vocabulary words. Use the ceiling or walls to show the elephant's height and trunk length. Show the children a globe and point out Africa.

<u>Seatwork</u> - "Parts Puzzle"

Label the parts of the elephant (head, ears, eyes, mouth, tusks, legs, body, tail) on the picture. The class uses a complete sentence to name each part such as "An elephant has a trunk," and so forth. Hand out crayons, scissors, and the "Elephant Parts" sheet. Direct the children to color and cut out the parts. Pass out glue and the "Elephant Outline" sheet. Tell the children to pick up the trunk of the elephant; after you are certain each child has the correct part, they may glue it in place. Repeat these instructions with each part of the elephant. The tail is only on the outline sheet. You will be progressing from the right to the left.

<u>Fingerplay</u> - "The Elephant"

The elephant has a great big trunk.   (Extend arm in front of nose)
He swings it to and fro.   (Swing from side to side)
He also has two tiny eyes   (Circle eyes with index finger & thumbs)
That show him where to go.   (Look from side to side)

His ears flop up, his ears flop down   (Lift shoulders to ears,
                                         wave arms up & down.)

And his feet go stomp! stomp! on the ground.   (Stomp feet.)

Name Recognition Activity - "A Peanut A Day. . ."

From tagboard, make a large elephant, a wooden tub, and a peanut for each child. Write names on peanuts. If you have a metal file cabinet, use two-sided carpet tape to cover with burlap. Stick strips of magnetic tape (available at craft stores) on the back of the elephant, tub, and peanuts.

Place the elephant near the top of the file cabinet. Put the peanuts above the bucket at the bottom of the display. Each day as each child arrives, he or she will give the elephant a peanut by finding his or her peanut and placing it near the elephant's trunk. You will need to assist at first.

Note: This also helps in taking attendance.

Rough-Smooth Sheet

Preparation - Buy one bag of miniature marshmallows and use peanut shells from "Open-Clown-Face Sandwiches" (see Kindergarten Kitchen - Day 2) or from "Peanut Hunt" (see Music - Movement - Games - Day 3). (You may substitute Froot Loop Cereal.) Duplicate "Rough-Smooth Sheet." Provide glue.

Procedure - Read Circus of Opposites by Emily Perl Kingsley (Sesame Street Book). Discuss opposites, ending with "rough and smooth." Pass around examples of each. Pass out the sheets. The children put a puddle of glue and the peanut shell half on the rough side of the sheet. The marshmallow is glued on the "smooth side."

Book - <u>Dumbo</u> by Walt Disney

Read <u>Dumbo</u>. Since the story is long, you may prefer telling the story or reading the shorter version.

Art

Performing Elephant

Preparation - Duplicate the "Performing Elephant" for each child. Collect the plastic rings from gallon milk jugs and tie an eight-inch piece of string on each. Keep the strings and rings hidden. Provide an elephant, crayons, and scissors for each child.

Procedure - Direct the children to cut out and color their elephants. They may also draw the features on the blank side and add polka dots, flowers, etc. Tell them if they do a super job, the elephant will do a trick for them. As the children finish, tie the strings and rings to the trunks. After everyone has a completed elephant, show them how to hold the elephant's ear, swing it in an upward motion, and catch the ring on the trunk. This is a true circus elephant!

Fingerpainted Elephants

Preparation - For each child, cut a piece of shelf paper fourteen inches wide. Stack four or five sheets at a time and make folds (as shown on illustrated page) about four inches from the left side, one and a half inches from the right side, and two inches from the bottom and top. Pass out the paper, pencils or crayons, scissors, and set out black and white fingerpaints. You will need a sponge and water or a spray bottle of water.

Procedure - Model on the board as you instruct the children to draw a line on each fold. Inside the large area (A), they should draw a large ellipse. Draw the trunk between the left side and the first line (B). Between the second line and right side of the paper is the tail area (C). The legs will go below the body (D). Cut out the elephant following the outside lines. Wet the elephants. Mixing on the elephants, use black and white fingerpaints to make gray. Fingerpaint the entire surface. Finally, use black to make eye and ear outlines.

Math

Feed the Elephant

Duplicate the sheet. Write different numerals on each sheet. Give each child a sheet. Provide glue. Pour piles of unshelled peanuts on the tables. The children read their numerals, shell the peanuts, and glue the correct number of peanuts on the sheet.

Variation: Substitute popcorn or cut out apples for the peanuts. Also the children can simply draw these on the sheet. Share with the class.

Music - Movement - Games

Action Song - "The Elephant" from Learning Basic Skills Through Music Volume I by Hap Palmer.
The children sing and act out the song.

Game - "Peanut Hunt"
Hide peanuts in the room. Divide the class into two teams, "Purple" and "Pink." Designate two elephants on each team. Put a bucket for each team in the center of the floor (preferably color coded). The children form a circle and march around the buckets. At the whistle, the teams

scatter, searching for peanuts. When team members find a peanut, they must call out to their elephants "Pink Elephant" or "Purple Elephant." Their elephants must come pick up the peanut, and put it in the bucket. (No one else can pick up a peanut!) At the whistle, everyone must return to the circle and march until the next signal. At the end of the game, the team with the most peanuts wins.

Story Time

Book - <u>The Circus Baby</u> - Maude and Miska Petersham

Book - <u>Little Wild Elephant</u> - Anna Michel

Book - <u>The Elephant Who Couldn't Forget</u> - Faith McNulty

Kindergarten Kitchen

Peanut Butter Cookies

Cream Together .... 1 cup butter or margarine

                                      1 cup peanut butter

                                      1 cup granulated sugar (extra needed-
                                                          see below)

                                        1 cup brown sugar

Add .... 2 eggs

                                        1 tsp. vanilla

Sift Together .... 2 1/2 cups all-purpose flour

                                        1 tsp. baking soda

                                        1/4 tsp. salt

Blend sifted ingredients into creamed mixture. Shape into 2" balls and roll in extra granulated sugar. Flatten each ball with the bottom of a glass, then crisscross with the tines of a fork. Bake at 350° on ungreased cookie sheet for 8-10 minutes. Cool slightly. Makes approximately 4 dozen.

Day 4 - Circus Animals

Concept Information

No circus would be <u>complete</u> without animals. A big circus may have many animals such as elephants, lions, tigers, horses, bears, camels, seals, monkeys, and dogs. A smaller circus may have only lions, horses, and dogs. Whatever the size of the circus, people always <u>look forward</u> to the animal acts.

Lions and tigers are both members of the cat family. The male lion has a <u>shaggy mane</u> which stands out around his neck. He can weigh more than 500 pounds and is sometimes called "the king of beasts." Lions are light brown or brownish-yellow in color. They have a <u>thunderous</u> roar. Their babies are called cubs.

The tiger looks much like the lion but the fur is bright orange with black stripes. Male tigers don't have manes like lions. The tiger is also longer and heavier than the lion and his roar is low. Lions and tigers are both strong. But in a fight the tiger would probably win. Lions and tigers are usually fed horse meat once a day. Lions and tigers were first found in <u>Africa</u> and <u>India</u>. But most of the circus animals were born in the circus, and know no other life.

Another circus animal is the bear. There are many kinds of bears such as the honey bear of <u>India</u>, the grizzlies of <u>America</u>, and the Kodiak of <u>Alaska</u>. Except for the white <u>Polar Bear</u>, bears are brown or black with heavy fur. In the winter, the female bear or "she-bear" digs a <u>cave</u> for herself; and there her cubs are born. In spring, she comes out of the cave with her cubs. She then takes care of them and teaches them until they are <u>full grown</u>.

Bears look friendly, and they are rather smart; but they are <u>dangerous</u>. Of all animals, a bear is the best fighter. Circus people who train and take care of the bears never trust them. Horses were on the <u>earth</u> long before man appeared. At one time, they were the size of medium-sized dogs. As time went by, horses grew and men began to ride them.

There are many kinds of horses but some of the most beautiful are in the circus. They are trained to <u>trot</u> to music, dance, <u>rear</u>, and to keep a <u>steady pace</u> as performers <u>balance</u> on their backs. A <u>newly-born</u> horse is called a foal and a young horse is a colt. Horses are trained for the circus when they are colts.

Horses eat green grass, hay, oats, and are fond of apples and carrots. They also need plenty of water. A horse wears shoes called "horseshoes" which are usually made from <u>iron</u>. They are attached to the horses <u>hooves</u> with sharp nails.

Camels are large animals which come from <u>Asia</u> and <u>Egypt</u>. The Bactrian has two humps on its back and the dromedary has one. They are often called the "Ships of the Desert" because they carry cargo across the <u>desert</u> like trucks and trains do in our country. A camel can go for a long time without eating or drinking water. Its hump is <u>stored-up fat</u>, and its stomach has <u>compartments</u> which hold water until it is needed.

Camels are mean, unfriendly, and <u>unintelligent</u>. They groan and sigh at any <u>task</u> and like to bite. A mother camel seems to love her babies, but dislikes everything else. Camels eat dates, beans, and shrubs. Like a goat, it will also eat cloth or leather if it is hungry. Camels have long eyelashes and an extra eyelid that they can see through. Both of these are used to keep desert sand out of their eyes.

Camels carry people in a "mohaffa" which looks like two wooden boxes on either side of the camel's back. It is very uncomfortable though, because the boxes sway and lurch as the camel walks. In the circus, camels are used to carry performers or walk around the rings. They cannot be taught any tricks.

At some circuses, you may see a seal balancing a ball on his nose, clapping his flippers or playing tunes on a set of horns. Seals live most of their lives in water but they are not fish. They are animals like horses or bears. Seals have sleek fur which helps them glide through the water. Their arms and legs are flippers which help them swim. The seal's eyes are large and their ears are hidden under their fur. Fish is their favorite food.

Seals come on shore to have their babies, then they return to the sea. The best known seals are the fur seals of the Pacific Ocean. In the spring, they live around the coast of Alaska.

One of the most friendly and intelligent of all pets is the dog. Dogs are devoted to their masters. Not only are they good companions but also they protect property and people. Dogs are used as shepherds, hunters, and guards as well as pets. Dogs do not see as well as humans. Also they do not see colors, only shades of black, white, and gray. But dogs can smell and hear much better than we can.

Baby dogs are called puppies. Like human babies, puppies love to play and explore. The dog's natural food is meat, and he needs plenty of water. He also needs to be bathed and groomed. There are many different kinds or breeds of dogs. Some are tiny such as the Chihuahua or huge like the

Great Dane. Many times the French Poodle, which is an intelligent breed, is used in the circus. As puppies, they are trained to do all kinds of tricks.

Language Arts - Social Studies - Science

Discussion

Relate the concept information and define vocabulary words. Use the globe, posters, pictures and transparencies as visual aids.

Note: Since the concept information is lengthy, you may wish to divide it between two days or among stations at Activity Time. One station could have a filmstrip on one animal; another, your tape recording set up as a Listening Center; one where you conduct a discussion, and so forth. Rotate.

Tiger Hunt Activity

Divide the children into groups and assign parts. Practice key words and responses until everyone understands. Each group should stand when responding, then sit back down. Everyone stands and pantomimes the dressing scene.

Word	Response	Motions
TIGER	"ROAR! ROAR!	(Act like tiger)
JAMMIES	"Mmm-Hmmm!"	(Smile and nod)
SAFARI HAT	"Knock! Knock!"	(Knock on hat)
GUN	"Boom! Boom!"	(Aim and shoot)
BOAT	(tune) "Row, row, row your boat!"	(Row)
JUNGLE	(Monkey sounds) "Eee! Eee!"	(Swing on vines)
WALK QUIETLY	"Pad! Pad!"	(Walk tiptoe)
BOA CONSTRICTOR	"Hiss! Hiss!"	(Head side to side)
LEG	"Squeeze! Squeeze!"	(Hug body)
VINE	"Ha-Ha! Ha-Ha!"	(Laughing)
RUN	Lickety-split! Lickety-split!"	(Run in place)

Would you like to go on a TIGER hunt? Okay! First we have to take off our JAMMIES, then get into our hunting clothes: shorts, shirt, boots, SAFARI HAT and GUN. Then we have to get in our BOAT and gee! we're already in Africa! Now we are in the JUNGLE. WALK QUIETLY! Oh, a giant BOA CONSTRICTOR! Help, he's got my LEG! Oh, it's just a VINE. Boy, it's dark in this JUNGLE. Wait, I see something--get your GUN ready. It's a TIGER! RUN, RUN! Jump in the BOAT! Bye TIGER! Gosh, I'm glad to be home and take off my hunting clothes--shorts, shirt, boots, SAFARI HAT and put up my GUN. Now I'll put on my JAMMIES and WALK QUIETLY to my warm bed--What's this? Oh, it's just a VINE. No! It's a giant BOA CONSTRICTOR--my LEG. . . .

Seatwork - "Dog Maze"

Duplicate and distribute the "Dog Maze" sheet. Direct the children to find the path from the dog's ear to the dog's tail.

Poem - "King Lion's Bet"

Read and enjoy the poem.   Ask follow-up questions.

Said King Lion of the Jungle to his jungle friends,

"I'll make you all a bet,

Whoever can guess how many ribbons I wear,

My crown he'll surely get."

"Twenty," yelled the tiger, "fifty," yelled the giraffe,

"Duh, one?" asked the big alligator,

And all the while, Mildred Monkey's child,

Was playing with his calculator.

"Pay attention!" Mildred said, "there's a crown for your head.

Listen to what I'm saying!"

But little Monkey Fred, just shook his head,

And continued with his calculator-playing.

"Well, I never!" said the zebra to Freddy's mom,

"That child is a total disgrace! Toys are for humans,

Those terrible things, but not for our superior race!"

"200!" guessed the snake, "forty!" squawked the bird,

"Ten!" yelled the tsetse fly,

"No, no," said the King, "all wrong, all wrong,

Does anyone else want to try?"

"We give up," said his friends, "uncle!" they cried,

"Tell us how many ribbons <u>do</u> you wear?"

But little Monkey Fred answered first instead,

"He wears 1900 ribbons in his hair!"

"Boo!" said the toucan, "hiss," said the snake,

"How'd you know?" said the King with a frown,

"Whenever I'm in doubt, I take my calculator out,"

Said Monkey Fred as he put on his crown.

Film

Show <u>Animals of the Circus</u> or similar film. Discuss favorite animals' characteristics, sounds, and tricks. Discuss which animals are not in the circus and give reasons why.

Rebus Activity - "The Circus Turtle"

Place the Rebus Story on the opaque projector. Use a pointer as you read each line of the story. Pause at the pictures and allow the children to supply the correct word.

Art

Animal Wagons

Preparation - Collect one small (individual serving) cereal box for each child. Tape the top shut, and cut out the front of each box. Collect two empty film spools for each child. (You may substitute thread spools and attach with hot glue.) Cut a forty-five inch piece of black yarn per child. Supply the children with the cereal box, playdough, and tools, pieces of cardboard, crayons or tempera paint, yarn, scissors, and tape.

Procedure - Demonstrate making a circus animal with playdough and tools. (Bread dough may be used. See Fall - Art - Day 5 for recipe.) The children choose an animal, make it with playdough on the pieces of cardboard, and put it aside to dry. Color or paint the inside of the box. Direct the children to cut a half-inch slit in the upper left corner and the bottom right corner. Stick the end of the yarn in the slit, and wrap around and around the box, spacing to represent bars, and ending in the bottom slit. Trim ends. Tape spool wheels to the bottom of each "wagon." Stand the box on its side and glue-dried animal in the "wagon." Display on a shelf and share.

Circus Seal

Preparation - Duplicate "Circus Seal" sheet on stiff paper. Provide crayons, glue, and scissors.

Procedure - Use crayons to color the seal, the ball, and the "cone." Cut out the seal, and the ball. Glue the ball behind the seal's nose. Allow to dry. Meanwhile, cut out the "cone"; and then cut on the dotted line to form slit. At the slit, bring one side over the other and staple to form a cone. With one hand, hold the bottom of the cone together. Snip an inch slit at the top of the cone beginning with the point. Insert the seal in the slit.

Burlap Lion

Preparation - Purchase enough gold burlap to cut an 8" x 7" piece for each child, pellon in orange, black, white, and fabric glue. Distribute supplies.

Procedure - Unravel the burlap about one and a half inches on all four sides. Cut features from pellon and glue. Work a piece of wire through the top and tie in back for a hanger.

Math

Roar-Two-Three-Four

Discuss and make the sounds of each circus animal. Call on each child to choose an animal to be. Give each a numeral or "number dots" card. Line up four or five "animals." When called on, each is to make the sound of the animal the number of times designated on his or her number card. (Example - A lion holding a "2" card will roar twice.) The other children count the number of sounds made and name the animal.

Circus Rings

Cut strips of poster paper to make ten-inch circus rings. Label each ring with a different numeral. Purchase packages of small plastic circus animals (similar to the green plastic army men). Call on a child to place the correct number of animals in a ring. Call on other children to check the "answer." Repeat so that all children participate.

Music - Movement - Games

Song - "The Lion" (Adapted from the Chilean Folk Tune "The Elephant") For words and music, see the sheet "The Lion" in pattern section.

We're Animal Crackers

Purchase a few small boxes of animal crackers. The box is designed like a wagon full of animals. Show the box to the class. Imagine that the box holds live animal crackers. Ask, "How would you feel if you were an animal cracker in this box?" Give each child one animal cracker which will designate the animal he or she will be.

Use four tables, an appliance box, or large blocks to form an animal cracker "box." Choose a group of children to become animal crackers. Tell a story of the animal crackers being put in the box at the factory, riding in a truck, being shelved at the store, being bought, shaken, opened, and eaten. The children dramatize.

Optional: Have the children make simple paper plate puppets by drawing the animals' faces on the plates and gluing a tongue depressor to the back. They may refer to the circus animal pictures or posters for facial details.

Story Time

Book - About Animals - Richard Scarry

Book - Bearymore - Don Freeman

Kindergarten Kitchen

Toasted Animals

1 slice of bread per child

butter

animal cookie cutters (large or small)

Cut animal shapes from bread. Put butter on each animal and toast.

Day 5 - Circus Performers

Concept Information

Circus performers train for many years to learn their acts. Sometimes whole families perform together. Some of the circus performers do their acts high in the air above the crowd. Trapeze artists swing and do stunts on a trapeze which is similar to a playground swing. Tightrope walkers or acrobats walk, ride bikes, and balance chairs on a rope or cable which is stretched tightly between two poles near the top of the circus tent. This is also called a tightwire or highwire. The ringmaster announces the acts in each ring as circus riders balance on prancing horses, Gymnasts balance on ladders, form human pyramids and perform tricks on unicycles. Jugglers juggle plates in the air; sword swallowers stick swords down their throats; and animal trainers order the animals to perform. All of these people must practice every day and continue to learn new stunts to give the audience a good performance.

Language Arts - Social Studies

Discussion

Refer to a circus poster or pictures as you share the concept information and define the vocabulary words. Ask the children to tell which circus performer they would like to be and why.

Circus Story

Help the class write a circus story on the board of experience chart. Think of a title such as, "The Elephant Who Wanted to be a Tightrope Walker," "The Trapeze Artist Who Wouldn't Swing," etc. The children may illustrate the story.

Film

Show The Circus Acrobats (or some similar film) without the sound. Call on children to narrate different parts. Show the film again with the sound.

Poems

Using the opaque projector, read and share the illustrations of "The Acrobats" from the book Where the Sidewalk Ends and "The Sword-Swallower" from A Light in the Attic. Both books are by Shel Silverstein.

Art

Trapeze Artists Accordion-Style

Preparation - Provide each child with a plastic drinking straw (a pencil or dowel may be substituted), one sheet of construction paper, and construction paper scraps. Distribute scissors, glue, and crayons.

Procedure - Show an example. Direct the children to cut a rectangle approximately 3" x 5" from the construction paper sheet. Fold accordion-style to form the body. Arms and legs are four strips cut approximately 1" x 5". Accordion pleat these also. (The children may swap leftover construction paper to vary colors or use construction paper scraps provided.) On the board, demonstrate drawing circles for faces and simple facial features, hands, feet, shoes, hair, and hats. The children draw and cut from scraps. Glue the arms and legs as shown in the illustration. Glue on head, hair, hands, and shoes, etc. Attach the hands by stapling to the straws or taping to dowels or pencils.

Toothpick Circus Picture

Preparation - Provide heavy paper, an ample supply of colored toothpicks, and glue.

Procedure - Show examples of simple shapes and objects made with toothpicks. Direct the children to make a circus picture. This may be one animal or object or a scene. Share with the class.

Circus Mural

As a culminating activity, supply the children with mural paper and crayons, markers or tempera paint to create a circus mural. Display in the hall or lunchroom.

Math

Flannel Board Activity - "Circus Hats"

Make flannel board figures as shown on the pattern page. Place the five performers on the flannel board. Place ten hats on the flannel board and ask, "Are there as many, more, or less hats as performers?" Have a child place one hat on each performer's head. Explain that there were more hats than performers. Repeat the activity varying the number of hats.

How Many?

Display circus scene posters or pictures. Call on a child to count the number of trapeze artists and write the number on the board. The class counts together to check the answer. Repeat, using the number of clowns, jugglers, lions, etc.

Variation: Divide the class into two teams. Alternate the procedure between the two teams. One point is scored for a correct response.

Music - Movement - Games

Song - "The Man on the Flying Trapeze" (record)

Teach the words to the song. Have the children choose partners.

Partners should face each other with arms outstretched and hands clasped.

Show the children the following movements:

Swing - Partners swing arms from left to right.

Swing-Rock - Partners swing arms from left to right while rocking on corresponding feet.

Swing Around - Partners swing around and around.

Turnabout - Partners both turn completely around with hands still clasped and arms "follow."

Slide - Partners hop and slide sideways across the floor.

To and Fro - Partners move (as one unit) two steps backwards and two steps forward.

Procedure - Play the record and call out the above movements to the "trapeze artists."

Story Time

Book - Clara Joins the Circus - Michael Pellowski

Book - Toby Tyler - based on the book my James Otis Kaler, adapted by Carl Memling (must be read in "installments")

"A Circus of Our Own" - (Culminating Activity)

Plan a class circus. This activity will depend on parental cooperation, so send a letter home and find out how many responses you have before informing the children.

With the children's help, decide what acts you will present. These will depend on the children's abilities and special talents. Examples:

Trapeze Artists - Children perform movement act. (See Music - Movement - Games - Day 5.)

Tumbling Clowns - Children do somersaults.

Trick Dogs - Children jump through hoops, dance, etc.

Racing Bears - Children ride tricycles or bikes through an obstacle course (wooden pins).

Tightrope Walkers - Children walk on balance beam or ladder.

Gymnasts - Children spin hoops on hands while walking.

Honking Seals - Children play horns to music.

Jugglers - Children toss bean bags to each other.

Circus Band - Children play rhythm instruments.

Decide on simple costumes and makeup, circus decorations (streamers and balloons are effective) and refreshments. Practice the acts. Invite another class and/or parents to watch the performance.

Kindergarten Kitchen

Mini Corn Dogs

1/2 cup yellow corn meal

1/2 cup sifted all-purpose flour

1 teaspoon salt

1/2 teaspoon pepper

1 egg

1/2 cup milk

1 Tablespoon liquid shortening

6 wieners

Also needed:

extra flour to coat each wiener

toothpicks

mustard

catsup

oil for frying

deep fryer

slotted spoon

paper towels

Sift together corn meal, flour, salt, and pepper into a bowl. Stir in egg, milk, and liquid shortening. Mix well. Cut each wiener in half and roll in thin layer of flour. Dip into batter and fry in hot deep fat until golden brown. Remove and drain on paper towels. Insert a toothpick in each mini corn dog and serve. Provide mustard and catsup.

<u>Concept Evaluation</u> - (See Introduction)

Dear Parents,

On _____, our class will begin our unit, "The Circus." Each day we will learn about the circus and the circus family with discussions, films, books, fingerplays, songs and other activities. Below are ways you can help.

Things to Send: _____

_____

_____

Volunteers Needed To: _____

_____

_____

Follow-Up: At the end of the unit, ask your child to share the following songs, fingerplays or stories.

_____

_____

_____.

The very best follow-up to our circus unit is an actual visit to a circus. The circus will be here on _____. If possible, take your child and join the fun!

Sincerely,

Copyright © 1987. Carol Taylor Bond

46

Copyright © 1987. Carol Taylor Bond

Circus Family

 Copyright © 1987. Carol Taylor Bond

Copyright © 1987. Carol Taylor Bond

Popcorn Booth

 Copyright © 1987. Carol Taylor Bond

Copyright © 1987.   Carol Taylor Bond

LEMONADE

   Copyright © 1987. Carol Taylor Bond

Cotton Candy

Copyright © 1987.   Carol Taylor Bond

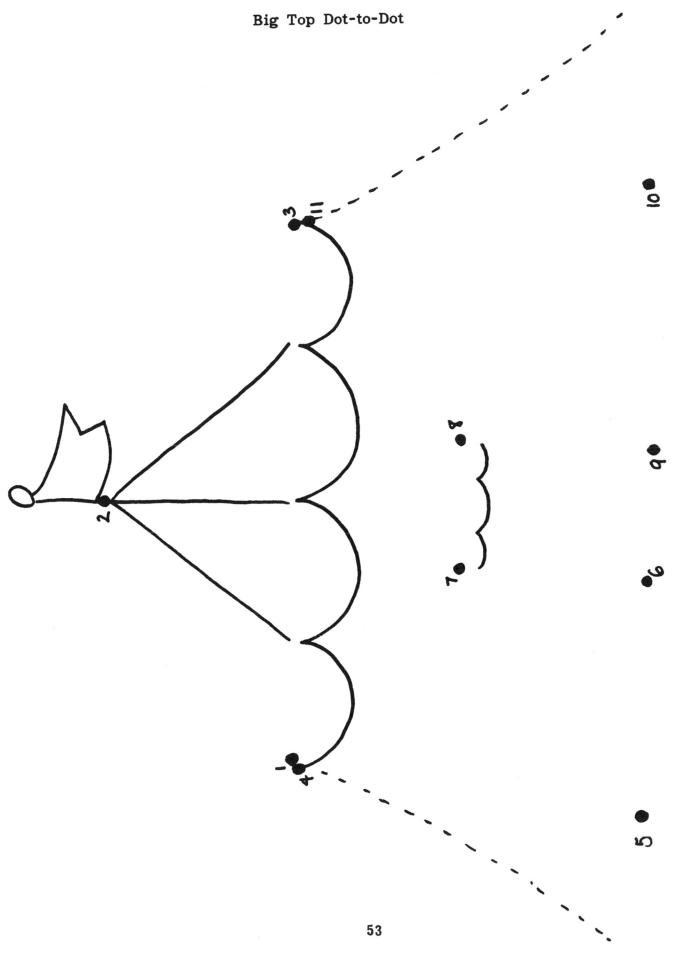

Copyright © 1987.   Carol Taylor Bond

Clown Sequence Sheet

Cut on dotted lines for two story strips. Then cut out squares. Beginning at the arrows, paste each story in order below.

 Copyright © 1987. Carol Taylor Bond

I'm A Clown!

Copyright © 1987. Carol Taylor Bond

Paper Plate Clown

Personalized Clowns

Beanbag Toss

Copyright © 1987. Carol Taylor Bond

56

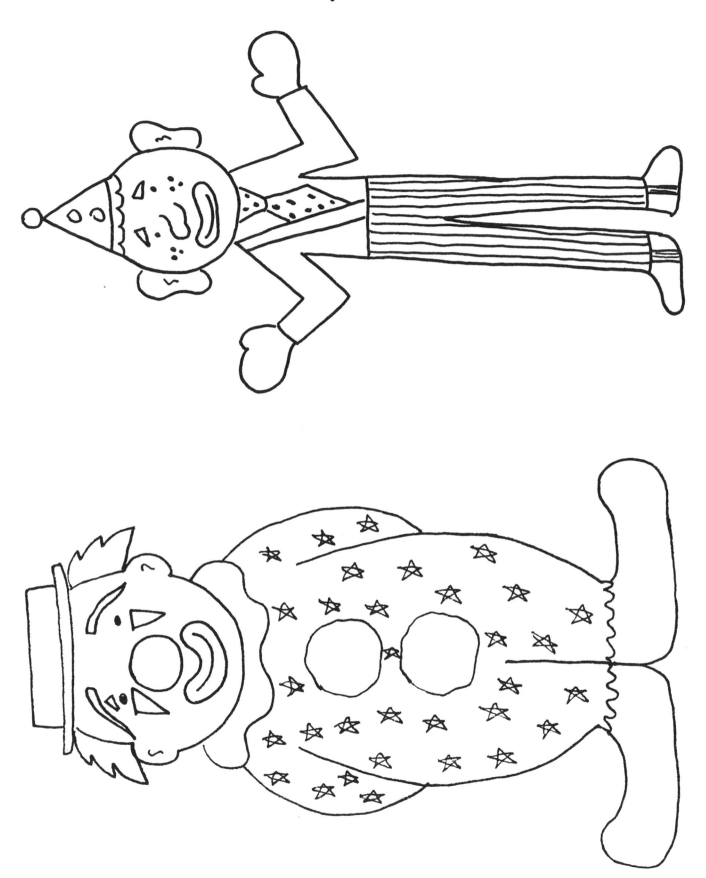

57 Copyright © 1987. Carol Taylor Bond

Silly Clowns

 Copyright © 1987. Carol Taylor Bond

What's Missing?

 Copyright © 1987. Carol Taylor Bond

Elephant

 Copyright © 1987. Carol Taylor Bond

Elephant Parts

61

Copyright © 1987. Carol Taylor Bond

Elephant Outline

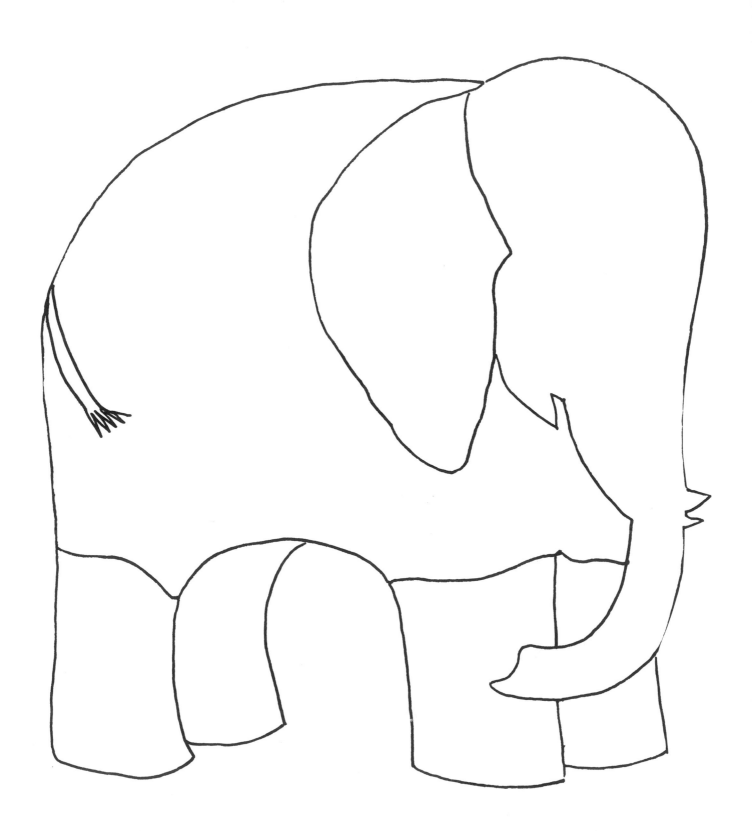

 Copyright © 1987. Carol Taylor Bond

Copyright © 1987. Carol Taylor Bond

Name _____

Can you find some things at home to add to the sheet?

Smooth

Rough

Copyright © 1987.   Carol Taylor Bond

Copyright © 1987. Carol Taylor Bond

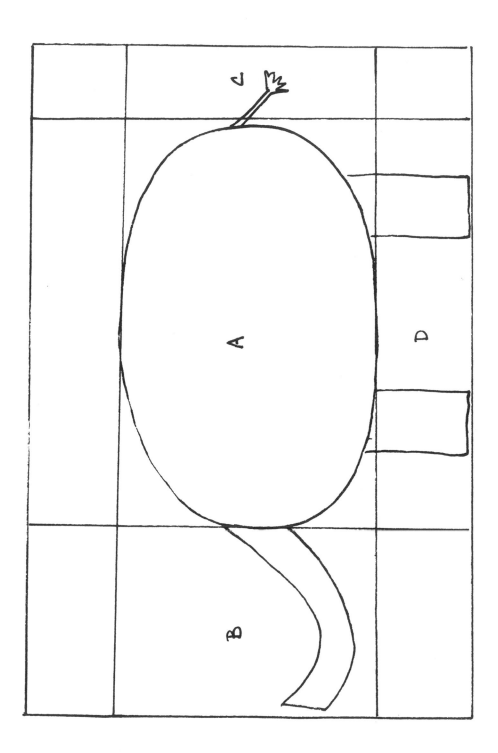

Copyright © 1987. Carol Taylor Bond

(numeral here)

Name _____

Copyright © 1987. Carol Taylor Bond

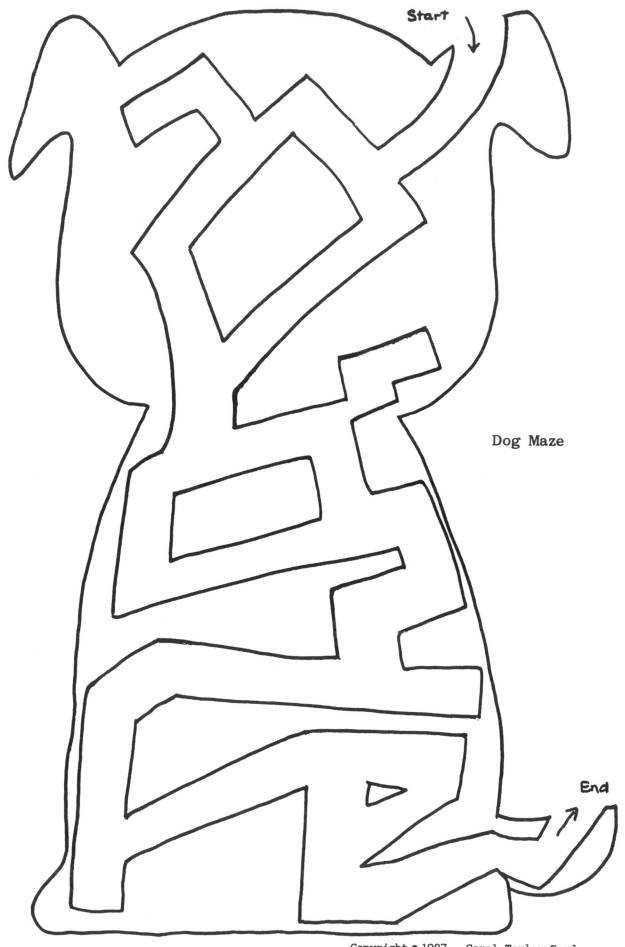

Start

End

Dog Maze

Copyright © 1987. Carol Taylor Bond

The Circus Turtle 🐢

[Tim] Tim and [Kate] Kate and [Little Joey] Little Joey went to the [circus tent] circus. [Tim] Tim and [Kate] Kate had learned about it in school. They especially wanted to see the [elephant][lion][tiger] animals. First they bought [peanuts] peanuts and [cotton candy] cotton candy. Then they sat down. [Kate] Kate said, "Look at the [tiger] tiger!" [Tim] Tim liked the [lion] lion best. [Little Joey] Little Joey said, "Where are the [turtles] turtles?" [Tim] Tim told him there were no [turtles] turtles in the [circus tent] circus. [Little Joey] Little Joey began to cry. [Kate] Kate had an idea. She ran to the [toy] toy stand. When she came back, she gave [Little Joey] Little Joey a toy [turtle] turtle. [Little Joey] Little Joey hugged it. Then [Kate] Kate and [Tim] Tim and [Little Joey] Little Joey enjoyed the show.

Copyright © 1987. Carol Taylor Bond

69

Burlap Lion

70

Copyright © 1987. Carol Taylor Bond

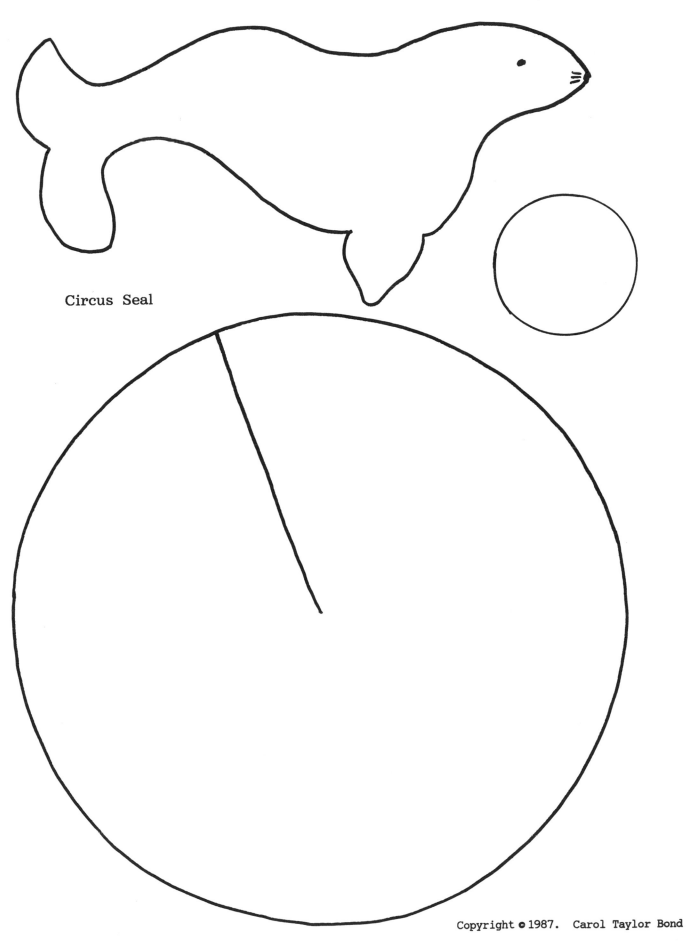

Circus Seal

Copyright © 1987. Carol Taylor Bond

The Lion

One big lion went out to play in the cir-cus

ring one day. He had such e- nor-mous fun, he

called for ot-her an - i - mals to come.

Verses:

2. Two huge tigers went out to play . . .

3. Three prancing horses . . .

4. Four frowning camels . . .

5. Five dancing bears . . .

6. Six barking seals . . .

7. Seven trick dogs . . .

8. Eight naughty monkeys . . .

Copyright © 1987. Carol Taylor Bond

Trapeze Artist -
Accordion Style

Toothpick Circus

Pictures

Copyright © 1987. Carol Taylor Bond

73

Circus Hats Activity

Copyright © 1987. Carol Taylor Bond

Copyright © 1987. Carol Taylor Bond

Circus Hats Activity

Copyright © 1987. Carol Taylor Bond

76

Circus Hats Activity

Copyright © 1987. Carol Taylor Bond

Family

Proposed Time: 5 days

Unit Objectives

To develop understanding of the family unit

To promote understanding of the roles of family members

To help the children explore and understand their immediate environments

To encourage positive self concepts

Room Environment - Bulletin Boards

"I Know Town"

Label the bulletin board "I Know Town." Cut the road from butcher paper and have the children color it. Staple on the bulletin board. Mount construction paper houses (see Day 5) along the road. Beside each house, place a construction paper telephone pole, mailbox pole, and apple tree. String yarn from the telephone poles to the houses, as shown.

Cut construction paper rectangles and label with names, addresses, and telephone numbers. These may be used for instructional purposes. Once each child learns the information, the name card is stapled under the house, the address card on the mailbox pole, and the telephone number card on the telephone wire. Small construction paper apples may be placed on each child's tree to signify other accomplishments.

"We Are Family"

At the beginning of school, ask the parents to send a family snapshot for display purposes. Have a co-worker take a snapshot of your class. Duplicate the house and apartment patterns on construction paper for the children to color and cut. At the top of the bulletin board, label "We Are Family." Make the "School House" and place in the center of the bulletin board. Staple houses and apartments on the bulletin board. Staple the class snapshot on the school house. Use stick pins or tacks to mount family pictures on each house or apartment. Extend colored yarn from the school to the houses and apartments.

Room Environment - Displays

"Welcome to Our Home"

From large paper, cut a triangular roof twice the width of your classroom door. Have each child choose a colored sheet of construction paper to fold and cut in fourths. During activity time, small groups glue their "shingles" to the roof. Guide them in overlapping each row and alternating colors. When complete, trim excess paper to follow triangular roof lines.

For the "front wall" of the house, cut two strips of large paper six inches longer than the length of the door frame. The children may add windows, window boxes, etc., to each strip.

Using duct or any similar strong tape, mount the strips on either side of the door and the roof above the door frame. Place a "Welcome Mat" in front of the door.

Day 1 - Introduction

Concept Information

Your father, your mother, your sisters and brothers, and you are all members of your family. All families are not alike. Some families are big with many members, and some are small with only a few members. Families share happy times and sad times. They also share work and play times.

Language Arts - Social Studies

Discussion

Use the "We Are Family" bulletin board or a poster depicting different families as a visual aid. Discuss the concept information and vocabulary words. Have each child name who is in his family, remove the snapshot from the bulletin board, and show the picture to the class. Discuss how family members help each other; how they work and play together.

Role Playing

Divide the class into groups. Act out and discuss the following scenes:

--The whole family raking leaves

--One family member raking leaves while the rest watch

--Family members doing their individual chores

--Feeding time for the baby

Film

Show a film on families. On the board list the family members, how they looked, and their roles. Ask the children to make mental comparisons to their own families. Call on some and list their responses on the board. Discuss similarities and differences.

Fingerplay - "My Family"

This is me. (Hold up thumb of right hand)

This is Mother. (Hold up pointer finger)

This is Father Tall. (Hold up middle finger)

This is Brother. (Hold up ring finger)

This is Sister. (Hold up pinky finger)

Oh, I love them all. (Clasp 2 hands together)

Art

Family Booklet

Preparation - Duplicate one of the Family Booklet sheets for each child. On the board demonstrate drawing people and their characteristics in the simplest forms. Provide scissors and crayons.

Procedure - Cut and staple the sheets together to form booklet. Draw and color a picture of your family on the cover sheet. Each day at Activity Time, work on the booklet.

Math

Sets of Family Members

Preparation - Provide old magazines, scissors, glue, and several sheets of mural paper. Draw lines to divide each sheet into squares. Provide one square for each child. Discuss the meaning of a set.

Procedure - Have each child find a picture of a family in the magazine. Cut out and glue in the square. Count the number of family members and write the numeral in the square. Share with the class.

Music - Movement - Games

"Who Is In Your Family?"

Tune - "The Bear Went Over the Mountain"

Oh, who is in your family?

Oh, who is in your family?

Some very special people,

I'm sure that you'll agree.

   I'm sure that you'll agree.

   I'm sure that you'll agree.

   Some very special people

   Are in your family.

(Spoken) Let's clap 1-2-3-4, 1-2-3-4

(Teacher) Okay! Keep clapping! I'm going to call on you to find out who is in your family! But first I'm going to call on myself to show you how!

(Teacher's Name)! Mother, Father, Jack, Susan, and I, (teacher's name)
Continue clapping and call on each child.

Story Time

Book - Papa Small - Lois Lenski

Book - Bedtime for Frances - Russell Hoban

Good Worker Sheet

Brainstorm for ways we help at school and at home. Explain the Good Worker Sheet. Send home the sheet with the explanatory cover letter. When the child returns the bottom portion, show it to the class. Then give the child a Good Worker necklace or any other appropriate reward.

Day 2 - Father

Concept Information

One of your parents is your father. When he was <u>younger</u>,--like you are now, he was a boy. Now he is a man. Every father is different. They look different. Some are tall; some are short. Some fathers have <u>brown</u> hair; some have <u>blonde</u> or <u>red</u>. Your father may like to <u>fish</u> or play <u>golf</u>. Your friend's father may enjoy <u>gardening</u> or watching television. Fathers have different hobbies. Fathers also have different jobs. Some are <u>policemen</u>; some are <u>salesmen</u>; some fathers work in <u>offices</u>; and some work at home.

Your father is not like anyone else's father. He is <u>special</u> just like you! Today we will talk about ways your father is special.

Language Arts - Social Studies

Discussion

Discuss concept and define vocabulary words. Call on children to point out fathers in family snapshots or in family posters. How can they tell the father from other members of the family? Discuss the concept of size. Show the difference in two toys and the difference in a student and you. Talk about the different ways people look. Poll the class for brown-eyed fathers, blue-eyed, blonde hair, etc. Take out clothes from the "Dress Up Box." Which clothes would father wear?

Sharing

Preparation - A week in advance, duplicate and send home the letter explaining the "Family Sharing Time." The day before "Family Sharing Time," send home the second letter. You will be asking for two representative objects from each parent and one from each child. One will represent the family member's hobby or pastime. The second object from each parent will represent his/her occupation. Examples and the delivery procedure are included in the letters.

Procedure - Direct the children to sit in a large circle with paper bags behind them. Call on one child to remove his father's objects from the bag and share them with the class. Encourage the child to elaborate on his father's occupation and hobby. Repeat the procedure for each child. Help the children to recognize similarities and differences. Stress the importance of each parent's occupation.

Note: Family Sharing Time will be continued each day throughout the unit.

Seatwork - "Johnny's Lost" Maze
Duplicate and follow directions as given on the sheet.

Book - The Daddy Book - Robert Steward (Illustrated by Don Madden)
Read the book to the children; go back through the book, encouraging the children to recall the information on each page.

Note: This may be used in correlation with the discussion.

Art

Preparation - Pass out art paper and paint brushes. Mix several colors of tempera paint. Set on tables.

Procedure - Paint a picture of your father doing something he likes to do. Label each picture with the child's explanation.

Math

Father Goes Fishing

Preparation - For each child, cut a twelve-inch length of string. Tie one end of the string to a small cork or a short piece of a drinking straw. Duplicate "Father Goes Fishing" sheet on different colored construction paper. You will need ten fish (one sheet) for each child. Laminate, if desired, and cut out. Punch a hole in each fish. Give each child the string and ten fish of assorted colors.

Procedure - Tell the children, "Father has gone fishing today and look what he has caught!" Put any two fish on your line and direct the children to do the same. Now ask, "How many fish did Father catch?" Call on a child to respond. Ask a child, "What color fish did your father catch? Are they big fish or small fish?" Take the fish off the line and begin again with a different number.

Note: There are many variations of this activity.

1. The teacher may write a numeral on the board or use flash cards to represent how many fish "Father should have on his line."

2. The child may choose how many fish to put on "Father's line" and the class counts them together.

3. The children repeat color patterns, such as red, blue, green, red, blue, green, as directed by the teacher.

4. Basic addition and subtraction may be taught by putting two fish on the line, adding two and counting the total, or by putting four fish on the line, taking away one, and counting the remainder.

Music - Movement - Games

Action Chant

Walk like your father.

Take big steps, big steps.

Walk like your father.

Take great big steps!

    Walk like your mother.

    Take medium steps, medium steps.

    Walk like your mother.

    Take medium steps, too!

Walk like you do.

Take small steps, small steps.

Walk like you do.

Take small steps, whew!

(Repeat replacing walk with run, hop, skip, jump, crawl, and so on.)

Procedure - Children form a circle and chant words as they perform actions.

Song and Flannel Board Activity - "Hush Little Baby"

Preparation - Cut out the flannel board figures. Sing the song, placing the figures on the flannel board. Repeat the song, allowing the children to place the figures on the board.

Note: The words to this song can be found in the book.

    American Folk Songs For Children by Ruth Crawford Seeger or on the following records:

<u>Folk Song Carnival</u> - Hap Palmer

<u>Lollipops and Spaghetti</u> - Miss Jackie (Weissman)

<u>There's A Hippo In My Tub</u> - Anne Murray

<u>Story Time</u>

<u>Book</u> - <u>Just Me and My Dad</u> - Mercer Mayer

<u>Book</u> - <u>Pinocchio</u> - Carlo Collodi

<u>Book</u> - <u>Father Bear Comes Home</u> - Else Holmelund Minarik

<u>Book</u> - <u>What Mary Jo Shared</u> - Janice May Udry

<u>Book</u> - <u>The Bear Scouts</u> - Jan and Stan Berenstain

Day 3 - Mother

Concept Information

One of your parents is your mother. She was once a little girl but now she is a woman. Your mother, along with your father, takes care of you and your brothers and sisters until you are an <u>adult</u>.

Your mother is not like any other mother. She looks different from anyone else and likes to do different things. Some mothers work in an <u>office</u> or a <u>store</u>, and some work at home. Today we will talk about ways your mother is special.

Language Arts - Social Studies

Discussion

Share the concept information and vocabulary definitions. Call on children to point out mothers in family snapshots or in the family poster. Discuss differences in appearance.

Book and Puppet Show - <u>Are You My Mother?</u> - Philip D. Eastman

Read the book. Set a table on its side for the puppet show. Using various hand puppets, take turns re-enacting the story.

Mom's Day at Kindergarten

Preparation - Duplicate the invitations. The children decorate, sign, and take them home. Enlist the children's help in organizing Mom's Day. Explain the purpose of the day is to have Mother join in the daily activities <u>just like she is a student</u>. Each child will be his or her mother's "student helper." The schedule will be the same, but the children help choose the activities. Be sure to choose the mothers as helpers, to answer questions, to run errands, and so on.

Examples for Activity Time:

a. Art Station - paper weave place mats

b. Manipulatives Table - clay, puzzles, pegboards

c. Listening Station - story record "The Wolf and the Seven Kids" - Brothers Grimm

d. Large Blocks - build a house

e. Sand Table

f. Housekeeping

g. Learning Centers - Learning Games

Procedure - Divide into groups and move in a circular direction. Post a number card in each area to signify "the capacity" of each activity.

Mother Shares

At the beginning of school, send home the Parent Helper explanation and information sheet. Find a mother with an interesting hobby or job to share. Prearrange a time for the mother to come to the class. Be sure to send home guidelines for her to follow. Explanations should be simple and discussions short. Demonstrations whenever possible should be followed by some kind of group participation. Cake decorating is an excellent hobby for this activity. Others can be found on the Parent Helper Sheet.

Note: Encourage this parent participation all year long. Read over the returned information sheets and insert Parent Helpers throughout your yearly plans.

Sharing

Repeat Day 2 procedure using the objects of each child's mother.

Art

A Jar For Mom

Preparation - From cardboard cut out a jar pattern for every three or four children. Provide white construction paper, scissors, and crayons. Draw a finished jar on the board.

Procedure - Brainstorm for things which we can put in jars. Encourage the unusual, such as rainbows, flowers, animals, etc. Choose something to put in your jar and demonstrate on the board. "We are going to make jars for Mom." The children should fill the jar with whatever they wish to give their mothers. It should be different from the ones on the board.

Note: The children can make name tags to tie around the neck of the jar from scrap paper and yarn.

Paper Weave Place Mats

Preparation - Supply scissors, glue, and two pieces of 9" x 12" construction paper for each child. Provide a variety of colors so that the children may choose. Demonstrate the whole procedure once. The class should do each step together.

Procedure - Fold one sheet of the construction paper in half widthwise. Cut the folded paper beginning at the folded edge and stopping about an inch before the paper's edge. Unfold the paper. This will be the loom. Now cut 9" (lengthwise) strips from the remaining piece of construction paper. The strips do not need to be perfectly straight or the same width. Weave or "thread" the loose strips over and under, over and under, the strips of the loom. If the first strip started under the edge of the loom, the next strip will start over the edge, or vice versa. When the place mat is completely woven, the ends should be glued to both sides.

<u>Math</u>

<u>Mother's Flower Pots</u>

Preparation - Duplicate a sheet for each child. Provide crayons, scissors, and glue.

Procedure - Follow the directions on the sheet.

<u>Fingerplay</u> - "Five Little Ducks"

Five little ducks went out to play (Hold up 5 fingers)

Over the hill and far away. (Walk hand up and down)

When the mother duck said, "Quack, quack, quack," (Other hand - open
                                        and close fingers to thumb)
Four little ducks came waddling back. (4 fingers walking)

(Repeat each time, decreasing number by one until no ducks come waddling

back. Crisscross hands and shake head for none.)

<u>Music</u> - <u>Movement</u> - <u>Games</u>

<u>Action Song</u> - "Mother's Cleaning Day"

Tune - "Here We Go Round the Mulberry Bush"

   Today is Mother's cleaning day.

   Today is Mother's cleaning day.

   Today is Mother's cleaning day,

   And everybody helps.

      This is the way we wash the clothes,

      Wash the clothes, wash the clothes.

      This is the way we wash the clothes

      So early Monday morning.

(Continue singing and acting out using standard verses.)

<u>Game</u> - "Mother, May I?"

Choose one child to play "Mother." The children stand side by side in a line about fifteen feet in front of "Mother." "Mother" calls on each child, giving directions such as "Take one giant step," "Turn around," "Take two baby steps," and so forth. The child must then ask, "Mother, may I?" to which "Mother replies, "Yes, you may." If a child forgets to say "Mother, may I?", he or she must return to the starting line. The first child to reach "Mother" is the new mother, or the teacher may choose someone to take "Mother's" place.

<u>Story Time</u>

<u>Book</u> - <u>Little Bear</u> - Else Holmelund Minarik

<u>Book</u> - <u>Even If I Did Something Awful?</u> - Barbara S. Hazen

<u>Book</u> - <u>My Mom Got a Job</u> - Lucia B. Smith

<u>Kindergarten Kitchen</u>

<u>Mom's Poppy Seed Loaves</u>

Read <u>The Little Red Hen</u>. Then follow the cooking procedure as outlined in the Introduction.

2 cups self-rising flour

1 1/2 cups granulated sugar

2 eggs

1/2 oz. almond extract

3/4 cup oil

1 cup milk

1/8 cup of poppy seeds

Preheat oven to 350°. Mix all ingredients well and pour into two greased and floured loaf pans. Cook for 45-60 minutes.

Day 4 - Brothers and Sisters

Concept Information

The other children in your family are your brothers and sisters. If you have a brother, he is a boy. He may be <u>older</u> than you or <u>younger</u> than you. If you have a sister, she is a girl. She, too, may be older or younger than you are. Two brothers or sisters who are born on the same day are called twins. Twins can be two boys, two girls, or a boy and a girl.

Your brothers and sisters may look like you or look very different. Brothers and sisters play together and work together. Sometimes brothers and sisters <u>disagree</u>, like all people. Brothers and sisters are special people, too!

Language Arts - Social Studies

Discussion

Discuss concept information and define vocabulary words. Call on children to point out brothers and sisters in family snapshots or in family posters. Discuss how they are different.

Book - <u>I'll Fix Anthony</u> - Judith Viorst
Read and discuss the book.

Poem - "For Sale" - Shel Silverstein
Read and show the illustrations of Shel Silverstein's poem "For Sale" from the book <u>Where the Sidewalk Ends</u>. Discuss why the boy is selling his sister. How do they each feel?

Experience Chart

On an experience chart, list the activities the children enjoy with their brothers and sisters. Examples: We play ball together. We like to make a tent from sheets.

On another sheet list reasons why brothers and sisters disagree. Examples: We argue over toys. My brother sometimes treats me like a baby.

Initiate a discussion on relationships. Guide the children to explore the different aspects of relationships, reasons for disagreements, and solutions to problems. Divide the class into two groups to "illustrate" each experience chart.

Transparency Activity

Call on a child and ask, "How many brothers and sisters do you have?" Determine the ages of the brothers and sisters. Using wipe-off markers, draw simple figures on the transparency to represent each child in the family. Write names under each figure, color their hair and eyes, and add an object to signify their interests. Encourage the class to note similarities and differences in appearances and pastimes.

Repeat with each child. If time is limited, the activity may be continued by the children at Activity Time.

Sharing

Repeat Day 2 procedure, using the objects of each child's brothers and sisters.

Art

Super Pilots

Preparation - This game is to be taken home for brothers and sisters to share. For each child provide one small paper bag, two pieces of string (each nine feet long), two paper cups, tagboard for wings, scissors, and glue. Duplicate and send home instruction sheet with the game. Assembly procedure is included in case additional plans are needed.

Procedure - Have the child write his or her name on the paper bag and put aside. In the bottom of each cup, punch a hole about a half inch from the edge. Cut a rectangular wing for each plane and glue on top of the cup. Thread one piece of string through the hole. Repeat this procedure for the other plane. Place both planes in the paper bag.

Playing the Game - Use the sample planes for class participation. Tie the strings (at chin level) between two chairs, trees, or poles. Two children race the planes by blowing into the open ends of the paper cups. The Super Pilot who reaches the end of the string first is the winner.

Math

How Many Kids?

Place large number cards, one through ten, about two feet apart on the floor. Ask the children, "How many kids are in your family? Keep the number in mind." Direct them to line up behind the corresponding numeral card. Once everyone is lined up, have each child name the children in the family as the class counts aloud. An abacus can also be used to help with counting.

Song - "I Get a Nice Feeling" - Sesame Street <u>Tenth Anniversary Album</u>

Game - "The Wolf and the Kids"

Use chalk, tape, or ropes as a line at each end of the play area. Choose one child to be the mother and another to be the wolf. The other children are the kids. The mother stands behind one line and the kids behind the opposite line. The wolf stands in the middle of the play area. The mother says, "Kids! Kids! Come home for dinner!" The kids reply, "We can't! We can't! The wolf will get us!" The mother answers, "Run as fast as you can!"

The wolf chases the kids as they run home. Any kids who are caught become wolves and help catch more kids as the game is repeated.

Story Time

Book - <u>The Cat in the Hat</u> - (Theodore Geisel) Dr. Seuss

Book - <u>When the New Baby Comes, I'm Moving Out</u> - Martha Alexander

Book - <u>When Everyone Was Fast Asleep</u> - Tomie De Paola

Book - <u>Hey, Don't Do That!</u> - Irene Heiz

Day 5 - The Home

Concept Information

The place where your family lives is called your <u>home</u>. Your home may be a <u>house</u>, an <u>apartment</u>, or a <u>mobile home</u>. Long ago, people lived in <u>caves</u>. <u>Indians</u> lived in <u>tepees</u>. Even today some <u>Eskimos</u> live in <u>igloos</u>.

We need homes to <u>protect</u> us from the <u>weather</u> and from <u>danger</u>. Also, a home is the place where our families work and play together.

Language Arts - Social Studies

Discussion

Share the concept information and define vocabulary words. Show pictures of different homes; Including Oscar the Grouch (trash can), Tarzan (tree house), and the possibility of living in outer space. Ask the children to tell about their homes.

Display an empty dollhouse. Call on children to name the rooms in the house and the function of each. Choose a child to pick a piece of furniture or household item, name it, tell its use, and put it in the correct room.

Block Walk

If your school is in a residential area, take the class for a walk around the block. Point out the different kinds of homes. Encourage observations of size, color, and so on. When you return, divide the class into groups. Each group uses blocks to build one of the homes they saw on the walk.

Fingerplay - "A Good House"

This is the roof of the house so good   (Make roof with hands)

These are the walls that are made of wood   (Hands straight, palms parallel)

These are the windows that let in the light   (Thumbs and forefingers form window)

This is the door that shuts so tight   (Hands straight side by side)

This is the chimney so straight and tall   (Arms up straight)

Oh!   What a good house for one and all.   (Arms at angle for roof)

Fingerplay - "Different Homes"

A sparrow's home is a nest in a tree,
    (Cup one hand, palm-up; perch other hand on edge)

An octopus' home is a cave beneath the sea.
    (Hook thumbs together; wiggle fingers)

In a hole in the ground a little rabbit hides,
    (Close fingers around thumb; slowly lift thumb, straighten,
    bend a little)

A sunflower is where a little gnome resides.
    (Palm flat, spread fingers, palm-up; perch other hand in center)

A hollowed-out log is for the porcupine,
    (Placed cupped palm palm-down on table; move other fist inside)

But the best home of all is the one that's mine.
    (Point to chest)

Flannel Board Story - "The House That Nobody Wanted"

From Story Telling With The Flannel Board (Book II) - Paul S. Anderson

Art

Houses

Preparation - Provide construction paper in a variety of colors.   Each child will need one sheet in the color of his or her choice and a pair of scissors.

Procedure - Fold the paper widthwise. The fold will be at the top and the open end at the bottom. Cut off the two corners at the top of the folded sheet as shown. This will make the roof of the house. Draw the windows and doors, etc., and color the outside. Open the house and draw a picture of your family inside.

Box House

Preparation - Obtain a large appliance box. Cut windows and a door. If a peaked roof is desired, tape two squares of cardboard together and tape or staple to sides.

Procedure - The house can be decorated in a variety of ways. "Bricks" can be cut from red paper and glued to the box. The walls can be colored with crayons, markers, or tempera. You may wish to make shingles for the roof or simply cover with brown paper. This is a good project for small groups at Activity Time.

Math

Counting Houses

Preparation - You will need fifty-five tongue depressors for ten houses (one through ten), ten milk cartons with the tops cut off, tempera paint, dishwashing liquid, crayons, white paper, and glue. Mix a small amount of dishwashing liquid with the tempera so the paint will stick to the cartons.

Procedure - Divide the class into groups to work on different parts of the project or, if you prefer, provide a milk carton and tongue depressors for each child. Paint the milk cartons. Cut out windows and doors from white paper. Write numerals on the doors. Glue on the "houses." Color faces on the tongue depressors. Line the houses up. Take turns putting the correct number of people in the Counting Houses.

Music - Movement - Games

Relation Song - "Up Goes the Castle" - Sesame Street Every Body's Record
Sing and follow the directions.

Story Time

Book - The Little House - Virginia Burton

Book - In a People House - Theodore LeSieg

Concept Review - Guessing Game

Ask questions concerning the concept information of the unit by giving the clues to the answers. Examples:

1. I am thinking of a member of your family who is a man. Who is he?

2. I am thinking of the place where you live with your family. What is it?

Concept Evaluation - (See Introduction)

Dear Parents,

On _____, we will begin our unit on "The Family." We will learn about family members and the home through discussions, songs, films, fingerplays, etc. Below are ways you can help.

Things to Send: _____

_____

_____

Ways to Volunteer: _____

_____

_____

Follow-Up Activities: At the end of the unit, ask your child to share these songs, poems, fingerplays, etc.

_____

_____

_____

Thank you for your cooperation.

Sincerely,

Dear Parents,

Next week our unit of study will be "The Family." On _____
                                                        (day)
_____, we will begin having "Family Sharing Time." During this time,
  (date)
we will discuss our family members--their occupations and hobbies. Your

child will need to bring the following:

1. An object which represents Father's work. (Examples: carpenter
    - nail; salesman - sales slip; policeman - whistle)

2. An object which represents Mother's work. (Examples:
    housewife - wooden spoon; teacher - red pencil; secretary
    - paper clip)

3. For each person in the household, an object which represents his
    or her favorite hobby or pastime. (Examples: Father likes to
    fish - cork; Mother likes to take pictures - film box; Joey likes
    to play baseball - baseball; Susie likes to paint - brush; Baby
    likes bathtime - rubber duck)

Please send these objects in a heavy paper sack. Label the outside

with the child's name and a list of the objects. Please do not send

anything which is fragile or valuable. The objects will be returned at the

end of the week.

I will brief the children on the nature of this activity. However, you

may want to discuss with your child what each object represents so that

he or she will feel comfortable at our sharing time.

Thank you for your cooperation.

Sincerely,

P.S. If you have not done so, please send the family snapshot.

- -

Dear Parents,

A reminder that tomorrow is our "Family Sharing Time." Your child
should bring two objects representing each parent's occupation and an
object for each family member's hobby or pastime. Please don't forget to
label the sack with the child's name and a list of the objects.

Sincerely,

103

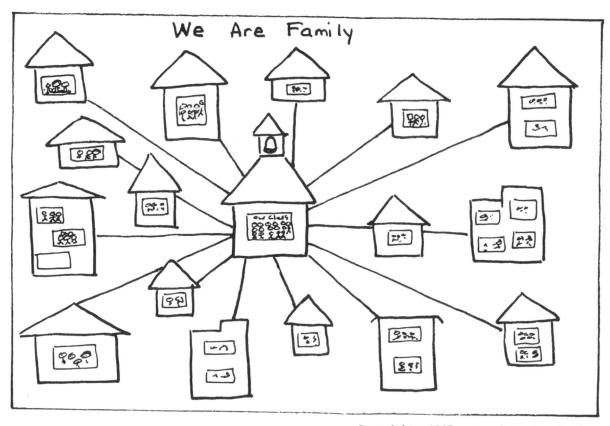

 Copyright © 1987. Carol Taylor Bond

WELCOME

Copyright © 1987. Carol Taylor Bond

105

My Family

Father

Mother

Brothers

106

Copyright © 1987.   Carol Taylor Bond

Sisters

Our Home

Grandparents

Pets

107 Copyright © 1987. Carol Taylor Bond

Dear Parents,

This week we are learning about "The Family," and the importance of sharing work as well as play. Attached is the "Good Worker" sheet for your child. Please post it in a prominent place such as your refrigerator or bulletin board.

For each day there is a job for your child to do. (Jobs can be switched to different days if it is more convenient.) As your child completes a task, draw a "smiley face" in the space provided. When he or she has completed a job for each day, please sign and clip the bottom portion <u>only</u> and return to me.

You can continue to use the "Good Worker" sheet at home until each space is filled with "smiley faces."

Thank you for your cooperation.

Sincerely,

Good Worker Sheet

Day	Chore	
Sunday	Go to bed when I'm told	
Monday	Try one food I do not like	
Tuesday	Set the table for a family meal	
Wednesday	Ask Mother what I can do to help (Mother's Free Choice)	
Thursday	Take out the garbage	
Friday	One outside chore (sweep, get mail, water plants, etc.)	
Saturday	Clean up my room without being told	

_____ has completed every
child's name

chore on this list!

_____
Parent's Signature

 Copyright © 1987. Carol Taylor Bond

110

Copyright © 1987. Carol Taylor Bond

Johnny's Lost!   Help Daddy Find Him!

Use a crayon to find the path from
Daddy to Johnny - then color them.

111   Copyright © 1987.   Carol Taylor Bond

Copyright © 1987. Carol Taylor Bond

Copyright © 1987. Carol Taylor Bond

113

Copyright © 1987. Carol Taylor Bond

Hush, Little Baby

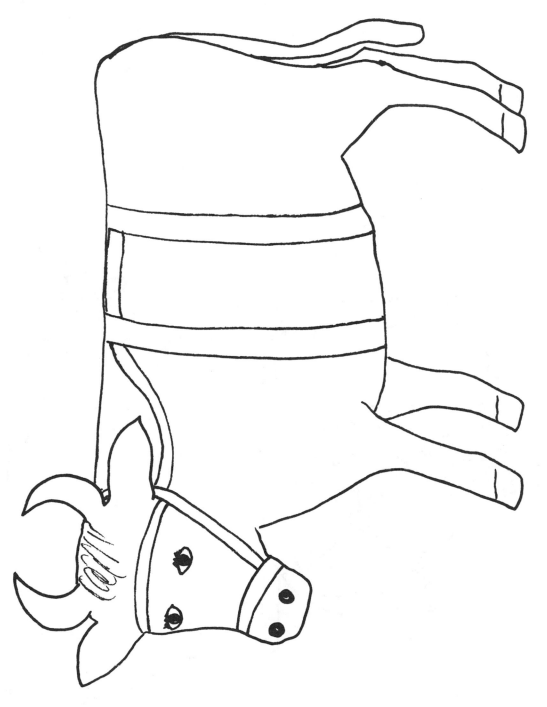

Copyright © 1987. Carol Taylor Bond

Reverse for Horse →

Copyright © 1987. Carol Taylor Bond

Hush, Little Baby

117

Copyright ©1987. Carol Taylor Bond

Calling All Moms !

Join Us For Mom's Day at School

Be a Student for a Day !

Date: _____   Time: _____

R.S.V.P.   Love,

Copyright © 1987. Carol Taylor Bond

Information Sheet

This is for my personal files on your child. Please fill out and return on the first day or as soon as possible. Thank you!

Name of Child _____ Birthdate _____
(month, day, year)

Name Child Goes By _____

Name of Mother _____ Occupation _____

Name of Father _____ Occupation _____

Address _____ Home Phone _____

Work No. - Mother _____ Father _____

If your child gets sick or hurt at school and I cannot reach you at the above numbers, I should call _____

Phone No. _____

Describe your child's personality (strengths, areas needing improvement)

_____

_____

_____

Your Child's Favorite Activities _____

_____

Responsibilities at Home _____

The Best Way You've Found to Discipline Your Child _____

_____

Allergies or Special Conditions _____

Parent Helpers - List any activities you would like to share with our class:

_____

_____

_____

When are you available to share with our class? (Days and Hours)

How You Can Help

Dear Parents,

Some of the best learning experiences are "real." Children learn so much more by seeing a baby duck or cooking and tasting pumpkin pie than by seeing pictures.

When we cook in _____, the children use their senses to see,
　　　　　　　　　　　　(grade)
touch, and taste ingredients; develop language with new vocabulary words; learn the concept of measurement; and many other prereading skills. Besides all of this, they enjoy it and, therefore, are more attentive.

In the past, I have asked if parents have any hobbies or occupations which they could share with our class. Some parents have felt their occupations or hobbies are not interesting enough, etc.; so I want to explain this in detail.

First some examples:

If you farm or plant a garden each year, you could bring the different seeds and tools to our class and demonstrate planting a seed (during our Plants unit).

If you drive a truck, you could drive it here and let the children see it. We could name the different parts, etc. (during our Transportation unit).

If you like to tell stories, we could set aside a time for you before naptime or at one of our parties. I read where one Mom dressed up as a friendly witch and came to the Halloween Party. If you're a housewife, you could describe the duties you have (during our Family unit) or cook your specialty in our classroom (fruitcake during our Christmas unit, corn bread, during our Thanksgiving unit--or we could coordinate your recipe with the Alphabet letter we're learning that week, such as Apple Pie during "A" week).

If you're an amateur or professional carpenter, you could bring your tools (the children love to look at these) and demonstrate building something simple (during our Community Helper Unit). If you're good with makeup, you could put clown faces on the kids (Circus unit), Indian warpaint (Thanksgiving), or Bunny faces (Easter).

If you decorate cakes, we'd love to watch. If you play a musical instrument, we can listen and maybe sing along. If you make your own Christmas wreaths, Easter baskets, etc., a short demonstration would be great! If your dog has puppies, your duck has ducklings, and so on, we'd love to see.

In other words, you need not be an expert to share with our class. Just let me know if you have something to share or any ideas. We'll work out a time and date, etc. Also, I'll give you some loose guidelines on what to do. This is_____ so we will keep it short and simple.
                    (grade)

Below is a list of the weekly units we will have this year:

We look forward to seeing you this year!

                    Sincerely,

Copyright © 1987. Carol Taylor Bond

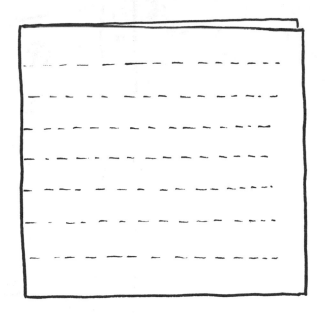

Paper Weave Place Mats

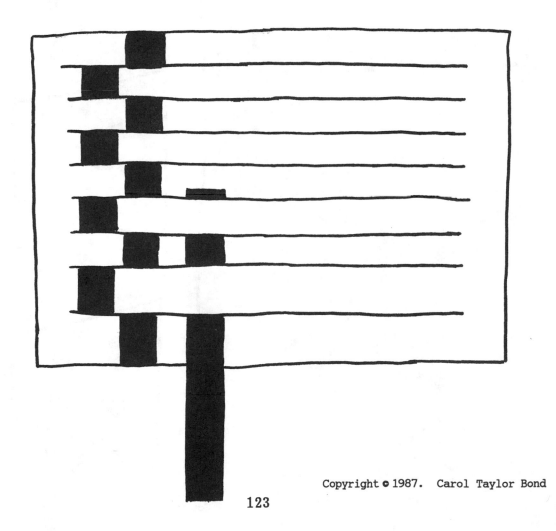

Copyright © 1987. Carol Taylor Bond

123

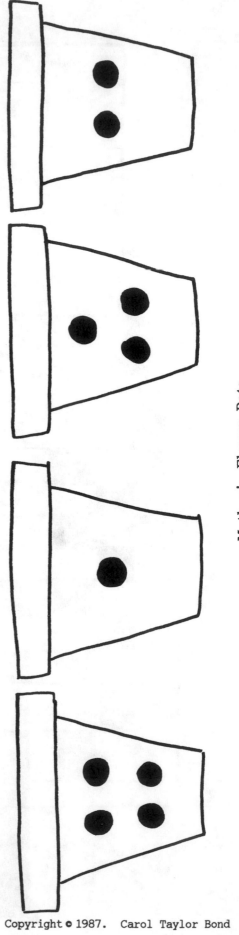

Mother's Flower Pots

124

Copyright © 1987. Carol Taylor Bond

Mother's Flower Pots

Help Mother plant the flowers in the correct pot. Cut out the flowers.
Glue to the pot with the same number of dots as the flower's petals.
Color.

Copyright © 1987. Carol Taylor Bond

Super Pilot Game

<u>Game Instructions</u> - Tie each child's string (and plane) at chin level between two chairs, trees, or posts. Slide both planes to the starting position. The children race to the end of the string by blowing in the open end of the cup. The Super Pilot who finishes first wins.

<u>To Make Additional Games</u> - Cut a nine-inch piece of string. Punch a hole in the bottom of the cup about a half inch from the edge. This will be the top of the plane. Cut wings from tagboard or cardboard and glue to the top of the plane. Thread string through hole.

Construction Paper Houses

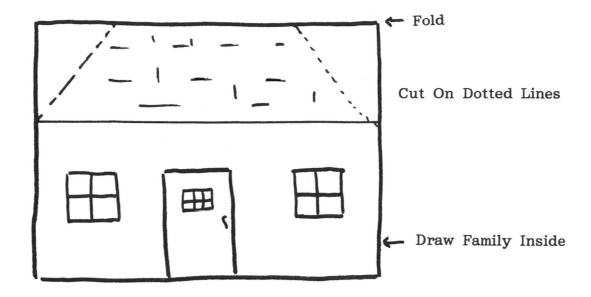

← Fold

Cut On Dotted Lines

← Draw Family Inside

Counting Houses

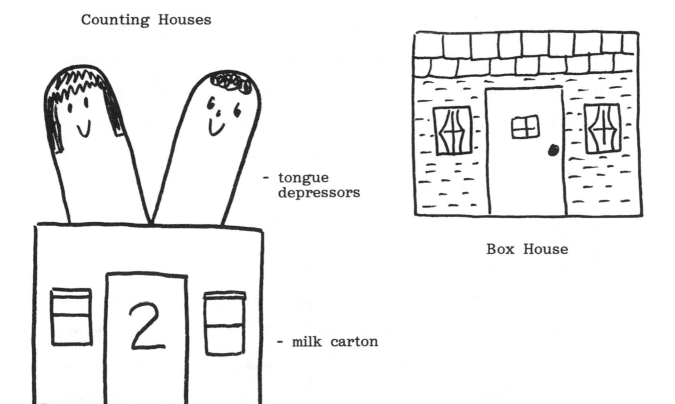

- tongue depressors

- milk carton

Box House

Copyright © 1987.   Carol Taylor Bond

127

The Five Senses

<u>Proposed Time</u>: 5 days

<u>Unit Objectives</u>

To define the five senses

To develop understanding of the senses and their corresponding body parts

To instill the importance of the senses in our daily lives

<u>Room Environment</u> - <u>Bulletin Boards</u>

"My Five Senses"

From tagboard make a large eye, ear, nose, tongue, and hand. At the top, label the bulletin board "My Five Senses." Mount the pictures in a line across the bulletin board, varying the heights of each. Staple pieces of colored yarn (or use colored tape) from each picture to the bottom of the bulletin board. Position a table below the bulletin board. Place objects relating to each picture on the table. For example: under the eye put a view master, a magnifying glass, a microscope, pictures of different scenes, and objects to examine. Under the ear put rhythm instruments, sound boxes (see Day 2), a tape of sounds, and a tape recorder.

"My Senses At Work"

Place the title in the middle of the bulletin board. Use large yarn to divide the bulletin board into five wedges. Make and mount an eye, ear, hand, tongue, and nose in each wedge. Direct the children to find pictures of things we see, hear, feel, smell, and taste from old magazines or catalogs. Glue on construction pieces and staple in the appropriate area.

Variation: For the "Touch Area," distribute squares of paper and direct the children to glue on objects with different textures such as cotton, macaroni, sandpaper. For the "Smell Area," spread glue on squares of paper and sprinkle with spices.

"Things We Like to Taste" - (Wall or Door Display)

Cut a large "plate" out of poster paper. Write the title in the middle. Direct each child to cut out a picture of a favorite food from an old magazine and glue on the "plate." Each child should write his or her name under his or her choice.

Note: This activity may be extended to include "Things We Like to See" (on a large eye), "Things We Like to Hear" (on a large ear), and so forth.

Day 1 - Introduction and Sight

Concept Information

(Introduction)

Each one of us has five senses. These five senses are sight, sound, touch, smell, and taste. Our eyes are used for sight or to see. We use our noses to smell and our ears to hear sounds. Our fingers are used to touch and our tongues to taste. We enjoy the world around us with our senses.

(Sight)

Today we will learn about the sense called sight. You see because your eyes work like cameras, but even better. Look at the person next to you. You can see this person because all the parts of your eyes are working together. With your eyes, you can see the size, color, and shape of things.

Language Arts - Social Studies - Science

(Introduction)

Discussion

Relate the Introductory concept information and define vocabulary words. Pass around a scented candle. Discuss how it looks, feels, and smells. Place the candle in an ashtray and light it. Encourage the children to observe and discuss how the candle looks, smells, and what changes are occurring. Pass around an apple or an orange. Discuss the color, shape, smell, and texture. Cut apples or oranges into quarters and give each child a piece. Observe the inside, then eat the fruit.

Book

Read My Five Senses by Aliki.

Films

Most Important Person Series "My Five Senses" by Sutherland Learning Associates, Inc., distributed by Encyclopedia Britannica.

This kit includes the films "My Five senses," "Seeing," "Hearing," "Tasting," "Touching," and "Smelling."

Fingerplay - "My Five Senses"

I have two eyes that see.   (Point to eyes)

I have a nose to smell.   (Point to nose)

I have two hands that feel.   (Hold up hands)

My tongue can taste so well.   (Point to tongue)

I have two ears that hear   (Point to ears)

And now I know you see   (Point to other person)

That my five senses   (Hold up five fingers)

Are very special to me.   (Point to self)

Poem - "Senses" by Shel Silverstein from A Light in the Attic

Make simple stick puppets of an eye, an ear, and a nose.   Use a hamburger box to make the mouth puppet.   Let four children act out the poem as you read it.   Repeat the procedure so others can participate.

Discussion

Share the concept information on Sight and define vocabulary words. Show a simple diagram of the eye and briefly explain the functions of the main parts.   Discuss things we see each day.

Overhead Projector - "What's Missing?"

Using wipe-off markers, draw simple objects on a transparency. Omit one part of the object such as the stem of an apple, the trunk of the elephant, and so on. Call on a child to identify what is missing on each object.

Book - Look Again! by Tana Hoban

Let the children guess the object from the revealed portion of the photograph. Then show the full photographs that follow.

Outline Game

While the children are out of the room, outline simple objects on the board, such as an eraser, a pencil, a ruler, a book, and a roll of tape. Put the objects back in or near their usual places. Ask a child to guess the object from the outline, find the object and fit it in the outline.

Art

Big Eye

Preparation - Duplicate the "Big Eye" sheet. Give each child a sheet, a 3" x 1" piece of black construction paper and a half sheet of different colored construction paper. Provide scissors and glue.

Procedure - Color the pupil black and the iris the color of your eyes. Cut out the two parts on the sheet. Glue the iris and pupil between the eyelids of the other part. Glue the "eye" on the half sheet of construction paper. Cut lashes from the black paper and glue on the top and bottom eyelids.

"Art in the Dark"

Preparation - Use the strips of an old sheet for blindfolds. Provide drawing paper and crayons.

Procedure - Blindfold the children and direct them to draw a face. Take off the blindfolds and share the results.

Variation: After the blindfolds are removed, direct the children to draw another face. Compare both pictures.

Eye Creatures

Preparation - Purchase plastic "wiggle" eyes at a hobby store. Provide paper and crayons or markers and glue.

Procedure - Glue the eyes on the paper. Make up a creature and draw around the eyes. Color in the creature. Share with the class.

Note: Gummed reinforcements may be used for the eyes.

Math

The Balloon Man

Duplicate the "Balloon Man" sheet for the follow-up activity. After the blackboard activity, pass out the sheets and crayons. Use colored chalk to draw the figures as you tell the following story. Let the children erase, and respond to questions. "The Balloon Man lives in a little house near the park. He enjoys blowing up balloons and giving them away to children. How many balloons has he blown up? The Balloon Man walks to the park. He gives one red balloon to Tommy for being nice to his little brother. (Erase one balloon.) How many balloons are left? Then he gives a pretty yellow balloon to Tommy's little brother. (Erase one balloon.) Now how many balloons does the Balloon Man have?"

Continue the story by having the Balloon Man give away all the balloons. Several balloons may "escape" into the air. End the story with the Balloon Man going home and blowing up more balloons for tomorrow.

Follow-Up - On the sheet count the balloons, and write the number on the line. Color the Balloon Man and the Balloons.

Music - Movement - Games

Song - "The Bear Went Over the Mountain"
Note: This song can be found on Disney's Children's Favorites, Volume II.

Game - "I Spy"
The children close their eyes while one child looks around the area and chooses an object. He or she then says, "I spy with my little eye something that is red (any color)." The children look around and try to guess the object. The child who guesses correctly gets to "spy" the next object.
Variation: An object may be identified by shape or by the beginning letter.

Story Time

Book - The Look Book - Jane Belk Moncure

Book - Flicks - Tomie de Paola

Book - Hugo and the Man Who Stole Colors - Tony Ross

Sharing Time

Send home the explanatory letter. The children bring objects from home to share with the class.

Day 2 - Sound

Concept Information

We hear sounds with our ears. The outside part of the ear which we can see helps <u>gather</u> in the sounds. The most important parts of the ear are inside the head. These parts let you hear sounds which are soft like a kitten's "meow" or loud like a fire engine's <u>siren</u>. We also hear sounds that are high, like some <u>alarm clocks</u>, or low, like the <u>hum</u> of the refrigerator, and sounds which we enjoy, like music, or sounds that we don't enjoy, such as <u>lawn mowers</u>.

<u>Language Arts</u> - <u>Social Studies</u> - <u>Science</u>

Discussion

Relate the concept information and define vocabulary words. Read and discuss the book <u>Sounds All Around</u> by Jane Belk Moncure.

<u>Seatwork</u> - Sounds Sheet

Duplicate and distribute the sheet. Provide crayons. Direct the children to circle in red the loud sounds and circle in blue the soft sounds.

Tape Activity

Use a tape recorder to tape sounds such as an alarm clock, a car starting, water dripping, a baby crying, a dog barking, and so on. Play the tape for the children. Call on different children to identify the sounds.

Note: This activity may be introduced by reading <u>Crash! Bang! Boom!</u> by Peter Spier.

Listening Exercise - I'm Hungry"

Choose one child to be Mr. or Miss Hungry, one child to be Mr. Restaurant Owner, and one child to be Mr. Cook. Mr. or Miss Hungry calls Mr. Restaurant Owner on an imaginary or play phone and places an order of three or four items for dinner. Mr. Restaurant Owner repeats the order to Mr. Cook. Mr. Cook repeats the order so he can remember what to cook. The phone call is terminated and three other children repeat the activity.

Following Directions

Give each child a paper plate, a chair, and directions as follows:
Place the paper plate over your head.
Hold the paper plate by your side.
Sit down and put the paper plate on your head.
Put the paper plate under your chair.
Stand up and hold the paper plate in front of your chest.
Place the paper plate on the seat of your chair.

Art - Rhythm Instruments

Preparation - Gather and provide materials for instruments. All of them may be decorated.

Procedure - (Horn) - Cover one end of a paper towel roll with a square of waxed paper. Secure with a rubber band. Make a hole in the roll approximately two inches from the opposite end. Hold the open end over the mouth and hum into the roll.

(Guitar) - Stretch three or four rubber bands over a shoe box (without the top). Pluck or strum the rubber bands.

(Shakers) - Staple together the edges of two paper plates so that they face each other. Leave an opening in which to insert dried peas or beans. Staple shut and shake. Or place dried beans or peas in an empty orange juice can. Tape the top shut and shake.

(Drum) - Tape shut the top of an oatmeal box. Use hand or a stick to beat the drum.

(Tambourine) - Staple together two paper plates so that they face each other. Punch holes at the edges around the plates. Punch holes in cold drink caps with a hammer and nail. String plastic-coated wire through the two or three caps and then through the holes in the plates. Twist to secure. Shake the tambourine and hit it with the palm of the hand.

Note: The children can all make the same instrument, or they can make different ones. Pipe cleaners can be used rather than wire.

The Moaning Stick

Preparation - Cut a piece of corrugated cardboard 2" x 7" for each child. Punch a hole in the center of one of the 2" sides. Provide the cardboard pieces, markers or crayons, and a piece of string about a yard long.

Procedure - Decorate the piece of cardboard. Push one end of the string through the hole and tie in a knot. Hold the other end of the string in one hand. Swing the Moaning Stick around in circles above the head.

Big Ear

Preparation - Duplicate and pass out the sheet, crayons, scissors, glue, and a sheet of construction paper.

Procedure - Cut out both parts of the ear. Color the ear opening black, and glue onto the ear. Then glue the completed ear on the sheet of construction paper.

Note: Pictures of things which make sounds may be glued around the ear.

Math

Ping Counting

Direct the children to close their eyes and count along with the "pings" (sounds). Drop one dried bean at a time into a tin pie plate. Vary the number of beans. Then have the children silently count the beans, and call on a child to tell how many beans were dropped.

Book - Oh, What a Noise! by Uri Shulevitz

Read the book. Go back through the book and let the children count the creatures on each page. Call on different children to respond by counting aloud.

Music - Movement - Games

Song - "Listen" - Every Body's Record - Sesame Street Records

Rhythm Instruments

Introduction - Introduce and play three or four rhythm instruments at a time. Have the children shut their eyes. Play one instrument and ask, "What is it?" Repeat until all instruments are introduced.

Procedure - Pass out the instruments and let the children practice playing them. Put on a record and demonstrate how to follow the beat. Let the children play to the music. Cues may be given for certain instruments to play alone.

<u>Action Song</u> - "The Teacher Who Couldn't Talk" and "Percussions" from <u>Creative Movement and Rhythmic Expression</u> by Hap Palmer

The children perform the actions as directed.

<u>Story Time</u>

<u>Book</u> - <u>Harry and the Lady Next Door</u> - Gene Zion

<u>Book</u> - <u>Drummer Hoff</u> - Adapted by Barbara Emberley

<u>Listening Walk</u>

Take the class on a Listening Walk through the school and around the school grounds. Emphasize that the children are to "collect sounds." When you return, call on each child to tell a sound he or she heard. On experience chart paper or the board list these in columns labeled "Inside Noises" and "Outside Noises."

Day 3 - Touch

Concept Information

We use our hands to touch or feel things. But we also have the sense of touch in all of the skin which covers our bodies, inside our mouths, and inside our bodies. Because of our sense of touch, we feel pressure and pain, textures, and heat and cold.

Language Arts - Social Studies - Science

Discussion

Relate the concept information and define vocabulary words. Read and discuss the book The Touch Book by Jane Belk Moncure.

Feely Boxes

Cover plastic frosting containers or margarine tubs with discarded socks. The containers will be in the foot part of the sock. In each container place different objects, such as: cotton balls, a pair of blunt-end scissors, rocks, dried beans, and rubber bands. Use tape to label the outside of each Feely Box with the initials or abbreviations of the contents. One child puts his or her hand in one Feely Box and guesses the contents. Variation: Place the two like objects and one different object in one Feely Box. The child feels all of the objects and names the two which are alike and the one which is different.

Poem Activity - "Sticky Is" - Author Unknown

Cut out pictures from old workbooks of the things mentioned in the poem. After reading the poem, hold up each picture. The children recall the descriptive word in the poem used for each. Examples: pudding - smooth; icicles - sharp.

Sticky is the paint Daddy put on the door.

Sticky is the chewing gum dropped on the floor.

Soft are the marshmallows so round and white.

Soft is the pillow for my head at night.

Smooth is the ice on which you skate.

Smooth is the pudding which you just ate.

Hard is the carrot on which you crunch.

Hard is the lollipop to lick after lunch.

Hot is the soup when your first sip you take.

Hot is the oven when a cake's to bake.

Sharp are the quills of a porcupine.

Sharp are the icicles in winter you find.

Rough are the edges of a sharp toothed saw.

Rough is Daddy's beard all around his jaw.

Seatwork - "Hard and Soft Sheet"

Duplicate a sheet for each child. Provide glue and cotton balls. Take the class outside to pick up small rocks. Each child puts a "puddle" of glue in the center of each block. The rock should be placed in the glue in the "Hard" block, and the cotton ball should be placed in the glue in the "Soft" block.

Art

Pudding Painting

Preparation - Prepare two large boxes of instant chocolate pudding. Provide fingerpainting paper.

Procedure - Use the pudding to fingerpaint. Discuss how the pudding feels. Divide and serve the remaining pudding.

Note: Substitute styrofoam meat trays for the paper. The children spread the pudding over the surface of the tray, then practice writing names, alphabet letters or numerals (with one finger) on the tray.

"Hands Are For Feeling"

Preparation - Provide scraps of nylon net, carpet, lace, cotton balls, packing "squiggles," paper doilies, and uncooked macaroni. Mix white tempera paint to a thin consistency and pour into a spray bottle. Give each child a sheet of different colored 12" x 18" construction paper, glue, and scissors.

Procedure - The child places one hand in the middle of the paper. The teacher sprays the paint on the sheet covering the child's hand. The child removes his or her hand. Allow the paint to dry while the children clean up. The children choose different scraps or materials to glue around the hand.

Math

Sand Numerals

Preparation - Duplicate the "Sand Numbers" sheets. Pour sand in a plastic bucket. Use a cup or scoop for sprinkling the sand. Pass out half-opened glue bottles and scissors.

Procedure - The children "write" over the first page of numerals with the glue and take the sheet to the sand bucket. The teacher holds the paper as the child sprinkles the sand over the page. The excess sand is shaken back into the bucket. Repeat the procedure with the second page of numerals. Once the glue has dried, cut apart the numerals following the lines. Stack and secure with a rubber band. Sand numerals may be used in class and then sent home.

Note: Direct the children to close their eyes and identify the numerals by touch.

Music - Movement - Games

Song - "Hands" - Every Body's Record - Sesame Street Records
The children sing the song with the record.
Action Song - "On Top of Spaghetti" from the book Eye Winker Tom Tinker Chin Chopper by Tom Glazer.

Game - "Hot Potato"
The children stand in a circle and pass around a potato as the music plays. The teacher stops the music periodically. The child holding the potato is out of the game. The last child in the game wins.

Story Time

"De Tar-Baby" - Walt Disney's America - Retold by Marion Palmer from the original "Uncle Remus" Stories by Joel Chandler Harris.

Kindergarten Kitchen

Raspberry Squish (Jello)
Read the poem "Squishy Touch" from the book A Light In the Attic by Shel Silverstein. Prepare raspberry jello. When it is ready, pass around one bowl for the children to feel. Then serve the rest in cups for a snack.

Braille Alphabet

Use dots of glue to make the Braille alphabet on a piece of poster paper. Explain the Braille alphabet to the children, and let them "read" each letter by touching.

Haunted House

Partition off an area of the room with a sheet. Place a long table in the Haunted House. Make posters using iridescent paints, and mount behind the table. Place a black light behind the table. Hang spiders, made from egg cups and pipe cleaners, and paper bats from the ceiling. Play a Halloween sounds record. On the table, place a bowl of wet plums for the eyeballs, wet spaghetti for intestines, a half-inflated balloon for the heart, Spanish moss or tangled string for hair, and so forth. A parent or older child, preferably in costume, should stand behind each bowl explaining in a "scary" voice that, "These are my eyeballs; hold them. Don't they feel wonderful?", etc.

Note: For very young children, explain beforehand that this is a pretend exercise.

Day 4 - Smell

Concept Information

We smell with our noses. Tiny particles or bits of whatever we smell travel through the air. We cannot see these tiny particles, but when we breathe them into our noses we smell them. There are many kinds of smells or odors. We enjoy the smell of good food, but we do not enjoy the smell of garbage.

Language Arts - Social Studies - Science

Discussion

Share the concept information and define vocabulary words. Read and discuss the book Follow Your Nose by Paul Showers.

Sniff Jars

Spray paint the outside of baby food jars. In separate jars, put substances with distinctive smells such as: perfume, peppermint candy, orange peels, coffee, soap, etc. Place a piece of gauze or paper toweling inside to cover the substance. Pass around one jar at a time. Direct the children to smell the contents and keep conclusions "in their minds." Call on children to guess the contents. Initiate a discussion about things which smell good but are harmful if swallowed.

Note: Pictures of the contents of each jar may be cut, mounted, and laminated. After each jar has been passed around, show the cards. Have a child pick out the correct card and place it on top of the Sniff Jar.

<u>Puppet Play</u>

Use the puppet play patterns to construct a stick puppet for each puppet in the play. Glue the nose so that it is inclined upward on the stick. Read the play and let the children take turns acting out the parts.

<u>Mr. Nose Misses Out</u>

Mr. Nose woke up and jumped out of bed.

"What a morning!" he said. "I'm so happy because everyone loves me. I'm such a wonderful nose--all the smells want to be my friend! And no wonder--I'm so beautiful!"

Mr. Nose decided to take a walk in the park.

"Hello, Mr. Nose," said Miss Orange. "Have you come to enjoy my fresh orange smell this morning?"

"Oh, I don't think so," replied Mr. Nose. "I've smelled so <u>many</u> oranges in my exciting life."

"What about me?" asked Mrs. Sweet Pea. "My fragrance is sweet today!"

"No, thanks," said Mr. Nose as he walked by.

"Hey, you!" yelled Mr. Wild Onion. "Come over here. I'm stronger than ever today!"

"Certainly not," answered Mr. Nose. "Once of <u>you</u> is enough!"

"H-h-hello there," said the shy Lady Grass. "Would you care to sit with me? I'm freshly cut--and, well--I've been told my smell is very refreshing."

"So ordinary!" replied Mr. Nose. "A nose like me deserves the best, and today the best I will smell!"

And on Mr. Nose walked, right over the grass! He walked right by Mr. Pine Tree, Miss Rose Bud, and the Strawberry Clan without a word. Soon he came to the edge of a pond. With a smile on his face, he walked over to the new home of the Bee Family. Honey was what he wanted to smell. Being a rude fellow, Mr. Nose did not knock or even say "please!" He just jumped right into the hive! But Mr. Nose did not stay long, and he did not get to smell any honey. For, as we all know, bees do not like visitors in their hives!

"Ouch! Ooh! Yow! Ouch!" yelled Mr. Nose. Out he jumped with the Bee Family following; and "PLOP," he jumped right into the pond!

The next day Mr. Nose was swollen and stopped up. He did not take a walk. He stayed in bed and thought of all the smells he was missing. Miss Orange and her friends did not miss him at all. They were too busy making other noses happy with their glorious smells.

Art

Smelling Sheet

Preparation - Duplicate and distribute the Smelling Sheet. Place crayons, glue, and shakers of spices such as rosemary, nutmeg, cloves, chives, cinnamon, chili powder, and allspice on the tables.

Procedure - Trace over the outlines of the nose and shapes. Spread glue within each shape. Shake different spices on each glued area. When the glue is dry, smell and discuss each area.

Paper Nose Mask

Preparation - Duplicate and pass out the sheet. Provide scissors, gummed reinforcements, and pieces of elastic to fit around the head.

Procedure - Cut out the nose, and punch a hole on each "x". Stick gummed reinforcements around each hole. Fold the nose in half so that a crease runs down the center. Knot the ends of the elastic after pulling through each hole. Wear the nose during different "smell" activities.

Math

"Add a Nose"

Duplicate the sheet. Demonstrate drawing different noses on the board. Pass out the sheet and crayons. Direct the children to give each person or animal a nose.

Music - Movement - Games

Song - "Smells"

Tune - Oscar Mayer "My Bologna Has a First Name"

Oh, smells can tell me many things

Like what I'm going to eat

Or if I'm in the country

Or on a city street.

The special smells of winter and fall,

Flowers of spring and summer baseball--

All these things I like so well

But holidays have the very best smell.

Game - "Hay Fever"

Draw a flower on a tagboard square. Punch a hole, string a piece of yarn through the hole, and knot to form a necklace. The rest of the children are the "noses." Position enough chairs for each "nose" in a circle facing outward. The "flower" walks around the circle and taps a "nose" on the shoulder. The "nose" puts both hands on the shoulders of the "flower" and follows him or her around the circle. As other children are tapped, they, too, join the line by putting their hands on the person in front of them. Once all the children are in the line, the teacher removes a chair and says, "HAY FEVER!" The children scramble for the chairs. The person left without a chair is the new "flower."

Story Time

Book - <u>What Your Nose Knows</u> - Jane Belk Moncure

Kindergarten Kitchen

<u>"Goody O'Grumpity" and Spice Cake</u> - The poem, by Carol Ryrie Brink, can be found in <u>It's Time for Thanksgiving</u> by Elizabeth Hough Sechrist and Janette Woolsey; also in <u>Favorite Poems Old and New</u> selected by Helen Ferris. Read the poem, then cook and enjoy the spice cake.

Aunt Charlotte's Spice Cake

1 teaspoon soda	1/4 teaspoon ground nutmeg
3 Tablespoons cold water	1 teaspoon allspice
3 eggs, separated	1 teaspoon ground cloves
1 cup butter	2 1/4 cups flour
1 cup granulated sugar	1/2 cup buttermilk
1 teaspoon cinnamon	3/4 cup blackberry jelly

Grease and flour a 13" x 9" cake pan. Preheat the oven to 325 degrees (Fahrenheit). Mix soda and water, and set aside. Beat egg whites until stiff, and set aside. In a mixing bowl, cream butter and sugar. Add egg yolks one at a time. Add cinnamon, nutmeg, allspice, and cloves. Gradually mix in flour and milk. Add jelly to mixture, and pour in soda water. Fold in egg whites. Pour mixture into cake pan. Bake for 30-45 minutes, or until toothpick inserted in the center of the cake comes out clean.

Caramel Icing

1/2 cup evaporated milk

3/4 cup granulated sugar

3/4 cup brown sugar

dash of salt

1/2 stick butter

1 teaspoon vanilla

Mix the first four ingredients in a saucepan, and bring to a boil. Cook gently, stirring occasionally, until a little mixture dropped into cold water forms a soft ball. Remove from heat. Add butter and beat until icing loses its gloss. Add vanilla; mix and pour on the cake.

Reward Booklets

Purchase scented stickers. Direct the children to fold several pieces of paper into fourths. Unfold and use the folds as cutting lines. Staple pages together to form a booklet. Decorate the cover. Spontaneously reward good behavior or accomplishments with scented stickers. The children stick the stickers on the pages. Discuss the scents of each sticker. When the booklet is filled, the children take them home.

Day 5 - Taste

Concept Information

We use our tongues to taste. There are four kinds of taste--sweet, salty, sour, and bitter. We have taste buds in the bumps on our tongues. The group of taste buds which can taste sweet foods are on the tip of our tongues. The taste buds which taste salty and sour foods are on the sides of our tongues. The taste buds at the back of our tongues taste bitter foods.

Our sense of taste and our sense of smell work together. When food smells good, it makes the taste even better. When we have a cold and cannot use our noses to smell, food does not taste as good.

Language Arts - Social Studies - Science

Discussion

Relate the concept information and define vocabulary words. Show a diagram of the tongue with locations of taste bud groups.

Tasting Jars

Pass around baby food jars containing sugar, salt, lemon juice, and unsweetened chocolate. After everyone has tasted one substance, call on a child to identify it. Discuss whether the substance is sweet, salty, sour, or bitter. Point out how substances can look alike but taste different.

Seatwork - "Tasting Tongues"

Preparation - Duplicate and distribute the sheet. Place bowls of sugar, crushed lemon candy, small pieces of orange peel, and salt shakers on the tables. Provide crayons, scissors, and glue.

Procedure - Trace over the X's with a black crayon. Color the lips and tongue. Fold the lips in half with ends together. Make a small cut on the line. Unfold, insert scissors in the cut, and cut in each direction on the line. Spread glue between the dotted line and the end of the tongue. Insert this portion into the slit of the lips and press to seal. Apply a spot of glue on each "X". Sprinkle sugar on the tip of the tongue, salt on the first X's on each side, lemon candy on the second X's on each side, and orange peel at the back of the tongue.

Book and Tasting Party

Read The Tasting Party by Jane Belk Moncure. Enlist parental assistance and have a "Tasting Party" following the guidelines of the book. Allow the children to participate in preparations. Follow up with an experience story.

Poem - "Tasty Things"

Read the poem and encourage the children to share their taste preferences.

Tasty things that I like most?

Popsicles, chocolate, and cinnamon toast,

Oatmeal and raisins, hot apple pies,

Crusty cheese sandwiches and golden fries,

Turkey and dressing and sweet potatoes,

Carrot curls and fresh tomatoes,

Ice cream and pudding and--I'll tell you more,

When Mom gets back from the grocery store!

Art

Flavor Creation

Preparation - Make patterns of the ice cream scoop and cone.

Read the poem to the children. Provide patterns, different colored construction paper, scissors, and glue.

(Poem) - "Eighteen Flavors" by Shel Silverstein from Where the Sidewalk Ends.

Procedure - Trace around and cut out the cone pattern. Choose four flavors for your ice cream cone. Trace around the ice cream scoop patterns on the different colors of construction paper and cut out. Glue the scoops in a "stack" on top of the cone. Cherries, chocolate chips, blueberries, etc., can be made by cutting pieces of scrap construction paper and gluing on the scoops. Share your ice cream cone creations with the class.

Tasty Mosaic

Preparation - Provide different types of breakfast cereal, uncooked spaghetti and macaroni, saltine crackers, and miniature marshmallows. Set out drawing paper, crayons, and glue.

Procedure - Draw a scene and fill in by gluing the food within the lines.

My Favorite Tastes

Preparation - Duplicate and distribute the sheets and a paper plate for each child. Provide scissors, old magazines, crayons, and glue.

Procedure - Color and cut out the tongue and set aside. Fold the paper plate in half to form the mouth. Color the top and bottom outside rim to represent lips. Make a small cut at the center of the fold to insert scissors. Cut along the fold, stopping at the inner circle line on each side. Open the "mouth." From magazines cut out and glue favorite foods in the mouth. Insert the tongue through the slit. Fold on the dotted line to prevent the tongue from slipping out of the slit. Hold this folded area and "wiggle" to make the tongue move.

Math

Raisin Count

Collect ten medicine cups and label 1-10. Purchase a large box of raisins. Put the raisins on a paper plate. Call on children to drop the correct amount of raisins in the cups. After checking the cups, let the children eat the raisins.

Variation: Make several sets of cups and give each child a cup. After the "raisin count," the children switch cups and repeat the procedure.

Music - Movement - Games

Song - "I Know an Old Lady" from Eye Winker Tom Tinker Chin Chopper by Tom Glazer

Action Song - "Making Pancakes"

Tune - "Did You Ever See a Lassie?"

We are making pancakes, pancakes, pancakes,

We are making pancakes for breakfast today.

We'll turn on the griddle, and then we'll start mixing,

We are making pancakes for breakfast today!

Now we measure flour, baking powder, and sugar

Add a little salt, and we're ready to sift,

Sift this way and that way, sift this way and that way.

We are making pancakes for breakfast today!

Break an egg and beat it, and beat it, and beat it,

Add the milk and butter, and stir with the rest,

Stir this way and that way, stir this way and that way,

We are making pancakes for breakfast today!

Pour it on the griddle, the griddle, the griddle.

Wait until it bubbles, then flip in the air.

Flip this way and that way, flip this way and that way,

We are making pancakes and now they are done!

Procedure - The children act out each line, making a stirring motion for "making pancakes." Or designate areas to be the mixing bowl and griddle. Assign one child to be the cook and the rest to be the different ingredients. For example, the cook sifts as the flour, baking powder, sugar, and salt do somersaults or log rolls. When the pancakes are flipped, the children jump in the air, then lie back down on the "griddle."

Story Time

Book - The Duchess Bakes a Cake - Virginia Kahl

Book - Strega Nona - Tomie de Paola

Kindergarten Kitchen

Lemonade (4 servings)

1/2 cup sugar

1/2 cup hot water

3 lemons

1 quart cold water

10-12 ice cubes

Cut the lemons in half. Cut one half into thin slices. Squeeze the juice from the remaining halves. In a pitcher, stir the sugar and hot water. Add the lemon juice, lemon slices, cold water, and ice cubes. Stir vigorously and pour into glasses.

Variation: Add several drops of red food coloring to make Pink Lemonade.

Crunch Munch (Culmination Activity)

2 quarts popped corn

2 cups peanuts

1 1/3 cups sugar

1 cup butter

1/2 cup light corn syrup

1 teaspoon vanilla

After popping the popcorn, mix in a bowl with the peanuts. Combine sugar, butter, and syrup in a 1-1/2 quart saucepan. Bring to a boil over medium heat, stirring until the sugar is dissolved. Continue cooking, and stir occasionally for 10-15 minutes or until the mixture turns a light caramel color. Remove from heat and stir in vanilla. Pour mixture over popcorn and peanuts, and mix rapidly.

Concept Review

On the board, draw various body parts including the eye, ear, nose, mouth, and hand. Call on different children to find and circle the part of the body which we use to smell, taste, touch, hear, and see. Erase the other body parts. Point out each of the remaining parts and have the children name things we see, hear, feel, taste, and smell. List these on the board.

Concept Evaluation - (See Introduction)

Dear Parents,

On _____, we will begin our unit on "The Five Senses." Each day we will have discussions and activities centering around one of the five senses. Please read below to see how you can help:

Things to Send: _____

_____

_____

Volunteers Needed To: _____

_____

_____

Follow-Up: At the end of the unit, ask your child to share the following songs, stories, etc.

_____

_____

_____

Follow-Up Questions: What are the five senses?

What part of the body performs each sense?

Name the parts of the eye.

How do ears hear, noses smell, hands feel, and tongues taste?

Family Activities: Have a quiet time, then name what you heard.

By the smell, guess what is for dinner? Describe the tastes of foods at dinner.

Name all the colors in one room.

Sincerely,

My Five Senses

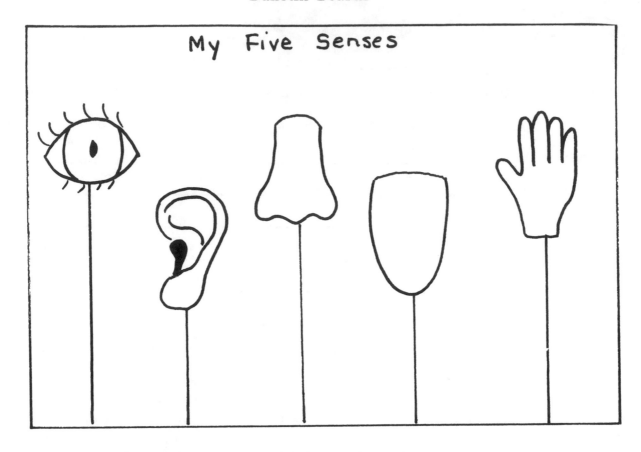

Copyright © 1987.   Carol Taylor Bond

Copyright © 1987. Carol Taylor Bond

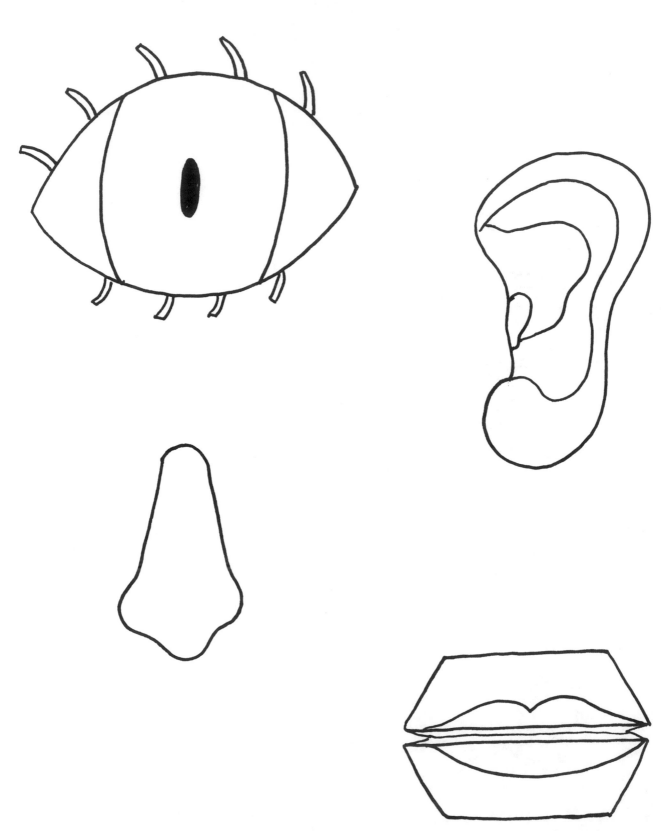

Copyright © 1987. Carol Taylor Bond

162

Big Eye

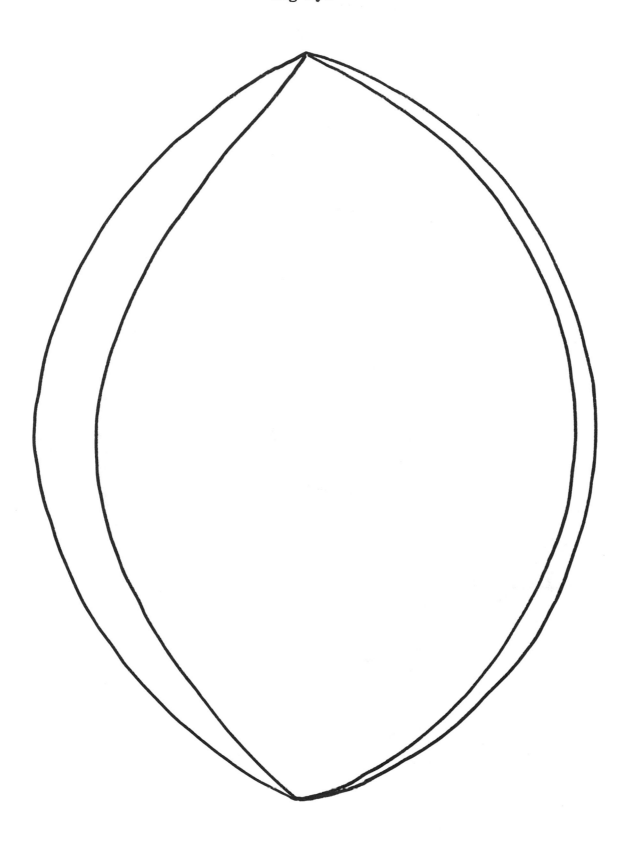

Copyright © 1987.   Carol Taylor Bond

163

Big Eye

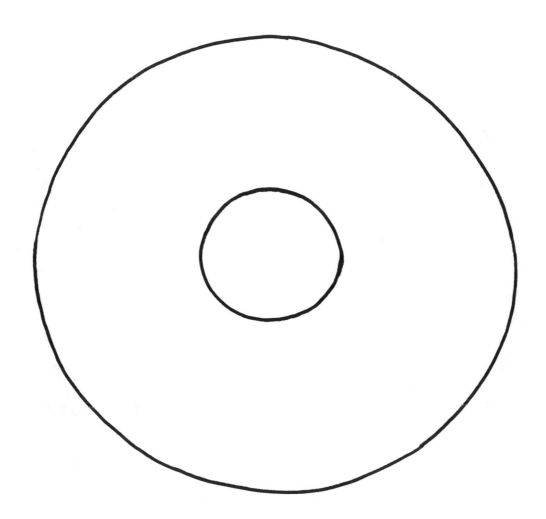

Copyright © 1987. Carol Taylor Bond

Eye Creatures

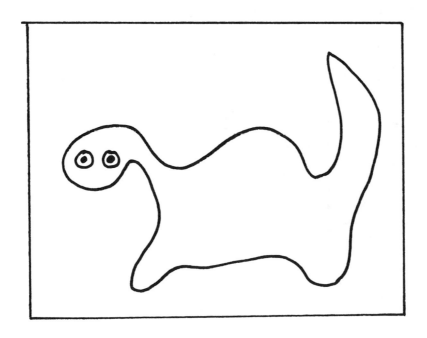

Copyright © 1987. Carol Taylor Bond

165

The Balloon Man

Copyright © 1987.   Carol Taylor Bond

Dear Parents,

_____ our class will learn about the Five
          (month and dates)
Senses - Sight, Sound, Touch, Taste, and Smell. Each day we will have

"Sharing Time" to help in recognizing and using our senses and to develop

social skills.

If your child would like to share an object, please place it in a paper

bag. Label the bag with your child's name and the identity of the object.

Please do not send anything that is fragile or valuable.

Objects may be things which we see, hear, touch, smell, taste, or

different combinations of the senses. It is helpful to discuss the object

with your child beforehand to insure self-confidence.

Thank you for your cooperation.

Sincerely,

Copyright © 1987. Carol Taylor Bond

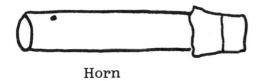

Horn

Rhythm Instruments

Shaker

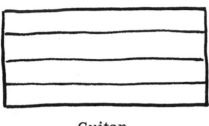

Guitar

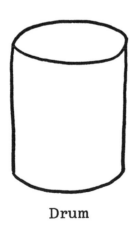

Drum

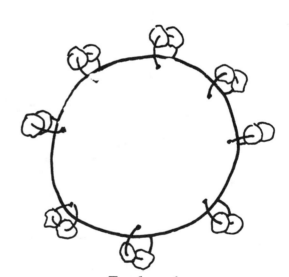

Tambourine

Moaning Stick

Copyright © 1987. Carol Taylor Bond

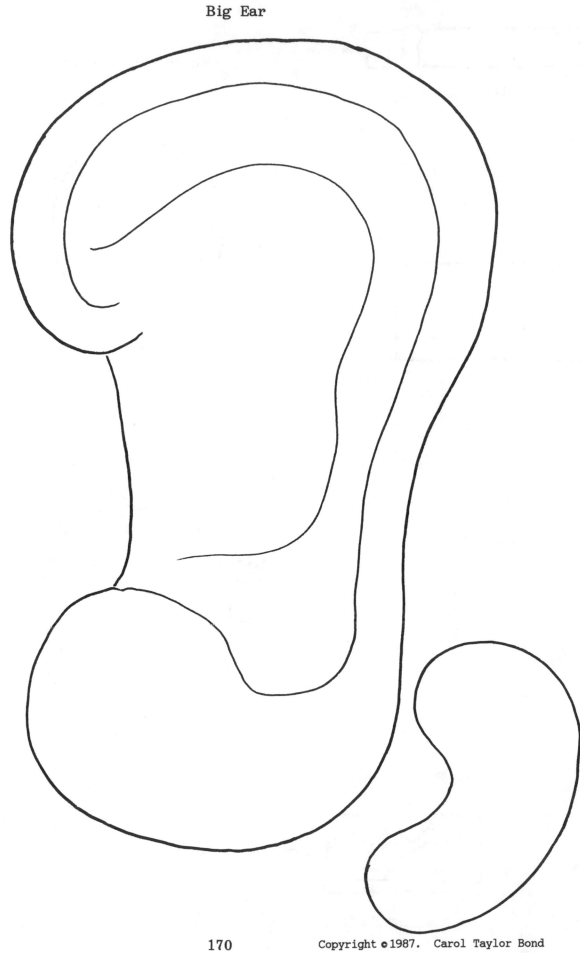

 Copyright © 1987. Carol Taylor Bond

Name _____

Hard and Soft Sheet

soft

hard

Copyright © 1987. Carol Taylor Bond

Hands Are For Feeling

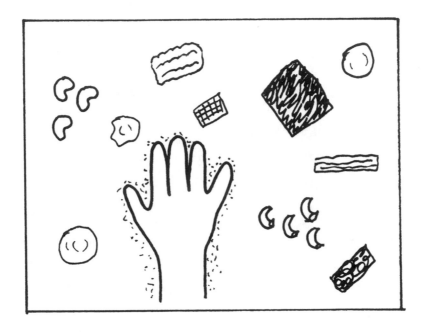

Copyright © 1987. Carol Taylor Bond

1	2
Sand Numerals	
3	4
5	6

 Copyright © 1987. Carol Taylor Bond

7	8
9	10

 Copyright © 1987. Carol Taylor Bond

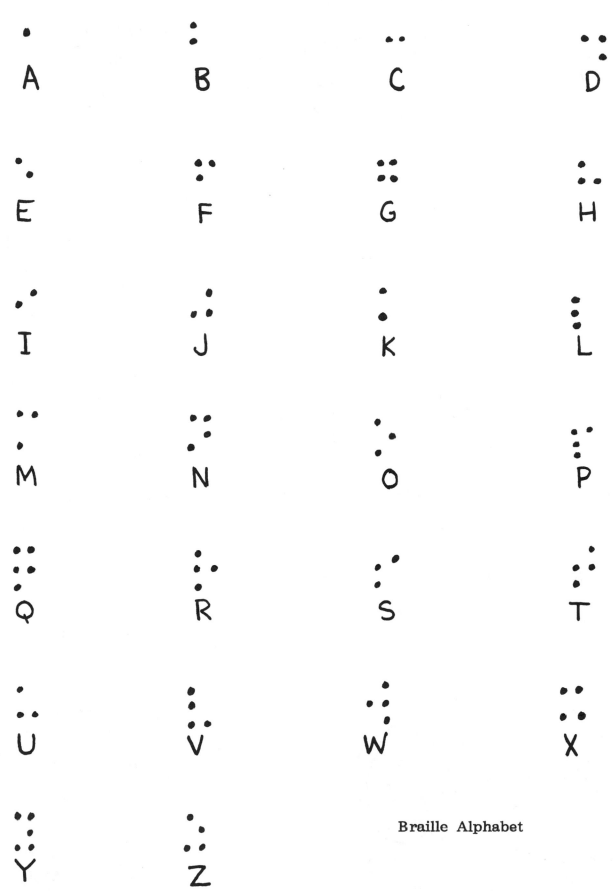

Braille Alphabet

Copyright ©1987. Carol Taylor Bond

Mr. Nose

Miss Orange

Mrs. Sweet Pea

Mr. Wild Onion

Lady Grass

The Strawberry Clan

Miss Rose Bud

176

Copyright © 1987. Carol Taylor Bond

Mr. Nose

Puppet Play

Mr. Pine Tree

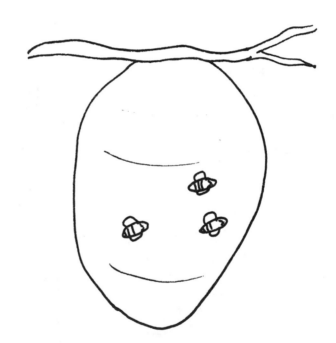

Home of the

Bee Family

Copyright © 1987. Carol Taylor Bond

Copyright © 1987. Carol Taylor Bond

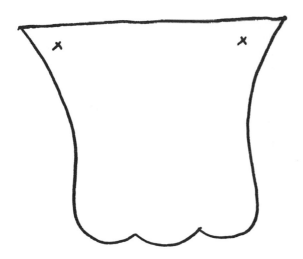

Paper Nose Mask

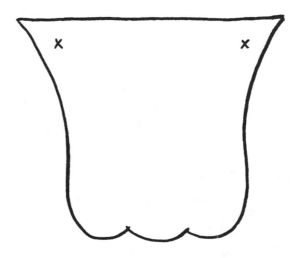

Copyright © 1987. Carol Taylor Bond

Add A Nose

Copyright ©1987. Carol Taylor Bond

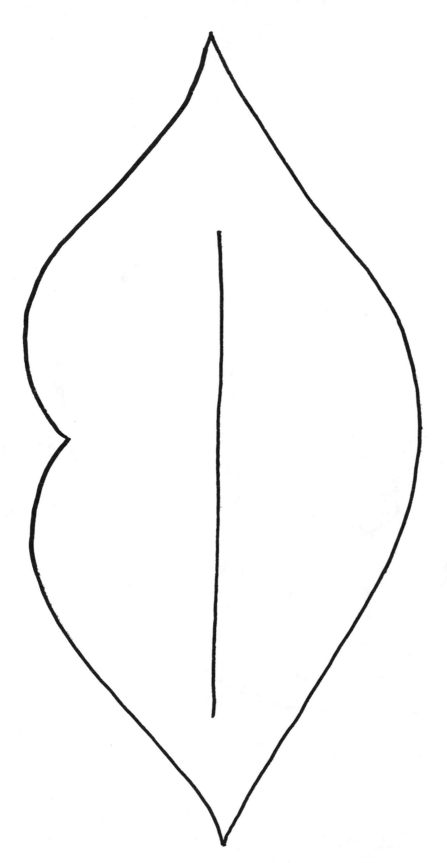

Copyright © 1987.   Carol Taylor Bond

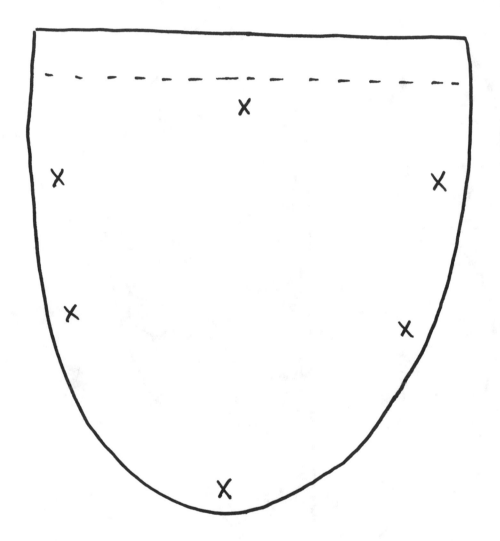

Copyright © 1987. Carol Taylor Bond

Flavor Creation

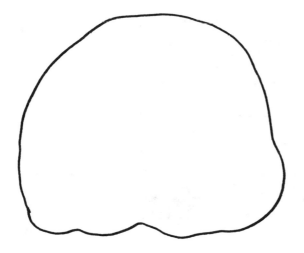

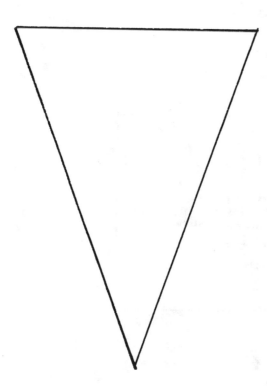

Copyright © 1987. Carol Taylor Bond

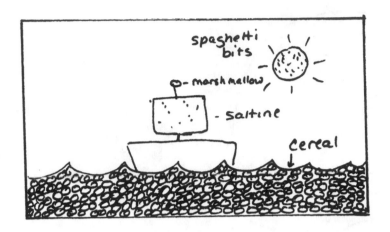

Tasty Mosaics

Copyright ©1987. Carol Taylor Bond

My Favorite Tastes

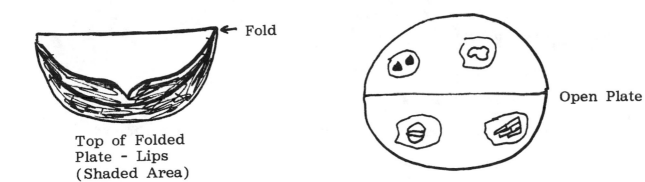

Fold

Top of Folded
Plate - Lips
(Shaded Area)

Open Plate

Tongue

Copyright © 1987. Carol Taylor Bond

185

Fall

<u>Proposed Time</u>: 5 days

<u>Unit Objectives</u>

To introduce the four seasons

To relate that fall is the season when all living things prepare for winter

To present the unique qualities of fall

To develop an appreciation for the fall season

<u>Room Environment</u> - <u>Bulletin Boards</u>

<u>"Fall"</u>

Cover the top three-fourths of the bulletin board with off-white paper and the bottom quarter with light brown paper. Use orange border trim and letters. Cut trees from dark brown paper. Staple the "Hand Leaves" (see Language Arts - Social Studies - Day 1) on the limbs of the trees and on the "ground." One tree should have red leaves; one should have yellow; and one should have orange. The leaves on the ground are mixed colors. Staple "Hungry Squirrels" (see Art - Day 3) on the ground and tree limbs.

<u>"Harvest Time"</u>

Cover the bulletin board with yellow paper. Cut a strip from tan paper to represent the ground. Pick tall weeds to represent the crop or cut corn plants from green paper. Tape the bottom of the plants to the back of the "ground" strip, leaving a space in the center for the scarecrow. Mount on bulletin board. From poster paper or tagboard, draw and cut out a scarecrow. Provide fabric glue for the children to fill in the shirt and pants with fabric scraps. Turn over and glue straw or pine straw at the bottom of the arms and legs so that it sticks out around the hands and feet. Add facial features with markers or fingerpaint and a hat cut

186

from felt, burlap, or brown paper. Staple a paper strip on the bulletin board for the pole. Mount the scarecrow on the pole. Staple "Footprint Crows" (see Art - Day 3) on the upper portion of the bulletin board.

Note: The Halloween Pumpkin Patch (see Halloween Unit - Room Environment - Displays) may be displayed in front of this bulletin board or construction paper pumpkins may be cut out and stapled on the ground strip.

Room Environment - Displays

"Classroom Tree"

Find a tree branch which is shaped like a tree. Put this in a coffee can, and fill with plaster of Paris to form a secure base. Collect a variety of autumn leaves, and press between the pages of books for several days. Remove the leaves, and tie to varied lengths of thread or thin fishing line. Tie to the branches of the tree. Place the tree where circulating air will twirl the leaves.

"Science Center"

Set up a Science Center on a large table. To make a standing display, cut away the front, top, and bottom of a large corrugated cardboard box. Cover the remaining section with burlap or felt. Staple pictures of the four seasons and fall scenes on the display board. Place at the back of the table. Suggested activities and objects to display are as follows:

1. Place a shallow box filled with different kinds of nuts on the table. For sorting, glue a picture and the name of each kind of nut on separate strawberry baskets.

2. A variety of leaves to examine

3. Fresh vegetables and fruits

4. On pieces of cardboard draw an outline of a pumpkin, an ear of corn, a watermelon, a peach, an apple, and so forth. Glue a seed of each in the middle of the outlines. Place a collection of these seeds in a box or basket on the table. The children sort and classify the seeds by placing the correct seeds in the outlines.

5. Bird feathers, animals, skins, squirrel tails

6. Books with colorful pictures of fall activities, animals and birds, and trees

7. Magnifying glasses and a simple microscope

8. Objects gathered on the Gathering Walk (see Day 1) and the Fall Outing (see Day 5)

Day 1 - Introduction

Concept Information

Each year has four seasons: Spring, Summer, Autumn or Fall, and Winter. In Spring, the days are longer; new leaves grow on the trees; and flowers bloom. Spring is the season when we fly kites on windy days or splash in puddles on rainy days. In Summer, the trees are green; and the weather is usually very hot. It is the season for swimming, playing baseball, and going on <u>vacations</u>. When the weather becomes cooler and the days are shorter, Autumn or Fall is here. The leaves on the trees change colors and fall to the ground. In Fall, we rake leaves, play football, and go "Trick-or-Treating."

Winter is the coldest season of the year. The days are short, and most of the trees are <u>bare</u>. In some places, it snows in the winter. This is the season for building a fire in the fireplace, drinking hot chocolate, and waiting for Santa.

Language Arts - Social Studies

Discussion

Share the concept information and define vocabulary words. Show pictures of the seasons from an encyclopedia, or from the book <u>Seasons</u> (a new True Book) by Illa Podendorf. Encourage the children to point out differences in the seasons. Collect items of clothing for each season, and put them in a paper bag or a box. Take out one item at a time, and ask in which season it is worn.

Book - <u>A Book of Seasons</u> by Alice and Martin Provensen

Duplicate one "Seasons Symbols" sheet for each child. Direct the children to cut out and color the symbols. Read the book, omitting or substituting the words "this season" for the name of the season mentioned. After each page, ask the children to hold up the symbol which represents the season described. Check responses and continue until the book is completed. Have the children volunteer characteristics of each season. List on the board.

<u>Fall Booklet</u>

<u>Poem</u> (for cover)

Write the following poem on a duplicating master. Make a copy for each child, and cut it out.

Here is an Autumn leaf so brown

And here is a red one I just found.

Put them together and you'll have two--

One for me and one for you.

<u>"Hand Leaves"</u> (for cover)

For Fall Booklet cover, distribute a half sheet of brown construction paper and a half sheet of red construction paper to each child. Direct the children to trace one hand (closed fingers) on each sheet. Complete the "leaf" by drawing in the open section (where the wrist was) and adding a stem. Cut out.

For the Fall Bulletin Board, distribute a half sheet of red, yellow, and orange construction paper. Follow the above procedure.

Cover Construction

Give each child two pieces of yellow or orange construction paper. Direct them to write "Fall" at the top of one page. One of the "Hand Leaves" should be glued below the title on the left side of the page. Below this, the poem is glued in the center, and the other leaf is glued at the bottom right-hand corner. Names may be written beside the bottom leaf.

Contents of Booklet

Include an activity sheet for each day of the fall unit. Suggested activities will be indicated by "(Booklet)."

Observe a Tree Activity

Pick a tree near the classroom, preferably one that can be seen from a window, to observe all year long. Hang a feeder in the tree for the squirrels and birds. On a piece of poster paper, make a Pictograph entitled "Tree Watch." List the nine months of school on the left side of the chart. Use the squares beside each month to draw observation symbols. These can include a red leaf, a squirrel, a bare branch, and so forth.

"A Tree In All Seasons" (Booklet)

Duplicate the sheet and distribute. Re-examine pictures of the seasons noting the appearance of the trees in each season. Decide how each tree scene should be completed and color.

Film

Show "Children in Autumn" or a similar film. Discuss the autumn scenes and activities.

<u>Art</u>

<u>Super Stuff Bucket</u>

Preparation - Collect a large plastic milk or bleach jug for each child.
Cut off the top, curving upward to leave the handle intact. Edges may be
covered with colored tape. Punch holes an inch apart around the opening,
and distribute the jugs. Provide scrap paper or scrap contact paper,
scissors, glue, permanent markers, and yarn pieces.

Procedure - Demonstrate drawing simple objects on the blackboard, such as
a leaf, a flower, a house, a sun. Direct the children to draw and cut out
objects of their choice to glue on their buckets. The yarn is laced
through the holes around the opening. Names are written on the buckets
with permanent markers.

Note: The buckets are used on the "Gathering Walk" to hold leaves,
acorns, etc. Throughout the year they are useful for carrying items to
and from school, such as gifts for parents and objects for sharing.

<u>"Weather Disc"</u>

Preparation - Duplicate the "Weather Symbols" sheet. Give each child a
sheet, a paper plate with a dot marked in the center, a metal paper
fastener, and a 12" piece of yarn. Provide pencils, colors, scissors, glue,
and a hole puncher.

Procedure - Color and cut out the symbols and indicator. Glue one symbol
at the top of the plate, one at the bottom, and one on each side. Punch
a hole near the end of the indicator (pointer). Insert fastener, then push
through the plate at the dot. Punch two holes in the top of the plate.
Knot an end of the yarn in each hole for a hanger.

Note: Weather Discs may be hung in the room for each child to use each day or sent home for use with an explanatory note.

Fall Crowns

Preparation - For each child, cut a "crown" strip 3" wide and 24" long from fall-colored construction paper. Duplicate the "Fall Crowns" sheet on construction paper of various fall colors. Cut the sheets into blocks with a leaf on each block. Allow the children to choose the colors of their crowns and leaves. Provide glue, crayons, and scissors. Have a stapler available.

Procedure - Cut out the leaves. Use crayons to color the stems and to lightly draw the veins of the leaf. Glue leaves on the crown. Staple to fit.

Math

"Alike and Different Pick-Up"

Put the materials from the "Science Center" and/or toys and kitchen utensils on a table. Ask a child to pick two things which are alike from the table. Discuss why they are alike. Ask another child to choose two things which are different. Discuss why they are different. Repeat the procedure so that each child has a turn.

Music - Movement - Games

Song - "Fall Is Here"
Tune - "Frère Jacques"

Fall is here

Fall is here

Time for fun

Time for fun

Piles of leaves for jumping

Carving out the pumpkin

Blackbirds fly

Apple pie

Movement - "The Treehouse Ladder"

Preparation - Place a wooden coordination ladder on the floor. Use a mat or rug under the ladder.

Procedure - One at a time the children perform these suggested directions:

1. Climb the ladder to the treehouse - walk forward on the rungs of the ladder.

2. Climb down the ladder - walk backward between the rungs of the ladder.

3. Hurry up the ladder - run between the rungs of the ladder.

4. Climb the ladder in a new way - walk sideways, using either the sides or rungs of the ladder.

5. Climb the ladder like a bear - walk on the rungs of the ladder, moving your right hand and foot for one step, and your left hand and foot for the next step.

6. Bounce a ball up the ladder - walk on the rungs as you bounce and catch the ball between each rung.

Story Time

Book - A Sunday In Autumn - Anthony Rowley

"Gathering Walk"

Take the class on a "Gathering Walk" around the school yard or, if it can be arranged, in nearby yards. Direct the children to pick up a variety of leaves, nuts, and so forth. Use Super Stuff Buckets or paper bags for collections. Discuss each child's collection and display in the Science Center.

Note: This is a good time to gather the extra items needed in the different unit activities.

"Our Class Through the Seasons" Photograph Album

Purchase an inexpensive photograph album. Label the first page "Our Class Through the Seasons." Label the second page "Fall" (or "Autumn"). Take snapshots of the children engaged in fall activities such as: the Gathering Walk or Fall Outing (see Day 1 and Day 5), playing football, and making leaf rubbings (see Art - Day 4). Mount in the book and label each snapshot. Continue this activity for each season. Summer snapshots may be sent from home, taken at the very beginning of school, or at the end-of-the-year outing.

Day 2 - Fall Weather, Clothes, Activities

Concept Information

In Fall, the days become cooler than in the hot Summer. If you <u>traveled</u> in a spaceship like the <u>astronauts</u>, you could see that from outer space our earth looks much like a globe. It moves in a circle around the sun. The <u>weather</u> is different in Fall because we are not as close to the sun.

In the fall season, we put away our shorts and wear clothes that will keep us warmer. We wear shirts with long <u>sleeves</u>, <u>jackets</u>, and <u>sweaters</u>.

There are many things to do in Fall. It is the season to <u>rake</u> and play in the leaves, watch the squirrels from a treehouse, and play football with friends. In Fall, we also enjoy "trick or treating" on Halloween and eating turkey with our families on Thanksgiving.

Language Arts - Social Studies

Discussion

Relate the concept information and define vocabulary words. Have one child stand and hold a paper plate painted yellow or a yellow ball. Rotate a globe as you move (revolve) around the sun. Show how our part of the earth is tipped away from the sun in winter and tipped toward the sun in summer. Encourage discussion and conclusions.

Book Activity - Caps For Sale - Esphyr Slobodkina

Read the book to the class. Make paper hats from sheets of newspaper, and paint with tempera. Choose one child to be the peddler wearing the stack of hats and four or five children to be the monkeys. The tree can be a table or an indoor gym set. Reread the book as the children act it out.

"Weather Charts"

Duplicate the "Weather Chart" sheet. On poster paper, draw the weather symbols to be used on the sheet. Post in a prominent place. Each day take the class outside, and observe the weather. Direct the children to draw and color the symbols on their charts for that day.

Fall Montage

Obtain a medium-sized (square) cardboard box. Label the top, "Fall Scenes." Label the sides, "Animals and Birds," "Weather and Clothes," "Activities," and "Harvest." Provide old magazines, scissors, and glue. Direct the children to cut out pictures for each category. Sort accordingly, and glue the pictures on the correct side of the box. Spray with fixative seal.

Note: This activity can be continued each day.

Book - Fall Is Here - by Jane Belk Moncure

Read and share the fall experiences.

Fingerplay - "Five Little Children"

Five little children on a fine fall day (hold up five fingers)

The first one said, "Let's all go play!" (hold up thumb)

The second one said, "Throw the football to me!" (hold up pointer)

The third one said, "No, I'll climb a tree!" (hold up middle finger)

The fourth one said, "I'd rather rake!" (hold up ring finger)

The fifth one said, "I'll pick apples to bake!" (hold up pinkie)

The sky turned gray and the wind blew cool (blow)

So they put on their jackets and ran to school. (pantomime)

Art

Football

Preparation - Make patterns of the football. Mix brown tempera paint, and cut 12" pieces of white yarn. Pass out white construction paper, patterns, crayons, scissors, and yarn. Set out tempera paint trays and small sponge squares.

Procedure - On the white paper, trace around the football pattern. Sponge paint with brown paint. When it has dried, punch four or five holes at the center top of the football. Lace with yarn.

"Time to Rake" (Booklet)

Preparation - Provide a sheet of white paper, a handful of fall leaves, crayons, and glue (for each child).

Procedure - Draw a line to represent the ground. Use crayons to color. Spread glue on the "ground" in the shape of a pile. Crumple leaves and sprinkle to cover the glue. Use crayons to draw a rake beside the pile of leaves.

Math

"Apple Count"

Duplicate the sheet. The children count the apples on the trees and circle the correct numeral below. Color the objects.

Music - Movement - Games

Song - "Raking Leaves"

For words and music, see the sheet in the pattern section.

<u>Game</u> - "Touchdown Relay Race"

Depending on the surface, use a rope, tape, or chalk for the lines. Divide the class into two teams, and line them up in single file behind the starting line. Give the first person in each line a small football. (This may be a rubber or sponge football.) At the signal, each player races to the finish line. When a player crosses this line, he or she must yell "touchdown," then turn around and throw the football back to the next team member. If the ball falls short, the player must run and pick it up and throw it until he or she reaches the next in line. He or she then returns to stand behind the finish line while the next team member repeats the race procedure. The game is completed when the last player on each team races for the finish line. The team whose player crosses the line and yells "touchdown" first, wins the race.

Story Time

<u>Book</u> - <u>All Fall Down</u> - Gene Zion

Poem and Snack

Read the wonderful poem "Animal Crackers" by Christopher Morley from his book <u>Chimneysmoke</u>. (This poem can be found in most collections of favorite poems.) Then prepare and enjoy hot cocoa with animal crackers.

Hot Cocoa

Drop marshmallows in paper cups (hot/cold). Heat chocolate milk in a saucepan. Pour in cups. Serve with animal crackers.

Day 3 - Birds and Animals in Fall

In Fall, people may buy winter clothes, take out <u>blankets</u>, and put up storm windows to <u>prepare</u> for winter. But birds and animals must work harder to get ready for the cold. Birds that cannot find food in the winter fly or migrate to warmer places. Tiny <u>hummingbirds</u> fly all the way to South America where it is warm, and <u>return</u> when winter is over. Birds that can find food in winter do not migrate. They grow more feathers to keep warm.

Animals grow <u>thicker</u> fur coats during the fall season. The raccoon and the bear eat more because all winter long they sleep or hibernate. Squirrels, beavers, and foxes do not hibernate. In the fall, these animals store food for the winter. The squirrel hides nuts and acorns in different places; the fox buries meat and fruit in the ground; and the beaver stores twigs and bark near his home. Some animals, like rabbits and deer, do not put away food in fall. They must spend the winter looking for food.

<u>Language Arts</u> - <u>Social Studies</u> - <u>Science</u>

<u>Discussion</u>

Discuss the concept information and define vocabulary words.

Display pictures of the animals mentioned.

<u>Book</u> - <u>Go With the Sun</u> by Miriam Schlein

Read the story. Go back through the book, letting the children explain each illustration.

<u>Fall Pantomime</u>

Preparation - Cut bits of orange, red, and brown construction paper; and divide among four paper bags marked "Fall." Cut bits of white paper and divide among four paper bags marked "Winter." Other items needed are: a football, a toy rake or broom, round tinkertoys for acorns, and jackets.

Actors - "The trees" are four children standing approximately three feet apart. They should hold the "Fall" bags and place the "Winter" bags behind them. On cue, they drop the leaves and snow.

"The children" are two or three children standing about five feet in front of the trees with jackets over their arms. One holds a football.

"The squirrels" are two children waiting on either side of the "stage" area. The rakes are placed near the squirrels for easy access.

Procedure - Read the following as the children act out the scene: Fall is here. Children put on their jackets and play football in the yard. The wind blows and the leaves of orange, red, and brown fall from the trees. Squirrels are busy looking for acorns to hide away for winter. It is time to rake the leaves into a big pile. And a big pile of leaves is perfect for jumping into! Isn't it fun! It is getting dark. The squirrels scamper to their nests, and the children go inside. The trees are bare. It is cold-- and the snow is falling! Fall is over, and winter is here!

Pathtracer Sheet

Duplicate and distribute the sheets. Ask the children to identify the animals and their homes. They should then trace the paths from each animal to its home, and color the pictures.

Fingerplay - "Five Little Squirrels"

Five little squirrels sat up in a tree; (hold up five fingers)
This little squirrel said, "What do I see?" (point to thumb)

This little squirrel said, "I smell a gun!" (point to pointer)

This little squirrel said, "Oh, let's run!" (point to middle)

This little squirrel said, "Let's hide in the shade!" (point to ring finger)

This little squirrel said, "I'm not afraid!" (point to little finger)

Then BANG went the gun (clap hands)

And away the little squirrels ran, every one. (make running motions with fingers)

Flannel Board Story - "The Mean Old Man"

Once upon a time, a little old man lived alone in a little house at the edge of a beautiful forest. He was a mean old man and, as we all know, mean people do not have any friends. But the little old man was not lonely because he did not like people. He did not like animals. In fact, there was not much he did like--except being mean.

Beside the mean old man's house was a giant pecan tree. Now, the old man did not like the taste of pecans, but he did like to throw them at the squirrels that came near his house in search of food.

On day three hungry children saw the pecan tree. They began picking up the pecans and putting them into the pockets of their ragged clothes.

"Stop!" croaked the little old man as he hobbled from his house. "Empty those pockets!" he cried. "Now shoo, beggars, shoo! Away with you!" he yelled.

"Please, Mister," said one of the children. "We are hungry. May we please have some of these pecans for our supper?" The little old man smiled a pretend-smile and picked up a big brown pecan.

"Is this what you would like, hmmm?" asked the mean old man as he cracked open the pecan and popped it into his mouth. "Yes, yes!" cried the hungry children.

"Or is this what you want?" he asked, eating an even bigger pecan. "Yes, yes," answered the children who did not know how mean the old man was.

"Well," the little old man said sweetly, "YOU CAN'T HAVE THEM!!!" "Now shoo, beggars, shoo. Away with you!" he yelled.

The hungry children began to run as the little old man began throwing pecans at them and laughing a horrible laugh. They hid behind a tree and watched as he laughed and laughed, and threw pecan after pecan.

But as they watched and the little old man laughed, something strange began to happen. The mean old man became smaller and smaller. Long whiskers grew from each side of the old man's nose, his hands and feet turned into paws, and a busy tail appeared from behind. Soon the old man was covered with short black hair.

After that, the three hungry children and their parents moved into the little house. They planted a garden for food and were never hungry again. They shared their food with the forest animals and always left some pecans for the squirrels--except for one. When the mean old black squirrel came looking for food, they threw pecans and yelled, "Now shoo, beggar, shoo. Away with you!"

Procedure - Use pellon to make the characters and tell the story.

Art

Footprint Crows

Preparation - Mix black tempera paint, and pour a thin layer in a tin pie plate or tray. Distribute white construction paper, small squares of orange construction paper, crayons, scissors, and glue.

Procedure - Follow the same procedure as the "Footprint Ghosts" (see Halloween Unit - Art - Day 6). When the footprints have dried, the children cut around the outside of the print. Color a white circle (with a white crayon) with a black dot in the center for the eye.

"Hungry Squirrels"

Preparation - Duplicate the "Hungry Squirrel" sheet on heavy paper. Hand out the sheets along with an acorn for each child. Provide crayons and glue. (If Hungry Squirrels are not used for the bulletin board, provide pine straw, leaves, etc., to cover the ground area on the sheet.)

Procedure - Color and cut out the squirrel. Apply a thick "puddle" of glue on the area marked "X". Place an acorn in the glue.

"Big Acorn" (Booklet)

Preparation - Duplicate the "Acorn Cap" on manilla paper and the "Acorn" on brown construction paper. Provide a copy of each and one sheet of yellow, red, or orange construction paper for every child. Supply scissors and glue.

Procedure - Cut out each acorn part. Glue the acorn with the cap on top to the sheet of construction paper.

Math

"Set of Acorns"

Duplicate and distribute the "Set of Acorns" sheet. Color the acorns, then cut the sheet in half on the dotted line. Next, cut out the acorns, and glue inside the closed curve. Count the acorns. How many acorns are in the set?

Music - Movement - Games-

Song - "Where Oh Where Is Pretty Little Susie?"

(Way Down Yonder in the Paw Paw Patch)

Where oh where is pretty little Susie?

Where oh where is pretty little Susie?

Where oh where is pretty little Susie?

Way down yonder in the paw paw patch.

Picking up paw paws, put 'em in your pocket.

Picking up paw paws, put 'em in your pocket.

Picking up paw paws, put 'em in your pocket

Way down yonder in the paw paw patch.

Come on boys, let's go find her.

Come on boys, let's go find her.

Come on boys, let's go find her

Way down yonder in the paw paw patch.

Come on boys, bring her back again.

Come on boys, bring her back again.

Come on boys, bring her back again

Way down yonder in the paw paw patch.

Procedure - The children move in a circle performing the following actions for each verse.

1. Shade your eyes and look from side to side as you walk in the circle.

2. Pick up paw paws and put them in your pocket - continue walking.

3. Make a waving motion and trot in the circle.

4. Choose a partner and skip in the circle.

Game - "Duck Duck Goose"

The children sit in a circle. One child is chosen to be "it." "It" walks around the circle touching each child on the shoulder and saying "duck." When "it" touches a child and says "goose," that child must chase "it" around the circle. If "it" is caught, he or she sits in the center of the circle; and the "goose" is the new "it." If "it" makes it around the circle and takes the "goose's" place without being tagged, he or she stays in the circle; and the "goose" sits in the circle. A new "it" is chosen. Repeat until everyone has a chance to run.

Game - "Feather Relay"

Use tape to mark the start and finish lines. These should not be over eight feet apart. Divide the class into two teams. Line the teams in two lines, single file, behind the start line. Place a feather on the floor in front of each team. The first player for each team crawls on the floor blowing the feather. When the feathers are blown past the finish line, the players pick them up, run back, and place them on the floor for the next players. The team's last player who blows the feather across the finish line first wins the game.

<u>Story Time</u>

<u>Book</u> - <u>Miss Suzy</u> - Miriam Young

<u>Book</u> - <u>Deep In the Forest</u> - Brinton Turkle

<u>Kindergarten Kitchen</u>

<u>Squirrel Stew</u>

1/2 box rice chex cereal

1/2 box corn chex cereal

1/2 box cheerios

1 cup pecans

1 cup peanuts (roasted)

1 box thin pretzels

2 sticks oleo

1 teaspoon garlic salt

1 teaspoon celery salt

1/4 teaspoon red pepper

1 Tablespoon Worcestershire sauce

Mix cereals, nuts, and pretzels in a large flat pan. In a saucepan, melt butter, and add remaining ingredients. Pour sauce over mixture in pan. Bake at 300 degrees (Fahrenheit) for one hour, stirring every 15 minutes.

Day 4 - Trees In Fall

Concept Information

One of the most beautiful things to see in Fall is the leaves on the trees. Many have changed from green to red, yellow, orange, or brown.

To prepare for winter, trees store water and food inside. So the leaves, which make food for the tree, are no longer needed. As they die, the leaves turn different colors and begin falling from the trees.

Fall is also the time when trees drop their seeds on the ground. If the seed gets pushed into the ground or covered with earth, it will grow into a new tree. But sometimes seeds such as acorns are eaten by animals. Some, such as pecans, are eaten by people.

Language Arts - Social Studies - Science

Discussion

Relate the concept information, and define vocabulary words. Make and show the children a poster which has different kinds of trees. Each may have a seed and a preserved leaf mounted beside it. Pass around some seeds and leaves. Discuss the colors, shapes, and textures.

Book

Read Johnny Maple-Leaf by Alvin Tresselt.

"Colors of Fall" Sheet (Booklet)

Duplicate the "Colors of Fall" sheet. Distribute the sheets, crayons, and glue. Put a pile of leaves on each table. The children trace the color word and glue a leaf of that color in the block. Repeat with each section.

Fingerplay - "Leaves"

The leaves are dropping from the trees, (Flutter fingers up and down)

Yellow, brown, and red. (Flutter fingers up and down)

They patter softly like the rain. (Tap fingers on floor)

One landed on my head. (Tap head)

"Leaf Match"

Duplicate a sheet for each child. The children find the leaves that are alike and draw a line from one to the other.

Art

Fall Collage

Preparation - Take the children outside to collect items for their collages or use items collected on the Gathering Walk (see Day 1). Make patterns of the Collage Acorn. Pass out patterns, brown construction paper, scissors, and glue.

Procedure - Trace the acorn pattern on the brown construction paper, and cut out. Glue fall items on the acorn.

Leaf Rubbings

Preparation - Supply an assortment of leaves, thin white paper, and crayons.

Procedure - Place a leaf under the paper. Anchor the leaf and paper with one hand. Color over the leaf with the side of a crayon. Lift the paper, and remove the leaf. Repeat the procedure with different leaves and colors.

Tiny Trees

Preparation - Collect half-pint milk cartons, rinse, and cut off the tops. Supply scissors, glue, rubber bands, scrap paper in fall colors, and a square of tissue paper.

Procedure - Go outside and fill the cartons with dirt. Find twigs that resemble tiny trees. Push into the dirt and pack. Return to the classroom, and set the carton on the tissue paper square. Bring up the sides to cover the box, and secure with a rubber band. Cut the scrap paper into small pieces, and glue these "leaves" to the branches.

Math

"Pumpkin Puzzle"

Duplicate both pages of the Pumpkin Puzzle. Hand out the "Pumpkin Puzzle Pieces" sheet first, along with crayons and scissors. The children color the objects and cut out the pieces. Distribute the "Pumpkin Puzzle" sheet. The children choose a puzzle piece, count the objects, and find the corresponding numeral on the puzzle page. The piece is then glued in place. Repeat this procedure with each piece until the puzzle is completed.

Music - Movement - Games

Action Song - "I'm a Nut" by Esther L. Nelson

For words and music, see the sheet "I'm a Nut" in pattern section.

Procedure - Sing the song, performing the actions as follows: "I'm a little acorn, small and round,"--A circle dance goes with it. Step to the right with your right foot. Then step behind it and put your full weight on that left foot. Continue this for seven steps. On the eighth step (the word "round"), stamp your left foot right near your right foot.

"Lying on the cold, cold ground" - Now reverse the entire step. Start to the left with your left foot, put your weight on your right foot behind it, and move to the left for seven counts, stamping your right foot on the eighth count (the word "ground"). When you do the circle walk, bend the knee of the leg that steps to the side (your right foot when you go right, your left foot when you go left). When you put your other foot behind it, get up on your toes so that you're moving down and up, like a fast horse on a carousel, as well as to the side.

"People come and step on me." - On this line, start from the beginning, but this time do only two side-behind steps. On the word "step," jump (with both feet in place) and land with a loud noise.

"That's why I'm so cracked, you see." - On this line, move to the left with the same side-behind step but this time speed it up double-time so it becomes almost a gallop to the side. Stop galloping on the word "see," which means you have taken thirteen steps. This stanza is difficult because it is not symmetrical as are the others. You really have to think ahead to each set of movements.

"I'm a nut!" - Drop hands and jump toward the center of the circle.
"Tch, tch" - Stand where you are and shake your head and shoulders.
"I'm a nut!" - Jump back to place.
"Tch, tch" - Repeat the head and shoulders shake again.

Game - "Tree Tag"

The play area must have several trees. One child is chosen to be the "Mean Owl." The rest of the children are "Squirrels." The teacher stands in the middle of the play area and calls out "red leaves." The "Squirrels" must run and touch the tree that has any red leaves to be safe from the "Mean Owl." Those tagged sit in an area to the side called "the Squirrel Pot." The teacher continues the game by calling out "yellow leaves" or "green leaves", etc. The last "Squirrel" in the game is the new "Mean Owl."

Story Time

Book - A Tree Is Nice - Janice May Udry

Kindergarten Kitchen

"Apple Sandwiches"

(Single serving recipe)

Break a large graham cracker in half and spread with ready-made applesauce. (For "class made" applesauce, see recipe below.) Top with a layer of whipped cream and the remaining half of the graham cracker. Chill for five minutes and serve.

Applesauce

6 apples

1/2 cup water

1/2 cup sugar

Cinnamon

Peel, core, and slice the apples into chunks. Cook in a saucepan in water until tender. Stir in sugar and sprinkle with cinnamon. Drain and mash with a fork. (Makes 6 servings)

Fall Mural

Preparation - Mix tempera of fall colors or use fingerpaints. Provide mural paper, half sheets of brown construction paper, glue, and paint.

Procedure - Tear the brown paper into the shape of a tree trunk. Glue on designated area of the mural paper. Dip one finger in the paint, and print leaves on the trees. Use one finger to paint your name under the tree.

Day 5 - Fall Harvest

Concept Information

Some plants grow <u>fruit</u>, berries, or <u>vegetables</u> which we eat as food. Corn, beans, tomatoes, blueberries, onions, and pumpkins all come from plants. Apples, plums, oranges, peaches, and pears grow on trees.

Farmers plant <u>seeds</u> in their <u>fields</u> which grow into <u>plants</u>. Trees are also grown from seeds. The tree or plant grows a fruit, vegetable, nut, or berry. At Harvest time, farmers pick the vegetables and fruit that they have grown on their farms. Later we buy this food at <u>grocery stores</u>.

Language Arts - Social Studies

Discussion

Relate the concept information, and define vocabulary words. Construct a simple puppet from a toilet tissue roll to be "Farmer Brown." Use burlap for his hat and denim for his overalls. Bring fresh fruit and vegetables and the seeds of each, and place in a wagon, if available. Farmer Brown pulls the wagon into the room. Conduct an interview with the farmer about his farm, crops, and fruit and vegetables in his wagon. Encourage the children to ask questions. The farmer then pulls his wagon around, letting each child touch, smell, and look at its contents.

Harvest Party

Preparation -

1. Enlist the aid of two or three parents for this activity. (If parents are unavailable, the children's participation will be limited to observing, tasting, and stirring.)

2. Assemble vegetables such as: corn, cauliflower, celery, onions, squash, bell peppers, and tomatoes (actually a berry); fruit such as: apples, peaches, pears, and raisins.

3. Divide the class into small groups and set up a station for each group.

4. Cover each table with newspapers or plastic.

5. Provide cutting boards, small knives, scissors, potato peelers, and bowls.

6. Set up a cooking station.

7. Assign a parent to each station.

Procedure - Peel and/or chop into small pieces the fruit and vegetables, and place in separate bowls. (Scissors may be used to chop pieces of some fruit or vegetables.) Put the bowls on one table. Let the children observe, smell, and then taste a small piece of each fruit and vegetable. Divide the class into two groups. One group prepares the "Fruit Salad" at a table. The other group prepares the "Fresh Vegetable Medley" at the cooking station. Eat on paper plates with plastic forks.

Note: Preparations for Fruit and Vegetable Prints (see Art) can be included in this activity.

"Fresh Vegetable Medley"

Fresh vegetables, chopped

3 Tablespoons salad oil

1/2 cup water

2 chicken-flavored bouillon cubes

1/2 teaspoon salt

1/4 teaspoon pepper

Heat salad oil in a large skillet. Add all vegetables except the tomatoes. Cook for about five minutes, stirring frequently. Add water, chicken-

215

flavored bouillon cubes, salt, and pepper. Cook for five minutes or until vegetables are tender. Add tomatoes, and continue cooking until heated.

"Fruit Salad"

Fresh fruit, chopped

Miniature marshmallows, 1 bag

Raisins and/or chopped nuts

4 Tablespoons mayonnaise

Milk (enough to thin mayonnaise to a cream consistency)

Mix all fruit in a large bowl. Add marshmallows, raisins and/or nuts. Mix milk and mayonnaise, and pour on the fruit. Mix and serve. (Chill, if time allows.)

Poem Activity - "The Apple Tree"

Duplicate "The Apple Tree" sheet for each child. The children cut out the apple, recite the poem, then punch holes on the dots. A piece of yarn is laced through the holes and tied in a bow at the stem. Note: Dip end of yarn in glue and dry, or use tape.

Book - Johnny Appleseed by Walt Disney

Read the book; then let the children act out the story.

Art

Fruit and Vegetable Prints

Preparation - Cut fruit and vegetables in half so that the insides are exposed. Allow any "juicy" fruit or vegetable to sit out and dry. Mix different colors of tempera paints, and pour thin layers in trays. Pass out newsprint.

Procedure - Dip fruit or vegetable in paint and print on paper. Vary the colors and vegetables and fruit.

Scarecrow

Preparation - Duplicate the "Scarecrow" sheet on white construction paper. Distribute sheet, crayons, scissors, and four paper fasteners to each child.

Procedure - Color and cut out the parts of the scarecrow. Push a paper fastener through the dot on the shoulder, then through the "X" on the arm. Turn the scarecrow over and press down the two stems of the fastener. Repeat with each appendage.

Bread Dough Vegetables and Fruit

Preparation - Cover the mixing table with a plastic bag. Set out flour, water, salt, and mixing bowl, wooden spoons and cookie sheets. Mix tempera paints of various colors. Provide paint brushes.

Basic Bread Dough Recipe   (Yield 4-6 vegetables or fruits)

2 cups flour

1 cup salt

3/4 cup water

Combine ingredients. Add water a little at a time. Stir, then use hands to form a ball. Knead for 7-10 minutes. If the mixture is too dry, add a little water; if it is too sticky, add flour.

Procedure - Mix one batch in each bowl. Help the children measure, mix, and knead the dough. Divide the dough. Direct the children to shape the dough into a fruit or vegetable. To join raw dough pieces together, moisten edges and press together. Place on foil-covered cookie sheets. Bake at 325 degrees. Allow 30 minutes for every quarter inch of thickness or bake until light brown. Cool. Paint with tempera paint. Coat with acrylic spray, if desired. Note: Warn children not to taste.

Math

Picking Blueberries

Preparation - Read Blueberries for Sal by Robert McCloskey, or tell the children, "Today we are going to pick blueberries." Duplicate the "Pickin' Blueberries" sheet. Hand out the sheets and scissors. The children color and cut out the bucket and blueberries.

Procedure - The child places the bucket on the table with the blueberries in a pile beside it. Give the class directions such as:

1. Put 5 blueberries in your bucket.

2. Take 2 blueberries out of your bucket--how many are left?
    (5 - 2 = 3)

3. Put 3 more blueberries in your bucket--count how many blueberries you have now in your bucket. (3 + 3 = 6)

4. Empty your bucket. Put a handful of blueberries in your bucket. Count how many you put in.

Continue in this manner. You may also wish to show the math operations involved (in parentheses) on the board.

Music - Movement - Games

Action Song - "The Farmer Picks the Corn"
Tune - "The Farmer in the Dell"
The children move in a circle and play the game as usual. But instead of "the farmer takes a wife," substitute the words "the farmer picks the

corn," "the corn picks the squash," "the squash picks the beans," etc., ending with "the scarecrow stands alone."

Game - "Fruit and Vegetable Salad"

One child is chosen as the Chef. The rest of the children sit in chairs in a circle. Two are corn, two are apples, two are beans, and so forth. The Chef calls out "Apples" and those two exchange seats. The Chef continues to call out the names of different fruits or vegetables. Whenever he or she feels like it, the Chef calls out "Salad Toss." All the children, including the Chef, scramble to find new seats. The person left without a seat is the new Chef.

Note: For identification, a picture-card necklace can be made for each child.

Story Time

Book - Autumn Harvest - Alvin Tresselt
Book - Hard Scrabble Harvest - Dahlov Ipcar

Kindergarten Kitchen

Blueberry Muffins

Purchase and prepare a Blueberry Muffin mix which contains real blueberries.

Fall Outing - (Culminating Activity) (Booklet)

Plan a walk through a nearby park. Observe and discuss all the signs of fall. After the trip, record these observations on an experience chart. Transfer to ditto, and duplicate for booklet.

Concept Review - "Happy Leaves"

Duplicate the "Happy Leaf" sheet. Cut out a leaf for each child, and punch a hole at the dot. String the leaf on a piece of yarn to make a necklace. Ask review questions about the unit. Award a "Happy Leaf" necklace for each correct answer. Be sure each child gets a necklace.

Concept Evaluation - (See Introduction)

Dear Parents,

Our class will begin our unit on Fall on _____.
Each day we will be learning about the weather, animals, and activities of
this special season of the year. Below are ways you can help:

Things to Send: _____

_____

_____

Volunteers Needed To: _____

_____

_____

Follow-Up: At the end of the unit, ask your child to share some of the
following songs, fingerplays, etc.

_____

_____

Follow-Up Questions for Your Child:

1. Name the four seasons.

2. Name things that happen in fall.

3. Describe the fall weather and clothing.

4. What does a squirrel do in the fall?

5. Why do most trees lose their leaves in fall?

6. What do farmers do at harvest time?

Family Activities: Share the objects found on the class Gathering Walk.

Each morning help your child "set" the weather disc.

Thank you for your cooperation.

Sincerely,

FALL

Harvest Time

 Copyright © 1987. Carol Taylor Bond

Science Center

Copyright © 1987.   Carol Taylor Bond

Seasons
Symbols

Copyright © 1987. Carol Taylor Bond

225

A Tree In All Seasons

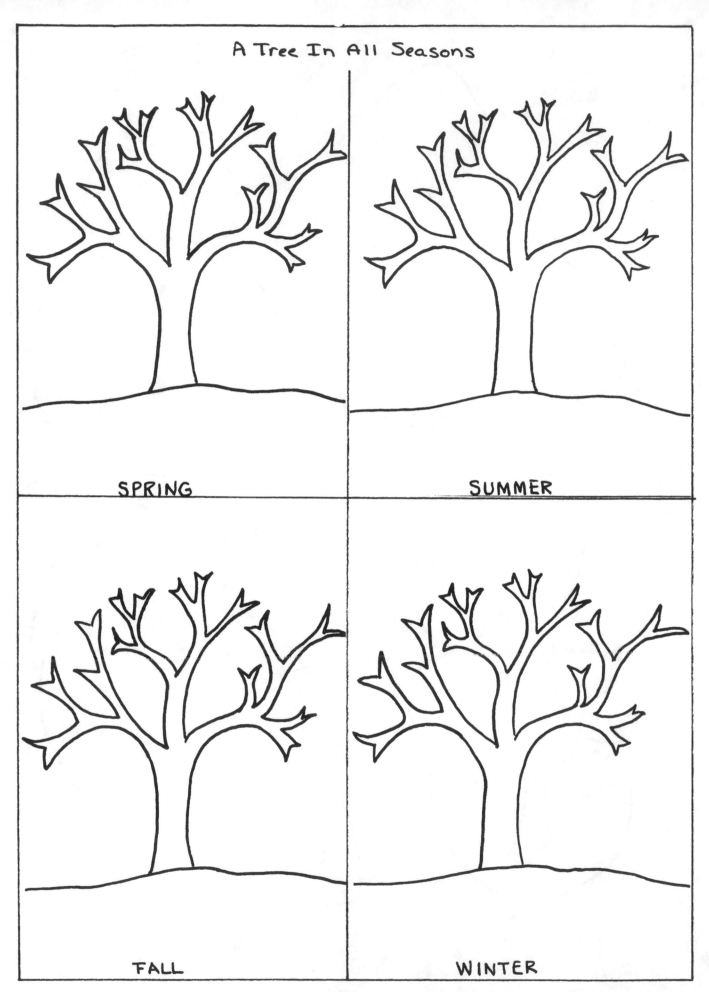

SPRING

SUMMER

FALL

WINTER

Copyright © 1987.   Carol Taylor Bond

Super Stuff Bucket

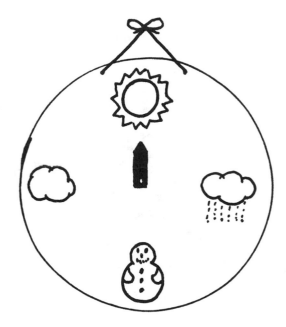

Weather Disc

Fall Crowns

Copyright © 1987. Carol Taylor Bond

227

Sunshine

Rain

Snow

Cloudy

Indicator

Copyright ©1987. Carol Taylor Bond

228

Copyright © 1987. Carol Taylor Bond

Weather Charts

Monday	
Tuesday	
Wednesday	
Thursday	
Friday	

 Copyright © 1987. Carol Taylor Bond

Football

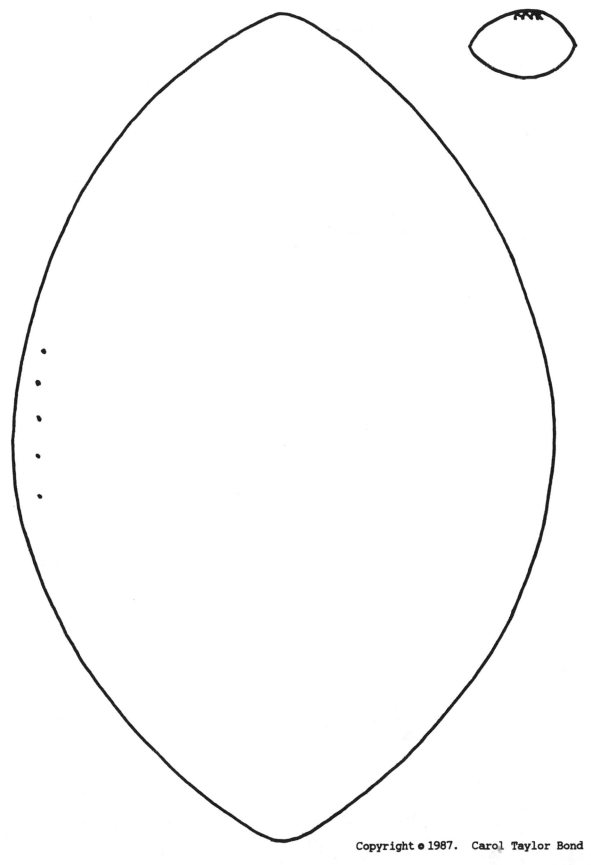

Copyright © 1987. Carol Taylor Bond

231

Time To Rake

Copyright © 1987. Carol Taylor Bond

Apple Count

Name _____

3   4   5

4   5   6

3   4   5

4   5   6

Copyright © 1987.   Carol Taylor Bond

Raking Leaves

I like to rake the leaves in-to a great big hump,

Back up just a lit-tle bit and bend my knees and jump!

Copyright © 1987. Carol Taylor Bond

Pathtracer Sheet

Copyright © 1987.   Carol Taylor Bond

235

Copyright © 1987.   Carol Taylor Bond

The Mean Old Man

Copyright © 1987. Carol Taylor Bond

237

Copyright © 1987. Carol Taylor Bond

Big Acorn - Acorn Cap

Copyright © 1987. Carol Taylor Bond

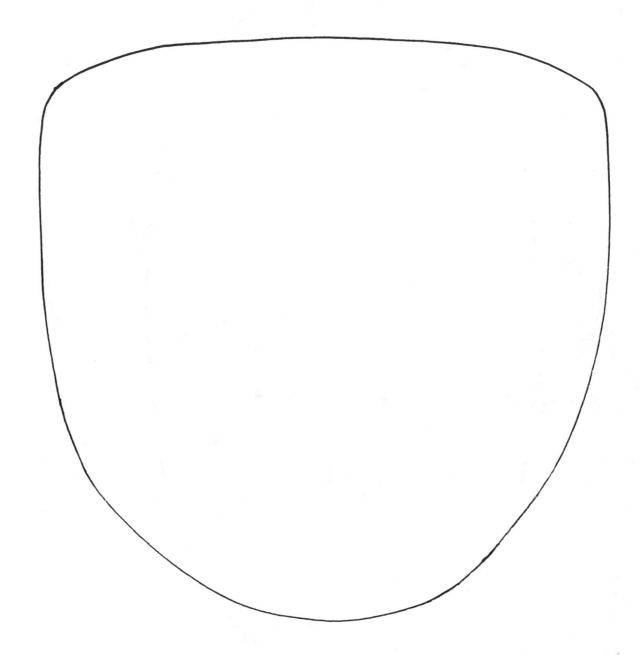

Copyright © 1987.   Carol Taylor Bond

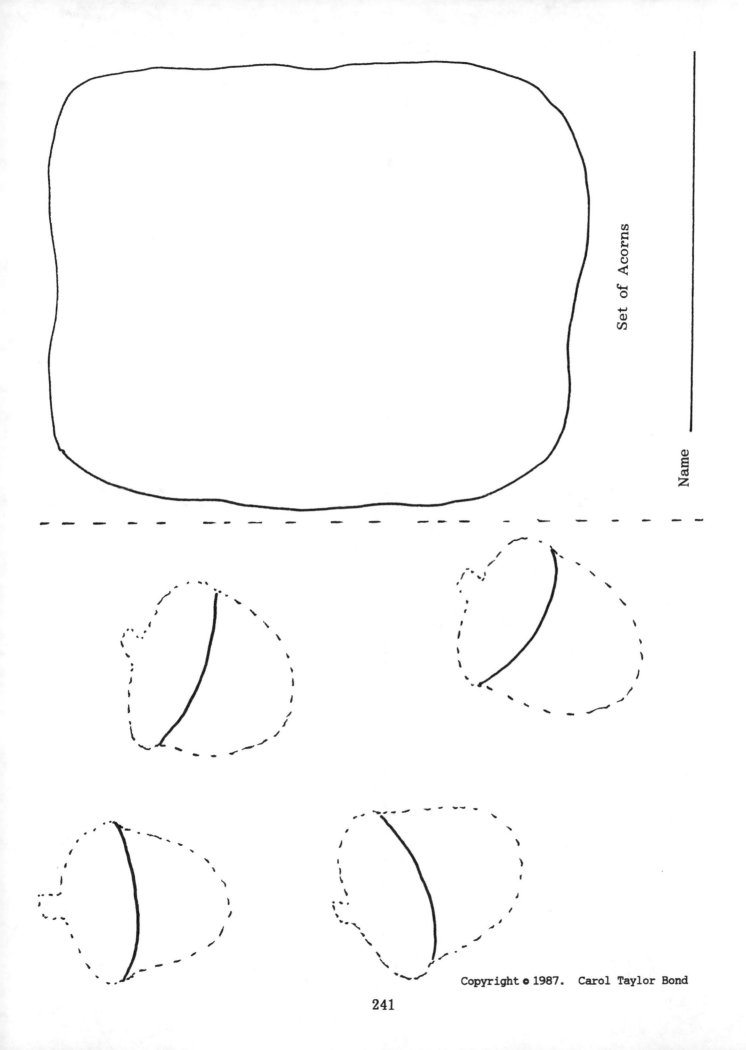

Set of Acorns

Name _____

Copyright © 1987. Carol Taylor Bond

red | brown

orange | yellow

Copyright © 1987. Carol Taylor Bond

Leaf Match

Copyright © 1987. Carol Taylor Bond

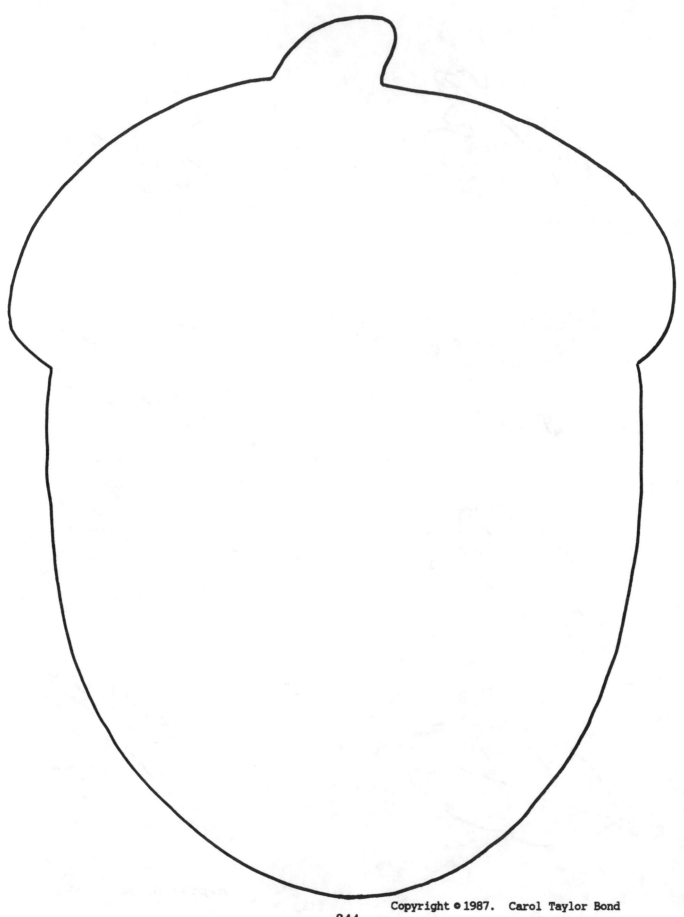

Copyright © 1987.   Carol Taylor Bond

Tiny Tree

Copyright © 1987. Carol Taylor Bond

Pumpkin Puzzle

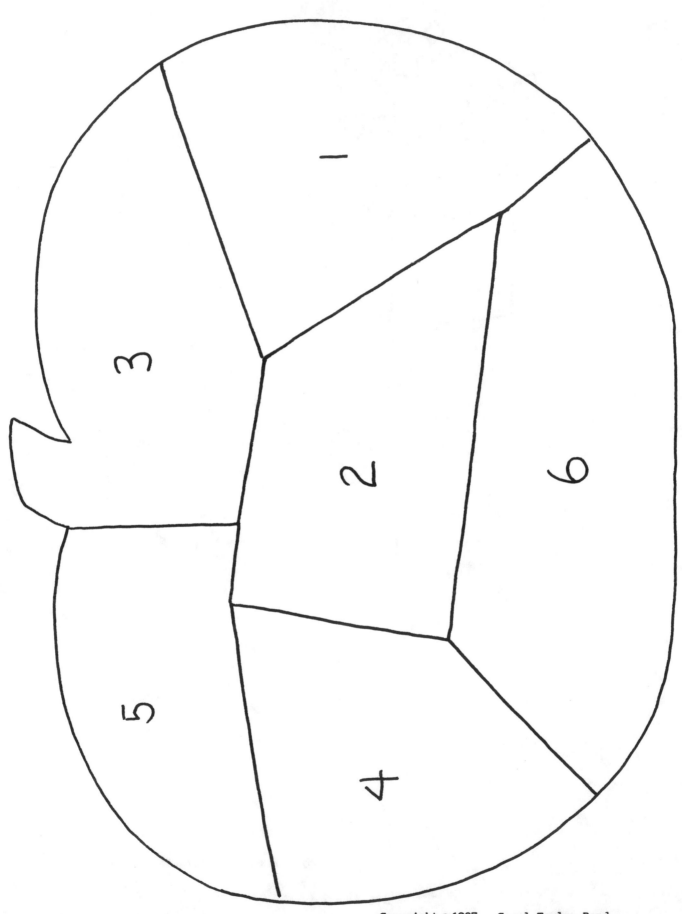

Copyright © 1987. Carol Taylor Bond

Puzzle Pieces

 Copyright © 1987. Carol Taylor Bond

I'M A NUT

Esther L. Nelson

Copyright ©1987. Carol Taylor Bond

248

Farmer Brown Puppet

Copyright © 1987. Carol Taylor Bond

249

The Apple Tree

Way up high in the apple tree,

A big, shiny apple, smiling at me,

I shook the tree as hard as I could,

Down came the apple, and

Ummm, it was good!

Copyright © 1987. Carol Taylor Bond

Scarecrow

Copyright © 1987. Carol Taylor Bond

251

Copyright ©1987. Carol Taylor Bond

Happy Leaves

Copyright © 1987.   Carol Taylor Bond

Columbus Day

<u>Proposed Time</u>: 1 day

<u>Unit Objectives</u>

To develop understanding of Columbus Day

To develop understanding of the life of Christopher Columbus

<u>Room Environment - Bulletin Boards</u>

<u>"Columbus and Crew"</u>

Cover the top portion of the bulletin board with light blue paper and the bottom with blue or green paper cut to represent the sea. Label the bulletin board. Enlarge the ship pattern, and make three ships of graduated sizes. Label the smallest the "Nina," the middle-sized, the "Pinta," and the largest, the "Santa Maria." Mount the ships on the sea. Give each child a piece of drawing paper, crayons, and scissors. Direct them to draw, color, and cut out a self-portrait. Staple the children's self-portraits in the ships.

Note: There must be room on the ships for all of the self-portraits. Therefore, the size of the drawing paper will depend on the dimensions of the ships.

<u>Room Environment - Displays</u>

<u>"Columbus Sails"</u> - <u>(Table Display)</u>

Place a long table next to a wall in the classroom or hall. On the wall above the table, make and mount a sign which says "Columbus Sails." Display the "Ships Upon the Sea" (see Art - Day 1) on the table.

<u>Day 1</u> - <u>Columbus Day</u>

<u>Concept Information</u>

On October 12th of each year, we <u>celebrate</u> Columbus Day. On this day, we remember a man named Christopher Columbus who first <u>discovered</u> America.

When Christopher Columbus was a little boy, he dreamed of being a sailor. At that time, everyone thought that the <u>earth</u> was flat. They believed if you sailed on a ship too far you would fall off the edge of the world. Columbus spent much time thinking and watching the ships sailing on the sea. He believed the earth was round like an orange, and he was right. He thought if he could sail across the ocean he would find <u>unknown</u> countries. Columbus asked the King of Portugal for ships and men to make the voyage. The king said no. Columbus then asked King Ferdinand and Queen Isabella of Spain to help him. They gave him three ships which Columbus named the <u>Nina</u>, the <u>Pinta</u>, and the <u>Santa Maria</u>, and the money for <u>crews</u> and <u>supplies.</u>

The three ships left Spain and sailed for two long months. The men on the ships grew tired and unhappy. They told Columbus that they would throw him in the sea if he did not return home. But Columbus told them that they would find land soon. On October 12, 1492, they landed on an <u>island</u> never before discovered. The King and Queen of Spain were so happy that they let Columbus make three more trips across the ocean. He and his men discovered Cuba, Haiti, the Dominican Republic, and the South American continent. Columbus died in 1506.

Language Arts - Social Studies

Discussion

Relate the concept information, and define vocabulary words. Show pictures from the book <u>Columbus</u> by Ingri and Edgar Parin d'Aulaire.

Seatwork - "Columbus' Voyage" Sheet

Duplicate and distribute the sheet. The children trace over the line of Columbus' first voyage with a crayon. While following the path, discuss the various locations.

Role Playing

Present different situations for the children to act out, such as: Columbus asking the king and queen for ships and money; Columbus telling his friends he thinks the world is round; Columbus facing an angry crew; and Columbus and crew meeting the natives.

Experience Story

Ask the children to dictate the steps leading to Columbus' discovery of America. Write the steps on an experience chart. When the story is completed, read it to the class. Let the children illustrate the story on the chart.

Art

Ships Upon the Sea

Preparation - Give each child a paper plate, an 11" square of blue or green crepe paper, three toothpicks, three walnut shell halves, and three 2" squares of white paper. Provide glue and scissors. Pass around a lump of modeling clay.

Procedure - Pinch off three bits of clay about the size of an "M & M," and roll into three balls. Press each ball into the bottom of each walnut shell half. Fold the 2" squares in half. Near the top and bottom of the squares, make a small cut on the fold. Insert the toothpicks through these two holes to make the sails. To complete the ships, insert each sail into the balls of clay. Cover the plate with glue. Lay the crepe paper on the glue. Pull up some portions to form waves. Put three "puddles" of glue on the "sea" and place a ship in each "puddle."

Note: A small amount of glue squirted around the base of the sail helps secure it.

Stand-Up Ships

Preparation - Duplicate and distribute the ships. Provide a piece of blue or green construction paper, scissors, crayons, and glue.

Procedure - Color, then cut out the ships following the dotted lines. Fold on the solid lines. Apply glue to the folded areas, and mount on the construction paper.

Math

Dot-to-Dot Sheet - "Crow's Nest"

Duplicate the sheet. As a group, follow the numbers connecting the dots with lines. Color the "Crow's Nest."

Music - Movement - Games

Action Song - "Columbus Sailed the Sea"
Tune - "The Farmer in the Dell"

Columbus sailed the sea,

Columbus sailed the sea,

Heave, ho, the sails do blow,

Columbus sailed the sea.

He had three sailing ships,

He had three sailing ships,

Heave, ho, the sails do blow,

He had three sailing ships.

The smallest was the Nina,

The smallest was the Nina,

Heave, ho, the sails do blow,

The smallest was the Nina.

Next came the Pinta,

Next came the Pinta,

Heave, ho, the sails do blow,

Next came the Pinta.

The Santa Maria was last,

The Santa Maria was last,

Heave, ho, the sails do blow,

The Santa Maria was last.

Columbus found new lands,

Columbus found new lands,

Heave, ho, the sails do blow,

Columbus found new lands.

Columbus sailed the sea,

We're thankful as we can be,

Heave, ho, the sails do blow,

Columbus sailed the sea.

The children sing the song while performing the following actions for each verse:

Verse 1: Move arms like waves.

Verse 2: Sway and hold up three fingers.

Verse 3: Form small ship with hands, sailing motion.

Verse 4: Form slightly larger ship and sail.

Verse 5: Extend arms in front, hands form the bow
of a large ship, sail it.

Verse 6: Sway from side to side with one hand pointing.

Verse 7: Sway from side to side with hands clasped.

Kindergarten Kitchen

Potato Ships

Bake a small potato for each child. Direct the children to make an "X" in the top of the potato with a plastic knife. Squeeze the potato with both hands (when cool enough). With a fork, mix in sour cream and butter. For the sail, stick a toothpick through a small slice of cheese; and insert in top of potato. Place prepared mushrooms around the sail to represent Columbus and his crew.

Concept Evaluation - (See Introduction)

Dear Parents,

    On _____, we will learn about Columbus Day. Below are ways you can help.

Things to Send: _____

_____

_____

Ways to Volunteer: _____

_____

_____

Follow-Up Questions: Who was Christopher Columbus?

    What did he do?

    Name Columbus' three ships.

    Thank you for your help.

    Sincerely,

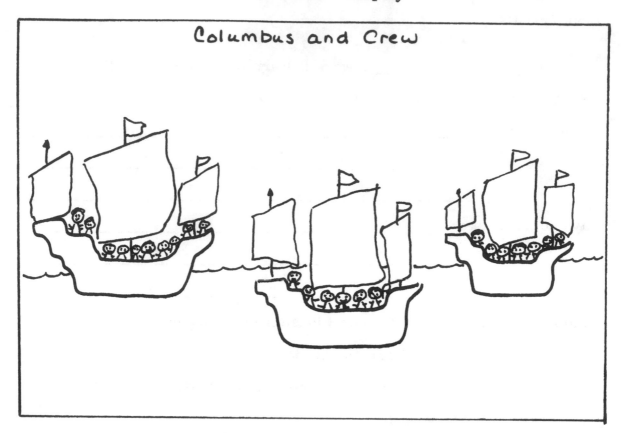

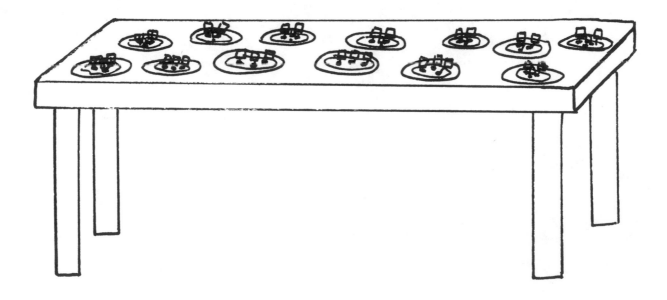

Copyright ©1987. Carol Taylor Bond

Ship Pattern

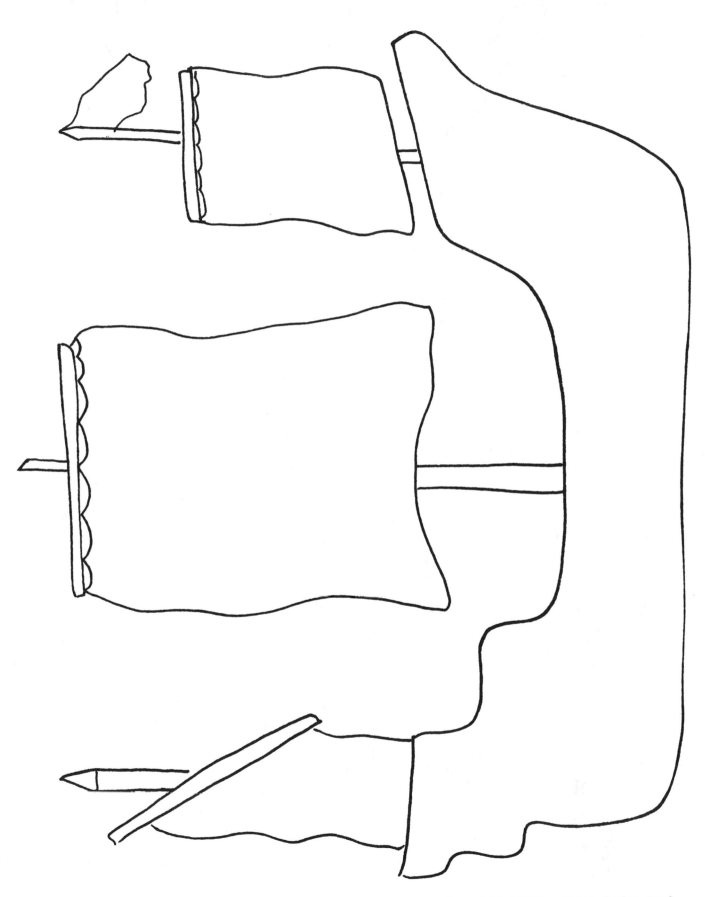

Copyright ©1987. Carol Taylor Bond

263

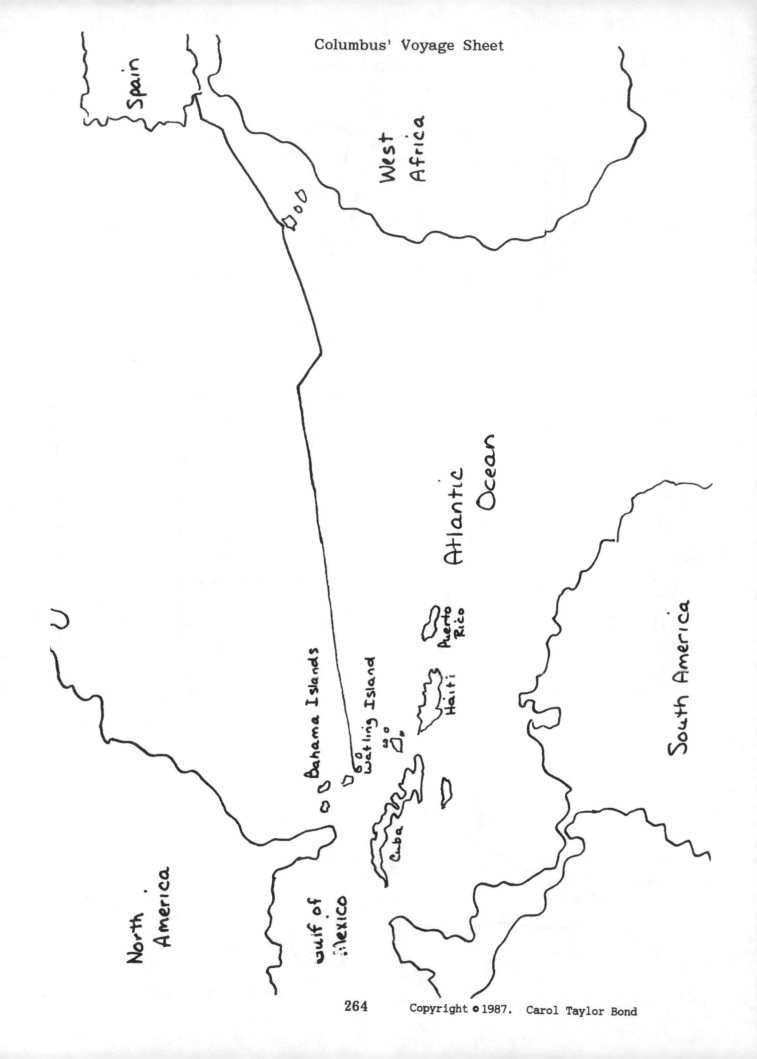

Columbus' Voyage Sheet

Spain

West Africa

Atlantic Ocean

South America

North America

Gulf of Mexico

Cuba

Bahama Islands

Watling Island

Haiti

Puerto Rico

 Copyright © 1987. Carol Taylor Bond

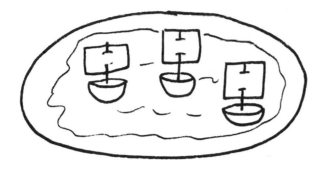

Ships Upon the Sea

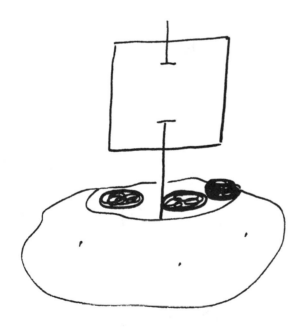

Potato Ships

Copyright © 1987.   Carol Taylor Bond

265

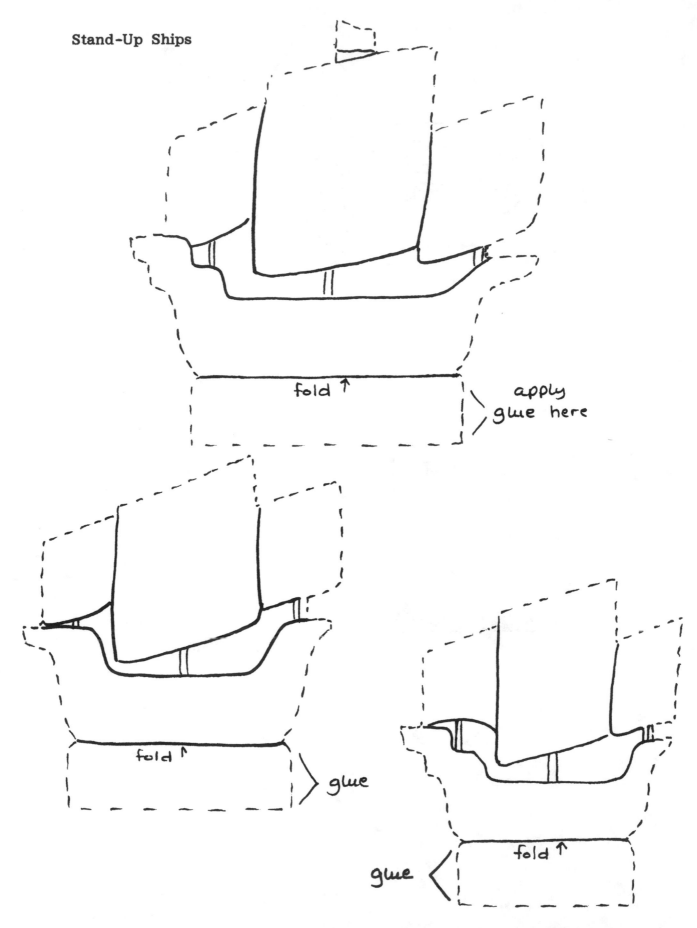

fold ↑

apply
glue here

fold ↑

glue

glue

fold ↑

Copyright © 1987. Carol Taylor Bond

266

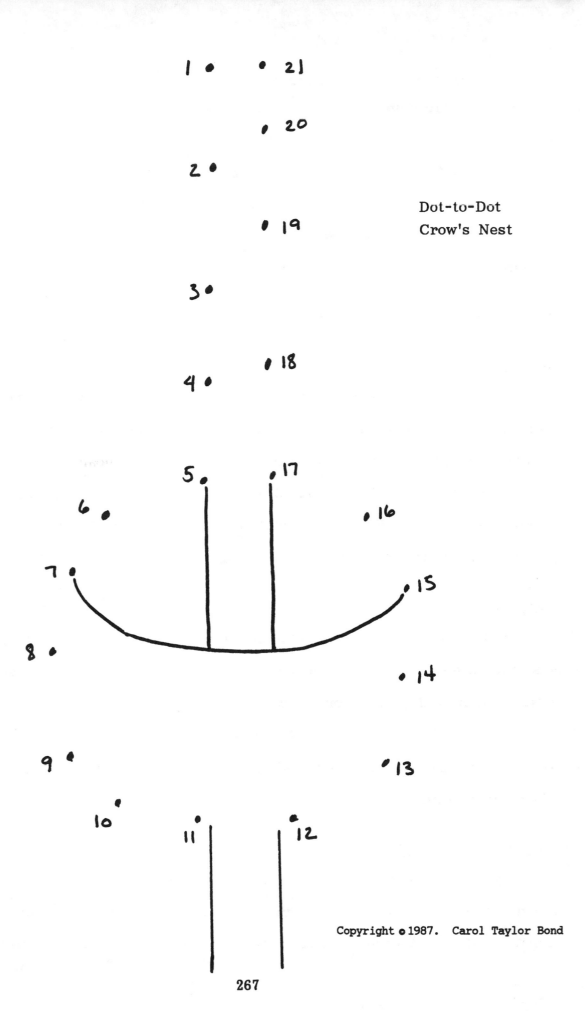

Dot-to-Dot
Crow's Nest

Copyright © 1987. Carol Taylor Bond

267

Halloween

Proposed Time: 10 days

Unit Objectives

To develop understanding of Halloween origins and symbols

To develop understanding of current Halloween customs

To emphasize the necessity of safety rules

To encourage enjoyment of Halloween

Room Environment - Bulletin Boards

"Happy Haunting"

Use orange bulletin board paper, black border, and black letters. To make the fence, fold black bulletin board paper accordion-style; and cut the top diagonally.   Staple to the bottom portion of the bulletin board.   Mount haunted house picture in the center. Cut out and mount black trees, black bats, and yellow moon. Staple the children's "Ghastly Ghosts" (see Art - Day 6) on remaining background.

"Ghostly Hosts"

Cover the top portion of the bulletin board with black and the bottom portion with brown, bulletin board paper. Use orange border and orange letters.   Mount orange moon on black sky and "Padded Pumpkins" (see Art - Day 8) on brown portion. Use green yarn for vines. Have the children cut around "Footprint Ghosts" (see Art - Day 6) as shown: .
Staple these to sky.

"Feed the Jack-O'-Lantern"

Use orange letters and border on a black background.   Cut a large pumpkin shape from white paper. Have the children paint this with orange tempera. Add features using black tempera. Be sure to make the mouth extra large. Cut out and laminate shapes, numerals, or alphabet letters. Place these around the Jack-O'-Lantern with stick pins. Each day one child feeds the Jack-O'-Lantern by finding and pinning a certain shape, numeral, or letter in the mouth.

Room Environment - Displays

"Pumpkin Patch"

Cut a three-inch strip of green paper long enough to fit around the sides of a shelf or table. The children can help "fringe" this strip to represent grass. Attach around the sides of the shelf or table with tape. Make a sign saying "Pumpkin Patch" from sturdy cardboard and attach at back of display. Fill the area with "Paper Bag Pumpkins" (see Art - Day 1). Tip: This looks especially good under your Halloween bulletin board.

"Owls in a Tree"

Draw and cut out a large tree from brown paper or burlap. Mount it on a door or wall. Staple or tack "Paper Plate Owls" (see Art - Day 3) on limbs.

Note: A tree may be a permanent part of your classroom. Decorate it with monthly symbols made by the children.

Day 1 - Introduction

Concept Information

Two thousand years ago in France and England, the Celtic people held a
festival for the dead on the last day of their year, October 31st. To
please their "Lord of the Dead," the Celtic priests would burn criminals
and animals. Witches also met on this night to cast spells and see into
the future.

Later a new religion, Christianity, began. Christians believed in God.
They did not like witches or festivals for the dead. The Christians started
a holiday to honor saints called "All Saints' Day" on November 1st. But
the Celtics still had their "Festival for the Dead." And since it was on
the night before the Christians' "All Saints' Day," the Celtics began calling
it "All Hallows' Eve." This meant "the evening before All Saints' Day." It
later came to be called "Halloween."

Language Arts - Social Studies

Discussion

Locate France and England on a large globe. Define and discuss
vocabulary words. Share the information on Halloween origins. Use
pictures whenever possible.

Film

Discuss the mood of Halloween and play a record of scary sounds (there
are several on the market). Show the filmstrip or film, "The Legend of
Sleepy Hollow." Direct the children to retell the story in proper sequence.

<u>Fingerplay</u> - "Five Little Pumpkins"

Five little pumpkins sitting on a gate,   (Hold up 5 fingers)

The first one said, "It's getting late!"   (Hold up thumb)

The second one said, "There's witches in the air!"   (Hold up index finger)

The third one said, "Oh, we don't care!"   (Hold up third finger)

The fourth one said, "Let's run and run!"   (Hold up ring finger)

The fifth one said, "Isn't Halloween fun!"   (Hold up fifth finger)

Wooooo went the wind and out (Clap) went the light,

And the five little pumpkins rolled out of sight.   (Roll hands)

Art

Paper Bag Pumpkins

Preparation - Mix twice as much orange as green tempera paint. It is helpful to draw a line around the bag, approximately two inches from the top, to distinguish between green and orange areas. Pass out small (lunch size) paper bags to the children.

Procedure - Shred old newspapers and stuff into the bags. Paint the tops of the bags green and the bottoms orange. Allow to dry. Twist tops and secure with rubber bands. Use pieces of green yarn to represent vines. Wrap these around the tops, and put pumpkins in the "Pumpkin Patch."

Math

Halloween Counting Booklet

Duplicate and assemble the booklets. Show the children a finished booklet, and read the complete poem. Reread the lines for number one, and direct the children to repeat these with you. Show the page for number one, and discuss the haunted house. Direct the children to trace

the numeral one and the number word "one" with a crayon. They may
then color the picture.

Music and Movement - "A Terrible Sight"

Tune - "Three Blind Mice"

One haunted house,

One haunted house,

See how it creaks,

See how it creaks,

(Chorus) These things we see on Halloween night,

       Love to give all the children a fright,

       Have you ever seen such a terrible sight,

       As one haunted house? (substitute subject of each verse)

Verse:

Two old witches, See how they fly	Seven gray ghosts, See how they groan
Three black cats, See how they screech	Eight gory goblins, See how they stalk
Four scary spooks, See how they BOO	Nine brown owls, See how they hoot
Five moldy monsters, See how they moan	Ten trick or treaters, See how they RUN!!!!
Six flying bats, See how they swoop	

Story Time

Book - Where the Wild Things Are - Maurice Sendak

Book - Little Monsters - M. Jean Craig

Book - Mommy Says There Aren't Any Zombies, Ghosts, Vampires, Creatures, Demons, Monsters, Fiends, Goblins or Things - Judith Viorst

<u>Day 2</u> - <u>Trick or Treat</u>

<u>Concept Information</u>

During the <u>Middle Ages</u> (500-1450 A.D.), Halloween was a time to pull <u>pranks</u> on neighbors. Men dressed up like women, and women dressed up like men. In Ireland, <u>peasants</u> went from house to house asking for food and gifts. Those who gave them something were wished good luck. It was thought that it you dressed like a witch or a ghost or a goblin a real witch, ghost, or goblin would think you were a friend and leave you alone. When some of the Irish people came to the United States in 1840, "trick-or-treating" began here also. Today children still dress up in <u>costumes</u> and go from house to house collecting candy.

<u>Language Arts</u> - <u>Social Studies</u>

<u>Discussion</u>

Point out Ireland on the globe, and define vocabulary words.

Discuss the origins of Trick-or-Treating and today's customs.

<u>Film</u>

Show the film, "Trick or Treat" (Walt Disney). Review highlights of the film.

<u>Safety Rules</u>

List the following rules on the board. Read and explain each rule. Review by beginning each rule and asking the children to complete. Review periodically throughout the unit.

1. Wear a <u>fluorescent</u> costume, <u>reflector</u> <u>strips</u>, or carry a flashlight when you are trick-or-treating.

2. Always have an adult with you.

3. Walk on sidewalks. If you have to walk on the side of the street, walk toward traffic.

4. Do <u>not</u> eat anything until an adult has checked it at home. (Anything that is not in a sealed package should be thrown away.) Many malls, clubs, etc., are now offering safe trick-or-treating.

<u>Art</u>

<u>Trick or Treat Bags</u>

Preparation - Several weeks beforehand, ask parents to send a medium or large (heavy) brown paper bag to school. Provide fluorescent crayons or fluorescent tempera paint for this activity.

Procedure - Review and draw simple Halloween symbols on the board. The children then decorate their bags with the fluorescent crayons or tempera paints.

<u>Halloween Snapper</u>

Preparation - Duplicate the snapper pattern on orange construction paper or use the pattern to trace on orange felt. (If you are using felt, you will have to cut out all of the patterns and Jack-O'-Lantern features.) Provide baby food jar lids, one for each child.

Procedure - Cut out the snapper. (Remind the children to cut only on the dotted lines.) Cover the circle with a generous amount of glue. Place a baby jar lid, top side down, in the center circle. Fold the flaps into the cap. Allow this to dry and then color a Jack-O'-Lantern face on top. Press on the center of the top to make snapping sound.

Note: Fabric glue must be used with felt. Features will be glued rather than colored on the snapper.

Halloween Shaker

Preparation - Collect an orange juice can and top for each child. Make sure you have a supply of pebbles somewhere near the school. Precut pieces of construction paper to fit each can. Provide construction paper scraps.

Procedure - Give each child a can and top. Make a trip outside to collect pebbles. Show the children how many pebbles they should put in their cans (about $\frac{1}{4}$ of the can). Put glue all around the rim and top of the can. Replace top, and tape closed. Glue precut paper on can, and decorate with scraps.

Math

Halloween Counting Booklet

Repeat the procedure used for Day 1, using the number two - Trick or Treaters sheet.

Candy Count

Seat the children in a circle in the large group area. Pour a bagful of assorted "penny candy" into the middle of the circle. Choose one child at a time to count out as many pieces of candy as you direct. Then have several children sort the candy into groups (sets). Have the class determine which attributes were used for each group (color, size, shape, etc.). Reward the children for their performance by passing out the candy.

Music and Movement - "If It's Halloween and You Know It"
Tune - "If You're Happy and You Know It"

If it's Halloween and you know it, be a cat,

If it's Halloween and you know it, be a cat,

If it's Halloween and you know it,

Then your face will surely show it (make a face)

If it's Halloween and you know it, be a cat.

2. Fly like a witch.

3. Float like a ghost.

4. Shout "Trick or Treat!"

Procedure - Children sing and act out each verse.

Story Time

Book - Georgie - Robert Bright

Book - Trick or Treat Halloween - Sharon Peters

Day 3 - Owl

Concept Information

Owls are birds which hunt for food at night. They are very <u>useful</u> to farmers because they eat mice, rats, and moles. Because of its eyes, the owl looks like it is very wise. The owl has a large head, thick body, <u>hooked</u> <u>beak</u>, and sharp <u>claws</u>. There are about 500 kinds of owls. But long ago, people in Europe were afraid of owls. The owls' big, <u>staring</u> eyes and <u>weird</u> <u>call</u> made people think of witches. Owls are mostly seen at night which make them even more <u>frightening</u>.

<u>Language Arts</u> - <u>Social Studies</u> - <u>Science</u>

Discussion

Define vocabulary words, and locate Europe on the globe. Share the information on owls. Show pictures of owls in an encyclopedia. Listen to the owl's call on the sound effects record.

Book

Read <u>The Owl Who Hated the Dark</u> by Earle Goodenow. Assign parts and reread the book as the children act it out.

Art

Paper Plate Owls

Preparation - Duplicate features on construction paper as directed on pattern pages. Mix brown tempera paint.

Procedure - Paint entire back of paper plate. As paint dries, cut out features. Glue these to the plate. Color inside of the eyes black.

Egg Carton Owl

Preparation - Collect cardboard egg cartons. You will need one half carton for every child. Cut each carton in half. Eyes can be made by cutting an egg cup for each eye, or by cutting circles from construction paper. Precut feet.

Procedure - Paint tops and bottoms of egg cartons with brown tempera paint. If egg cups are used for eyes, paint yellow or orange. Use markers to make the black center of eyes. Glue eyes on top of carton, and feet to bottom. Front "ruffles" can be made with paint or markers.

Stretchy Owl

Preparation - Duplicate head, wings, and tail on brown construction paper. Duplicate eyes of Paper Plate Owl. Collect one coat hanger per child and stretch into oval shape. Provide each child with one pantyhose leg.

Procedure - Slip pantyhose leg over the hanger. (Children may work in pairs.) With string, rubber band, or twistee, tie hose at "neck" of coat hanger. Color center of eyes black, cut out. Cut out and fringe wings and tail. Cut out head, and glue on eyes. Glue head, wings, and tail to hose body. Cut out and glue triangular beak.

Math

Halloween Counting Booklet

Repeat Day 1 procedure, using number three - Owls sheet.

Music and Movement - "Not Me"

Tune - "Skip to My Lou"

An old owl sat in the big oak tree, (Stand like a tree)

Big eyes staring to see what he could see, (Circle eyes with
                                              thumbs and index fingers)
He looked all around and WHOOO said he, (Keep eyes circled)

All I could say was (pause) NOT ME! (Shake head, look scared,
                                          point to yourself)

Action Game - "The Wise Owl Says"

This game is played just like "Simon Says." Choose one child to be the Wise Owl. He/she stands in front of the group and gives directions for different movements. The children listen for the key words, "The Wise Owl says," before performing actions. If they perform actions without hearing the key words, they are out. The last child standing is the new Wise Owl.

Story Time

Book - Happy Owls - Celestino Piatti

Book - Owl at Home - Arnold Lobel

Day 4 - Black Cat

Concept Information

Long ago people thought that cats had magical powers. They thought cats had once been human beings, but had been changed by evil spells. Witches were known to have cats. And although the cats were not all black, at night they looked black. So people believed that all witches' cats were black. The yellow eyes and quiet movements of the cat made them frightening.

Language Arts - Social Studies - Science

Discussion

Show pictures of cats. Define vocabulary words and share concept information. Play sound effects record. Identify the screeching cat. How does this differ from cat sounds the children have heard?

Book - The Tale of the Black Cat - Carl Withers

This book lends itself perfectly for "drawing as you tell it." Therefore, tell the story rather than read it. Use a large sheet of white paper and a black marker to draw the cat.

Fingerplay - "The Witch's Cat Am I"

The witch's cat am I, (Make a fist with 2 fingers extended for cat)

On the witch's broom I fly, (Hold broom and "fly")

My glowing eyes are a fearsome sight (Circle eyes with fingers)

My screech can wake you in the night (Pop open eyes)

The witch's cat am I. (Make fist with two extended fingers and stroke fist with other hand)

280

Art

Black Cat

Preparation - Using white chalk or light colored crayon, trace around pattern as shown on pattern page. Each cat requires one sheet of black construction paper and a portion of another sheet for the tail and whiskers. You may cut out eyes, nose, whiskers, and tail yourself or duplicate for the children to cut.

Procedure - Cut on the lines. Glue features to face. Insert head and tail in slits. Display on shelf or table.

Milk Carton Black Cat

Preparation - Collect one half-pint milk carton for each child. Rinse and dry. Cut top of milk carton, as shown, to form ears. Staple closed. Use glue to cover with white paper. Duplicate yellow eyes, blue whiskers, and red nose and mouth on construction paper. Mix black tempera paint.

Procedure - Paint the milk carton black. Cut and glue on features.

Note: Carton can be left open to hold party favors.

Math

Halloween Counting Booklet

Repeat Day 1 procedure, using number four - Cats sheet.

Black Cat Drill

Draw a black cat at the top of the blackboard. Beneath the cat, divide the board into three sections. Divide the class into three teams. Label each section on the board with the team name. Using flash cards, call on one member of each team to name the numeral. For each correct response, draw a portion of the cat under the team name. Repeat the procedure. The team with the first completed cat is the winner.

Story Time

Book - <u>Wobble the Witch's Cat</u> - Mary Calhoun

Book - <u>The Witch of Hissing Hill</u> - Mary Calhoun

Day 5 - Witch

Concept Information

A witch is a woman who is believed to have <u>magical</u> powers. Many years ago, witches used magic to try to change the weather or to keep bad things from happening. Witches were not thought of as scary or evil. Later when churches were built, <u>religion</u> took the place of witches. <u>Laws</u> were passed to stop the use of <u>magic</u> <u>spells</u> by witches. So witches began having <u>secret</u> meetings. One special meeting time was on Halloween. The witches would dance around a fire, <u>chanting</u>. People were frightened. Now witches are one of our most famous <u>symbols</u> of Halloween.

Language Arts - Social Studies

Discussion

Explain the vocabulary words. Discuss the concept information. Ask for children's descriptions of witches. Show pictures.

Note: A most effective method for accomplishing the same objectives is to ask a parent or friend to dress up like a witch and visit the class. Explain before the visit that this is a "friendly witch." Help the children interview the witch.

Book - ABC Witch by Ida Delage

Read the book to the children. Go through the book again and ask the children to name the representative object for each letter.

Art

Egg Carton Witch

Preparation - Collect cardboard egg cartons. You will need one-third (4 cups) for each child. Cut into sections. Discard the top. Cut black construction paper hats and yarn for hair.

Procedure - Use markers to color eyes in the top to egg cups. Draw lips across the bottom two cups. Glue or tape yarn at top of carton. Glue hat on top of yarn.

Math

Halloween Counting Booklet

Repeat Day 1 procedure, using number five - Witches sheet.

Music and Movement

Action Song - "Halloween Witches"

Tune - "Ten Little Indians"

One little, two little, three little witches (Wiggle thumb, index,
                                                third fingers)
Flying over haystacks ("Fly" hand in up and down motion)

Flying over ditches (Same motion)

Sliding down the moon without any hitches ("Glide" hand down)

Hi-Ho, Halloween's here!

Action Game - "The Witch"

The class is divided into four groups with one student designated as the witch. A rectangular area should be set out so that there are four corners for use as a "safe" section. The witch will stand in the center of the play area and call out, "The witch needs company." At this signal, the four groups of students will try to change places by running from one "safe" section to another. The witch will try to tag the students as they pass by. Once tagged, those students will go to the sidelines. The witch will have three attempts at catching the students. Then a new witch is chosen, and all students start again. The witch that has caught the most students is the winner.

Story Time

Book - Humbug Witch by Lorna Balian

Book - The Old Witch Finds a New House by Ida Delage

Day 6 - Ghost

Concept Information

A ghost is the <u>spirit</u> of a dead person which is said to live in another world. Years ago, the people of Scotland, Ireland, and England believed that ghosts came back to the earth on Halloween to look for warmth and cheer. <u>Bonfires</u> were built to welcome the ghosts. People thought they would be punished if they did not please the ghosts. Later, when some of these people came to America, they brought their <u>belief</u> of ghosts with them.

Language Arts - Social Studies

Discussion

Use the globe to point out the countries mentioned in the concept information. Explain the vocabulary words. Discuss the information, and show pictures of how ghosts are supposed to look.

Flannel Board Story - "Country Ghost and City Ghost"

Preparation - Purchase pellon at any fabric store. Place pellon over flannel board figures on pattern page and trace. Color with permanent markers. Cut out. Colored felt may also be used, but figures must be drawn on the felt or outlined around a pattern. Tell the story as you place the figures on the board. Divide the board with a piece of yarn.

Story

Country Ghost lived on a farm in the country. His room was in the attic at the top of a farmhouse.

City Ghost lived in a building in the big city. His room was in the basement at the bottom of a skyscraper.

Country Ghost sent a letter to City Ghost asking him to visit. City Ghost packed his suitcase, put on his derby hat and red scarf, and flew to the farm.

Country Ghost put on his cowboy hat and his kerchief and opened the window for City Ghost.

City Ghost liked his cousin, Country Ghost, but he thought to himself, "My, Country Ghost lives a strange life!" Each morning Country Ghost helped the farmer milk the cows, feed the chickens, and drive the tractor. For lunch they had fried chicken and something called corn bread. City Ghost had never eaten such food! At night they sat on the roof, looked at the stars, and listened to the farmer play his guitar. City Ghost had never heard a guitar, and being so high made him dizzy!

Country Ghost packed his backpack and went home with City Ghost. He thought, "My, City Ghost lives a strange life!" Each morning City Ghost helped the workers mop the floors, burn the trash, and drive the street sweeper. For lunch they had pepper steaks and something called egg rolls. Country Ghost had never eaten such food! At night they sat in the park, watched the city lights, and listened to the cars honking. Country Ghost had never heard cars honking, and the city lights made him dizzy.

At the end of his visit, Country Ghost said, "City Ghost, soon it will be Halloween. In the country we fly around and watch the Trick or Treaters. Then we scare a few cats and go trick-or-treating ourselves. It is great fun. Won't you join me?"

City Ghost said, "Country Ghost, on Halloween in the city we fly around and watch the Trick or Treaters. Then we scare a few cats and go trick-or-treating ourselves. It is great fun. Won't _you_ join _me_?"

Country Ghost and City Ghost both laughed. They had found out they were not so different after all. On Halloween they went trick-or-treating in the country and trick-or-treating in the city and had the best Halloween ever!

Story and Record

I Can Read About Ghosts by Erica Frost, illustrated by Frank Brugos
Follow along in the book as the record "reads" the story.
Ask the children to recall the story.

Art

Ghastly Ghosts

Preparation - Draw and duplicate three-inch circles on white paper. Give one circle to each child.

Procedure - Cut out the circle. Color ghost face with black crayon or marker. Turn the circle over. Glue the corner of a tissue to the bottom of the circle. (See example: "Happy Haunting" bulletin board)

Footprint Ghosts

Preparation - Supply one piece of black construction paper for each child Mix white tempera and put in a shallow pan. Place the shallow pan and a small bucket of water on newspapers on the floor. Have a towel handy.

Procedure - Dip each child's foot in the tempera paint and press on the black construction paper. Then place the child's foot in the bucket of water, and towel dry. The heel of the footprint will be the ghost's head. When the prints are dry, the facial features may be drawn with a black crayon. (See example: "Ghostly Hosts" bulletin board)

<u>Coat Hanger Ghosts</u>

Preparation - Collect one coat hanger for each child. One sheet of tissue paper is required for each ghost. Stretch out each hanger. Shape like a pear.

Procedure - Place the hanger on the tissue paper. Fold excess toward the center and tape. Color features on the opposite side.

<u>Math</u>

<u>Halloween Counting Booklet</u>

Repeat Day 1 procedure, using the number six - Ghosts sheet.

<u>Ghost Sheet</u>

Count the ghosts in each section and circle the correct corresponding numeral.

<u>Music and Movement</u>

<u>Action Song</u> - "I Am the Ghost"

Tune - "Here We go 'Round the Mulberry Bush"

I am the ghost who lives in your house, lives in your house,

   lives in your house,

I am the ghost who lives in your house, all year long.

2. This is the way I fly 'round the room...

3. This is the way I bump and thump...

4. This is the way I rattle the house...

5. This is the way I scare the kids...
    This is the way I scare the kids, just on Halloween Night, BOO!!

Procedure - The children perform appropriate actions with each verse.

<u>Story Time</u>

<u>Book</u> - <u>The Ghost in Dobbs Diner</u> - Robert Alley

<u>Book</u> - <u>Georgie and the Robbers</u> - Robert Bright

Record (LP) - "A Graveyard of Ghost Tales" - Vincent Price (Caedmon Albums)

Concept Information

A skeleton is the <u>connected</u> bones which <u>form</u> the <u>frame</u> of the <u>human</u> body. But at Halloween, skeleton is the word for a dried-up body. It comes from the Greek word "skeletos" which means "<u>withered</u> or dried up."

Language Arts - Social Studies - Science

Discussion

Define vocabulary words; share information; and show a picture of a skeleton. Discuss why skeletons are frightening.

Film

Show a film on the human skeletal system.

Activity

Purchase a large cardboard (Halloween) skeleton and take it apart. Label the backs of the bones to prevent confusion. On a bulletin board or large piece of corrugated cardboard, put the skeleton back together again. Use stick pins to secure each piece. Give the simple name for each skeleton part. Repeat the names. Disassemble the skeleton once again and distribute the parts. Starting with the skull, call out the names of the parts. The child who has that part pins it in place.

Art

Skeleton Mask

Preparation - Duplicate a mask for each child. Use heavy construction paper. Cut a small slit in the center of each eye, nose, and mouth with a razor blade so that the children can insert blunt scissors. Cut two pieces of string, yarn, or thin elastic for each mask. Have a hole puncher available.

Procedure - Cut out the mask and features. Punch holes for string. Tie a piece of string in each hole.

Foil Skeleton Faces

Preparation - Provide several thicknesses of tin foil for each child. Mix black tempera.

Procedure - Demonstrate the procedure, using one child. Open your mouth in an "O" position. Put foil carefully over your face. Be sure to close your eyes. Mold to show all the facial features. Remove and fold the edges into a face shape. Push in the tip of the nose to resemble skeleton. Paint indented areas with black paint mixed with soap flakes.
Tip: This works best as a "partner activity."

Paper Bag Puppet

Preparation - Provide a lunch-sized paper bag for each child. Duplicate the pattern on white paper.

Procedure - Cut out pieces. Glue the top of the skull to the bottom of the bag. Glue the bottom piece under the bottom flap of the bag. Slide your hand inside the bag. Four fingers will fit inside of the flap and make the skeleton "talk."

Math

Halloween Counting Booklet

Repeat Day 1 procedure, using number seven - Skeletons sheet.

Music and Movement

Action Song - "Hokey Pokey"

Sing and perform the actions, using body parts. Wear the skeleton masks.

Game - "Simon Says"

Play Simon Says. Directions should include the names of skeleton parts.

Story Time

It Hardly Seems Like Halloween - David S. Rose

Day 8 - Pumpkin

Concept Information

A pumpkin is a gourd-like fruit. It is large, round, and orange in color. Pumpkins grow on vines. The word "pumpkin" comes from the Greek word "pepon" which means ripe. Pumpkins were one of the early American Indians' main crops. They planted pumpkins between the corn plants to keep the weeds from spreading. Pumpkins are ripe in the fall at Halloween time.

Language Arts - Social Studies - Science

Discussion

Before the children arrive, put one large and one small pumpkin in the middle of the class "Pumpkin Patch." Ask the children if they see anything new in the class. Discuss how they got there. Place the pumpkins in the center of the group area. Let each child feel the pumpkins. Then ask for descriptive words. Compare the pumpkins in size, shape, and color. Define vocabulary words and share the information on the pumpkin.

Seatwork - "The Stages of a Pumpkin"

Pass out duplicated sheets. Draw, label, and number six squares on the board. Using colored chalk, draw and explain each stage of the pumpkin's growth. The children then fill in their sheets.

Art

Make Your Own Jack-O'-Lantern

Preparation - Duplicate the two pattern sheets and distribute. Supply scissors and glue.

Procedure - Choose and color the features to be used on the jack-o'-lantern. Cut out and glue to pumpkin.

Padded Jack-O'-Lanterns

Preparation - Duplicate two pumpkin shapes for each child. Provide scissors, glue or stapler, and tissue paper.

Procedure - Color a face on the pumpkin. Cut out and glue or staple together leaving a two-inch opening. Stuff with tissue paper and glue or staple shut.

Math - "Halloween Counting Booklet"

Repeat Day 1 procedure, using number eight - Bats sheet.

Music - Movement - Games

Song - "The Pumpkin in the Patch"

Tune - "The Farmer in the Dell"

The pumpkin in the patch,

The pumpkin in the patch,

Hi-ho, it's time to go,

The pumpkin in the patch.

    The pumpkin gets a face,

    The pumpkin gets a face,

    Hi-ho, it's grinning so,

    The pumpkin gets a face.

The pumpkin gets a light,

The pumpkin gets a light,

Hi-ho, his face does glow,

The pumpkin gets a light.

The pumpkin makes a pie,

The pumpkin makes a pie,

Hi-ho, I can't say no,

The pumpkin makes a pie.

<u>Story Time</u>

<u>Book</u> - <u>Trick or Treat</u> - Louis Slobodkin

<u>Kindergarten Kitchen</u>

<u>"Your Own Jack-O'-Lantern Cookies"</u>

Purchase any kind of cookies, preferably those which are large and "plain," such as sugar cookies. Spread ready-to-serve orange frosting on the cookies with plastic knives. Decorate the "jack-o'-lanterns" with chocolate chips, raisins, nuts, or any small candy.

Day 9 - Pumpkins

Concept Information

When we <u>carve</u> faces on pumpkins, they become jack-o'-lanterns. Jack-o'-lanterns are named after a man named Jack. Jack could not enter heaven because he was a <u>miser</u>. He played tricks on the devil so he was punished. The devil made him walk forever on <u>earth</u> carrying a <u>lantern</u>. He became known as "Jack of the Lantern." So our jack-o'-lanterns are named after him.

Language Arts - Social Studies - Science

Carving the Pumpkin

Draw the face on the large pumpkin with a crayon. Cut and remove the top. Let the children look inside. The children then take turns scooping out the pulp. Discuss how the pulp looks, feels, and smells. Cut out the features. (Save these for art.) Wash the seeds well. Put the seeds on a cookie sheet which has been coated with a thin layer of cooking oil. Toast these in the oven until golden brown. Salt and eat.

Experience Chart

Guide the children in recalling the sequential steps of the above activity. Write each step on experience chart paper. Include a quick illustration at the end of each sentence. Read the chart to the children.

Art

Pumpkin Prints

Preparation - Use the pieces of pumpkin saved from various projects. Scrape each piece clean, wash, and dry. Mix different colors of tempera paint.   It is a good idea to have different "stations" for each color. Provide newsprint.

Procedure - Dip pumpkin pieces into trays of tempera.   Print the designs on the paper.

Pumpkin Men

Preparation - Duplicate pattern sheet on orange construction paper.   Cut out arms and legs from black construction paper.   Arms should be one inch by six inches.   Legs should be one inch by twelve inches.   Provide glue, colors, and scissors.

Procedure - Cut out head, hands, and feet.   Draw face.   Fold arms and legs accordion-style.   Glue to head.

Math

Halloween Counting Booklet

Repeat Day 1 procedure, using the number nine - Jack-O'-Lantern sheet.

Seatwork - "Sets of Pumpkin Seeds"

Save pumpkin seeds from large or small pumpkin activities.   Wash and spread on paper toweling to dry.   Direct the children to glue a circle of yarn or draw a circle with crayons on a piece of paper.   Assign different numbers to each table or group.   The children write their number within the circle.   Place seeds on the tables.   The children count out the pumpkin seeds to match their numbers and glue inside the circle.

Music - Movement - Games

Song - "My Little Pumpkin"
Tune - "Paw Paw Patch"

Where oh where is my little pumpkin,

Where oh where is my little pumpkin,

Where oh where is my little pumpkin,

Way down yonder in the pumpkin patch.

(Chorus) Picking up pumpkins, put them on the gateposts,

Picking up pumpkins, put them on the gateposts,

Picking up pumpkins, put them on the gateposts,

Now we're ready for Halloween night.

Procedure - Children sing and act out the song.

Kindergarten Kitchen

Pleasin' Pumpkin Pudding

Cut the small pumpkin into eight pieces. The children can help scrape the pumpkin. Put the pieces in a pan with a small amount of water. Cover tightly and steam the pumpkin until it is tender. Chop the steamed pieces in a blender. Then, letting the children help, mix:

2 cups cooked pumpkin	1 1/2 teaspoon cinnamon
1 egg	1/2 teaspoon nutmeg
1 cup milk	Dash of salt
1 teaspoon cloves	3/4 cup sugar
1/2 teaspoon allspice	

Place this mixture in a saucepan. Cook for about 15 or 20 minutes. Serve in cups.

Note: You may also use the small pumpkin to make your favorite pumpkin pie recipe.

Day 10 - Culmination

Concept Evaluation

Each child should be evaluated individually, as explained in the Introduction.

Concept Review

Thirty Pumpkins

Draw thirty pumpkin shapes on the blackboard. Ask questions concerning the daily topics covered in the Halloween unit. Call on one child at a time. If the response is correct, the child may draw a face on one pumpkin and write his/her name underneath.

Art

Self-Portrait

Preparation - Mix different colors of tempera paint. Provide art paper for each child.

Procedure - Paint a self-portrait in your Halloween costume.

Math Booklet Cover

Preparation - Duplicate Halloween Counting Booklet cover on orange construction paper.

Procedure - Outline the pumpkin, and color in the letters of the booklet cover.

Math

Halloween Counting Booklet

Repeat Day 1 procedure, using the number ten - Trick or Treat Bags sheet. Put booklets together and staple.

Music and Movement

Sing Along

Light a candle in the jack-o'-lantern; turn off the lights; and sing all of the songs learned in the unit.

Halloween Party

If you choose, the children may bring their costumes to school and dress up for the party. Recognize each child. Let them "share" their costumes. Suggested activities include: apple bobbing, a ghost story told by a parent volunteer, refreshments, the "Witchey Visit" (see Day 5 - Witch), and "Pin the Nose on the Jack-O'-Lantern." (Cut a large pumpkin out of orange paper. Color on the eyes and mouth. Make an "X" for the nose. Cut out noses and label with each child's name. Blindfold one child at a time and pin the nose where the child places it. The nearest to the "X" wins a prize.)

"Care Trip"

The children dress in their costumes and visit a hospital or nursing home. They can sing Halloween songs, recite poems, visit with patients, and present goodies.

Note: All details of the visit should be worked out well in advance with the administrator in charge. You will need a chaperon for every three or four children. Goodies could include the jack-o'-lantern cookies or candy placed in the Milk Carton Black Cats.

Concept Evaluation:

Dear Parents,

We will begin our unit on Halloween on _____. Some of our topics will be "Trick-or-Treating," "Owl," "Witches," "Black Cat," "Ghosts," "Pumpkins," and "Skeletons." The activities for each day will center around these topics. Please read below to see how you can help.

Things to Send: _____

_____

_____

Volunteers Needed To: _____

_____

_____

Follow-Up: At the end of the unit, ask your child to share the following fingerplays, songs, etc.

_____

_____

_____

Community Activities Scheduled for Halloween:

_____

_____

_____

Thank you for your cooperation.

Sincerely,

Copyright © 1987. Carol Taylor Bond

Feed The Jack-O'-Lantern

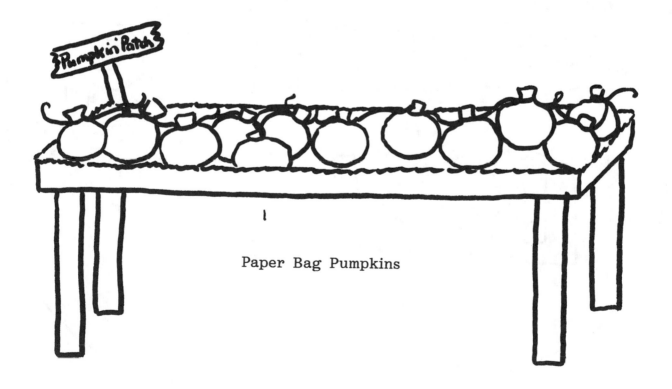

Paper Bag Pumpkins

Copyright © 1987.   Carol Taylor Bond

305

My Halloween Counting Booklet

Copyright © 1987.   Carol Taylor Bond

Halloween Counting Poem

One Haunted House standing all alone,
The tall black trees bend and sway and moan.

Two Happy Children run out to the street,
Dressed in costumes, it's time for Trick or Treat!

Three Owls staring, eyes shining bright,
"Who! Who!" they say, "Who is out tonight?"

Four Black Cats with backs arched high,
Watch the Trick or Treaters as they go by.

Five Witches flying in the light of the moon,
Circling and shrieking, "We'll be there soon!"

Six ghostly ghosts with empty black eyes,
"Oooooooooooooooo," the children hear their cries.

Seven Skeletons from their graves so deep,
Rise in the night to dance and groan and creek.

Eight Bats screeching and away they fly,
Sweeping and gliding across the starless sky.

Nine Jack-O'-Lanterns sitting in a row,
Making Halloween faces that flicker and glow.

Ten Trick or Treat Bags that grew and grew,
A Happy Halloween to You and You and You!

1

one

Copyright © 1987. Carol Taylor Bond

2

two

Copyright © 1987. Carol Taylor Bond

309

3

three

Copyright © 1987. Carol Taylor Bond

310

4

four

Copyright © 1987. Carol Taylor Bond

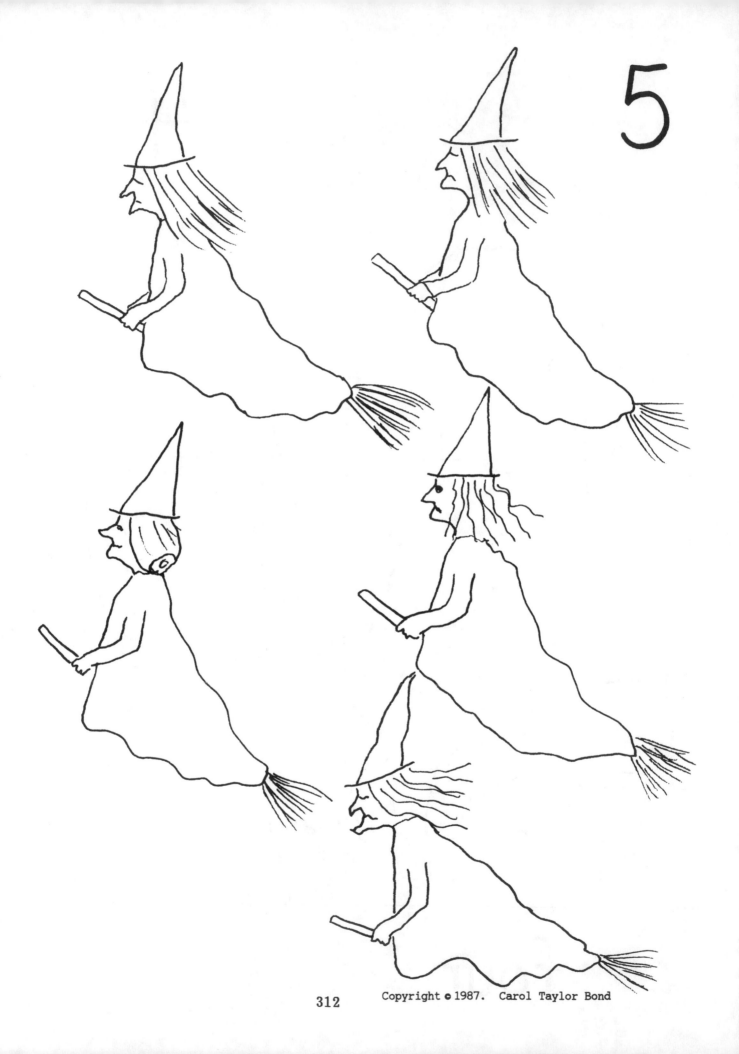

5

 Copyright © 1987. Carol Taylor Bond

6

six

313

Copyright © 1987. Carol Taylor Bond

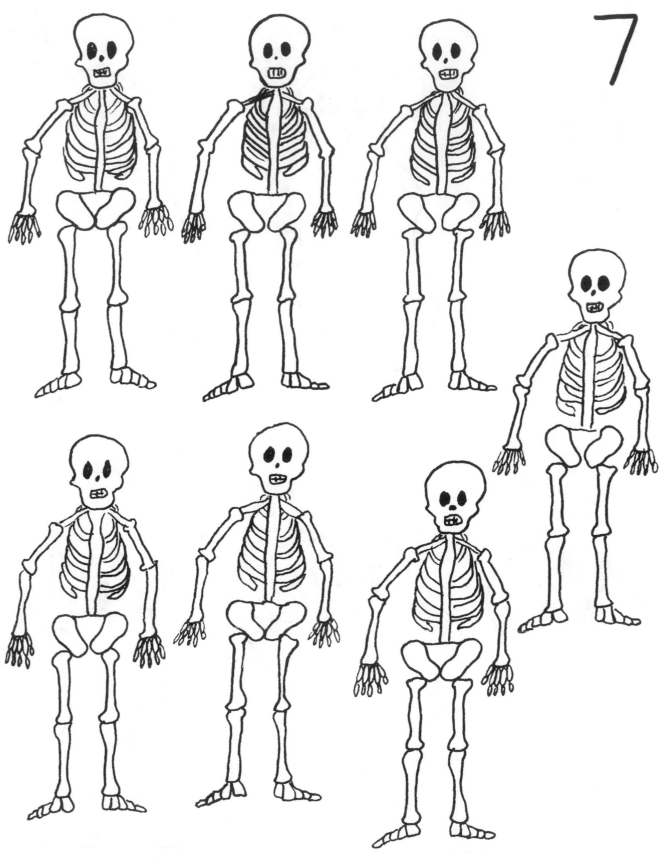

seven

Copyright © 1987. Carol Taylor Bond

8

eight

Copyright © 1987. Carol Taylor Bond

9

nine

Copyright © 1987.   Carol Taylor Bond

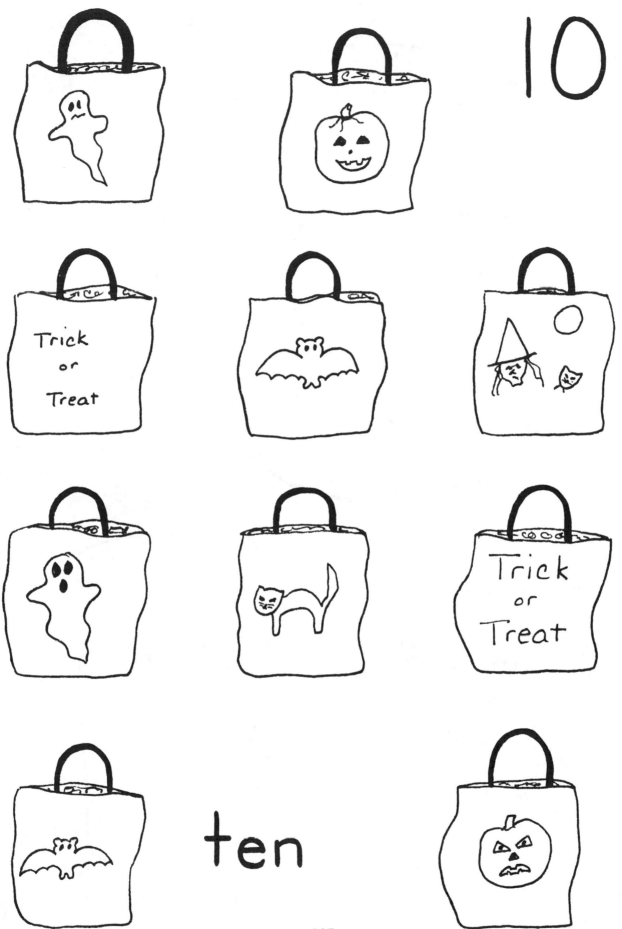

10

Trick
or
Treat

Trick
or
Treat

ten

Copyright © 1987. Carol Taylor Bond

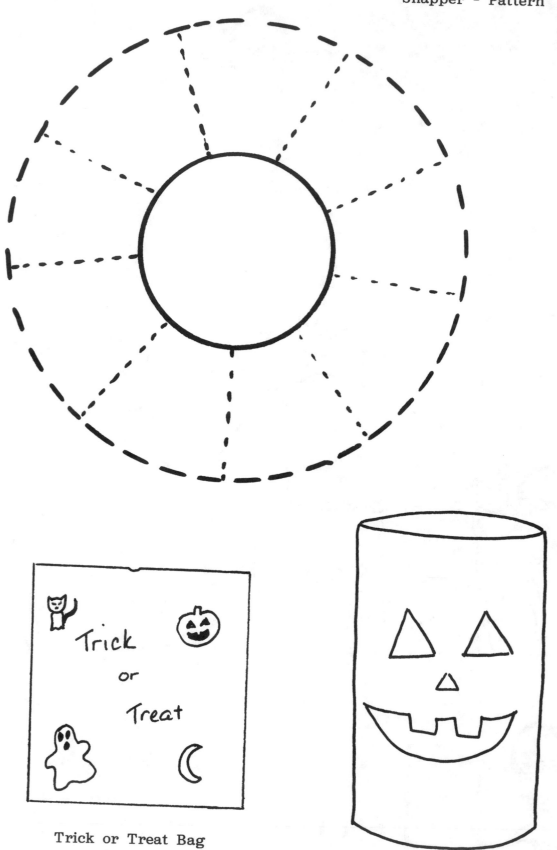

Trick or Treat Bag

Shaker - Example

Copyright © 1987. Carol Taylor Bond

Owls -
Paper Plate

2 Patterns
Duplicate on orange
construction paper.

Copyright © 1987. Carol Taylor Bond

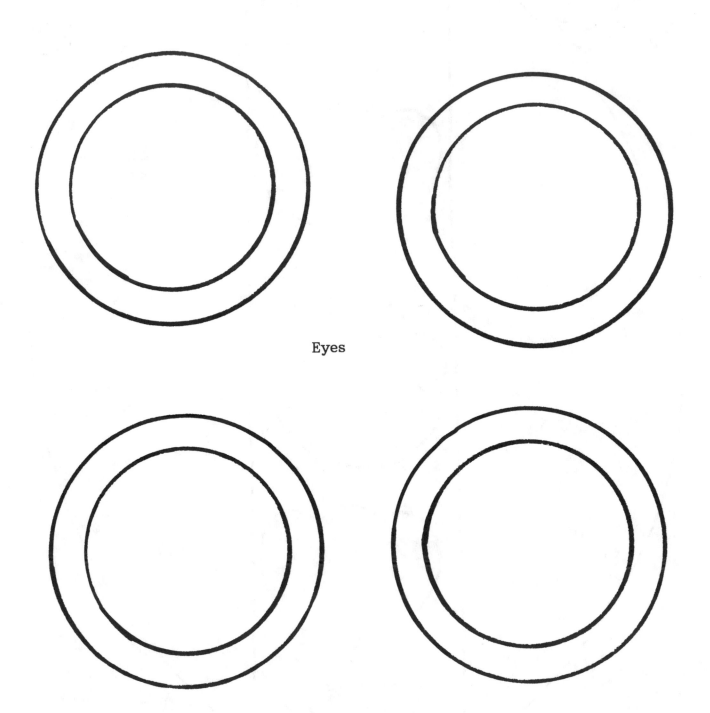

Eyes

2 Patterns
Duplicate on yellow
construction paper.

Copyright ©1987. Carol Taylor Bond

Stretchy Owl

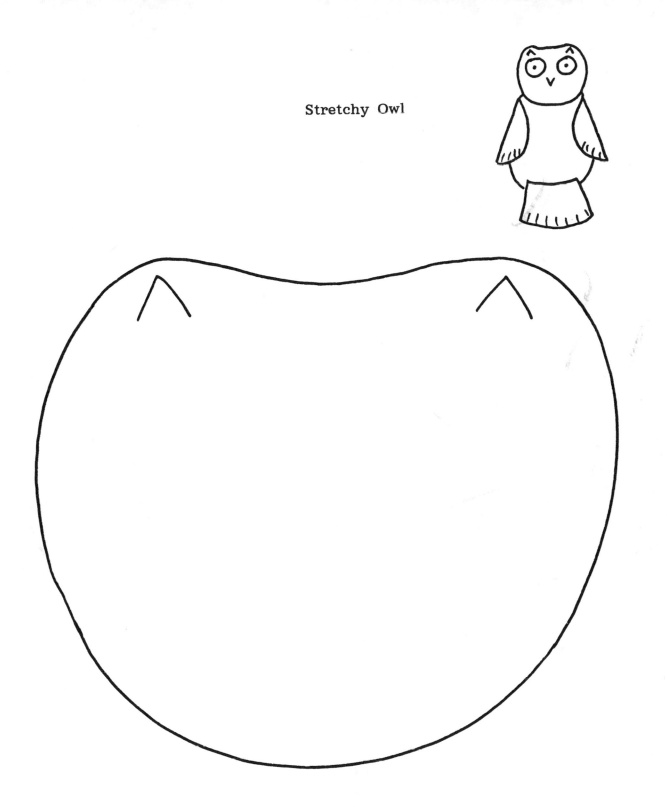

Owl Face - Duplicate 1
Eyes - may use those from
Paper Plate Owl

Copyright © 1987. Carol Taylor Bond

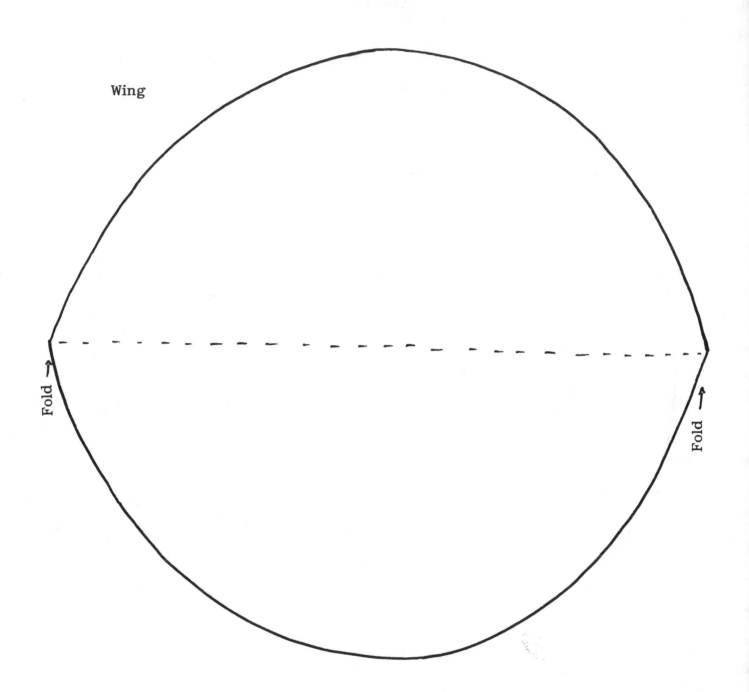

Wing

Fold

Fold

Duplicate 2 per owl

Copyright ©1987. Carol Taylor Bond

Stretchy Owl

Tail

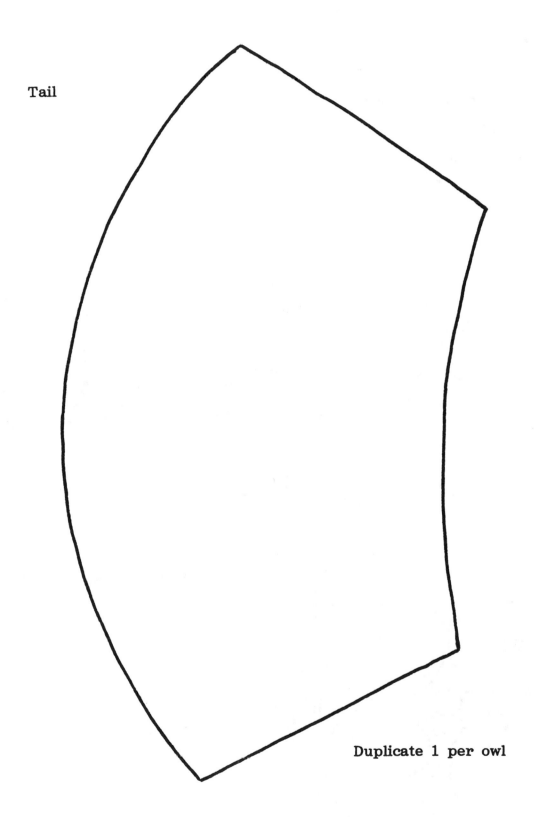

Duplicate 1 per owl

Copyright © 1987. Carol Taylor Bond

Examples

Milk Carton
Black Cat

Egg Carton Owl

Egg Carton Witch

Copyright © 1987. Carol Taylor Bond

Black Cat Pattern

Heavy Black Construction Paper - Folded in Half

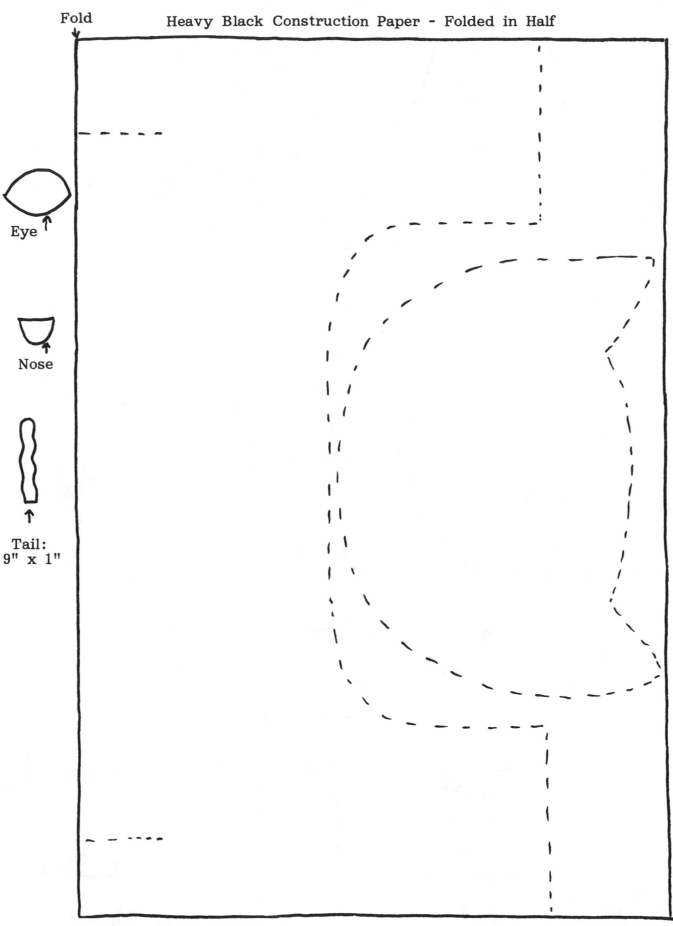

Fold

Eye ↑

Nose ↑

Tail:
9" x 1" ↑

Cut on Dotted Lines

Copyright © 1987. Carol Taylor Bond

Country Ghost

Farm House

Chicken

Corn Bread

Chickens

Cowboy Hat

Guitar

Kerchief

Trick or Treat Bag

Feed

Back Pack

Copyright © 1987. Carol Taylor Bond

City Ghost

Skyscraper

Mop

Derby

Scarf

Trash

Trick or
Treat Bag

Pepper
Steak

Egg Rolls

Car

Suitcase

327

Copyright ©1987. Carol Taylor Bond

Coat Hanger Ghosts

Copyright © 1987. Carol Taylor Bond

328

GHOSTS

Name:

1 2 3

3 4 5

1 2 3

4 5 6

329

Copyright © 1987. Carol Taylor Bond

Skeleton Mask

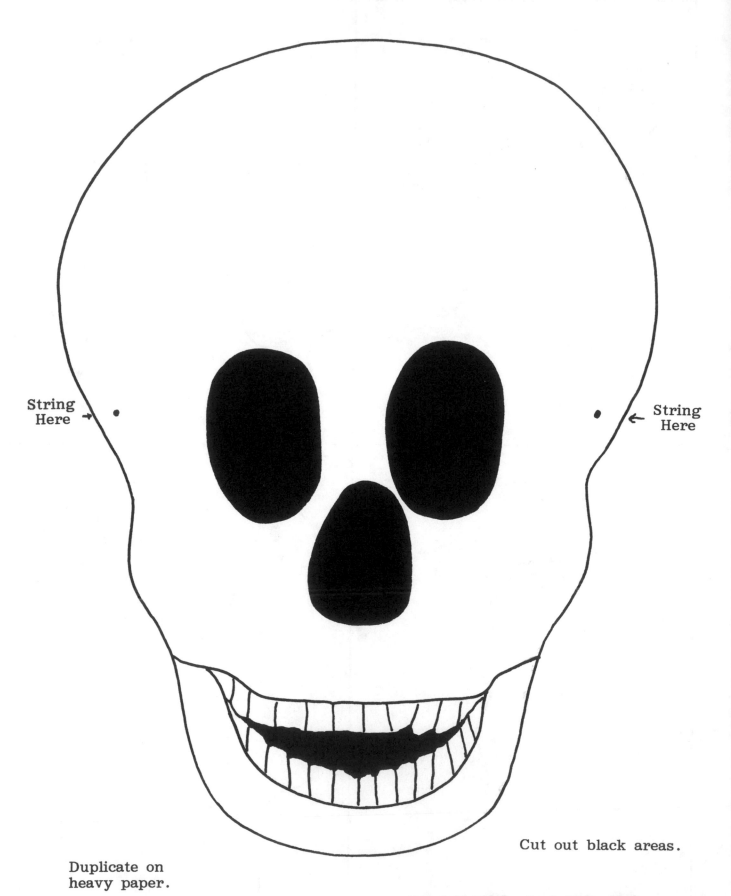

String
Here →

← String
Here

Cut out black areas.

Duplicate on
heavy paper.

Copyright © 1987. Carol Taylor Bond

Paper Bag Puppet

Copyright ©1987. Carol Taylor Bond

Stages of a Pumpkin - Example

1	2	3
O O O O O Seeds	✷ Plant	✷ Blossoms

4	5	6
✷ Pumpkins	🎃 Ripe	🎃 ⟍ Jack-O'-Lantern

Copyright © 1987. Carol Taylor Bond

Stages of a Pumpkin

1	2	3
	Plant	Blossoms
Seeds		
4	5	6
	Ripe	Jack-O'-Lantern
Pumpkins		

Copyright © 1987.   Carol Taylor Bond

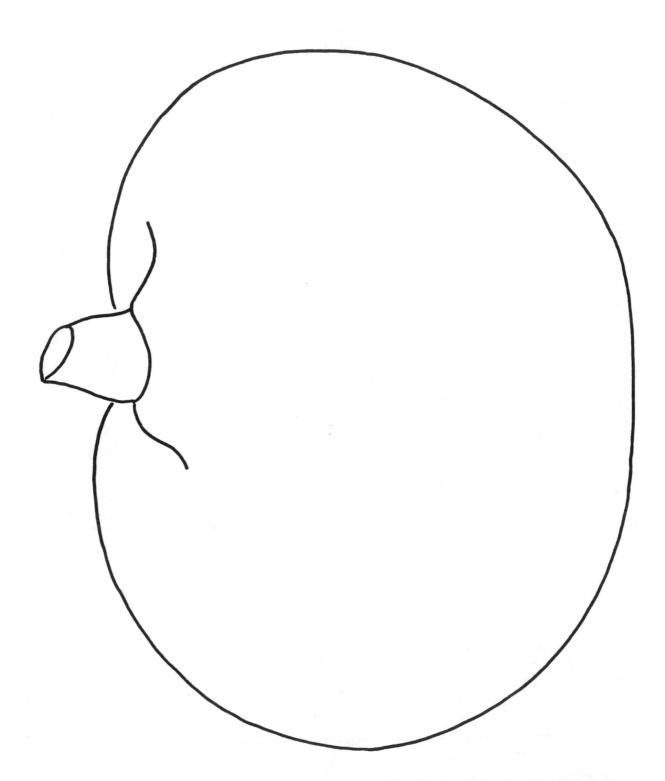

Copyright © 1987. Carol Taylor Bond

Make Your Own
Jack-O'-Lantern

 Copyright © 1987. Carol Taylor Bond

Duplicate 2 per child.

Copyright ©1987. Carol Taylor Bond

Duplicate on orange paper.

Copyright © 1987. Carol Taylor Bond

Indians

<u>Proposed Time:</u>   5 days

<u>Unit Objectives</u>

To instill appreciation of the American Indian

To promote interest in the history of the American Indian

To develop understanding of the customs of the American Indian many
  years ago

To present background material for understanding the American Indian's
  role in the First Thanksgiving

<u>Room Environment - Bulletin Boards</u>

<u>"America, Long Ago"</u>

Cover the top portion of the bulletin board with light blue paper and the
bottom with brown or green.   The bottom portion should be cut to
represent a landscape.   Cut out a portion on the right side of the
landscape for the sea.   Fill this in with blue or green "water."   At
Activity Time, allow the children to tear strips of brown construction
paper and circles of green construction paper for the trees.   Place on the
landscape.   Add an Indian village, using Paper Tepees (see Art - Day 1)
and Egg Carton Totem Poles (see Art - Day 2).   Put several Indians
around the village and by the shore.   (These may be stick figures.)   The
"Mayflower" will be added on the bulletin board during the Pilgrims unit.

<u>"Proud of Our Feathers"</u>

Make a tagboard pattern, using the "Proud of Our Feathers - Indian
Pattern" sheet.   Increase or decrease the size, if necessary.   Duplicate the
"Feathers" page on construction paper of various colors.   Each child makes
an Indian on kraft paper by tracing around the pattern, cutting it out, and

338

decorating it. The child's name is written on the headband. Mount the Indians on the bulletin board. Cut out the feathers. When a child masters a concept such as numeral or alphabet recognition, the numeral or letter is written on the feather. The feather is then stapled behind the head of that child's Indian.

Room Environment - Displays

Door Display - Tepee

Cut a large tepee from kraft paper. Measure the classroom door and cut out this portion of the tepee. The children decorate with fingerpaints, referring to the Indian picture-language. Cut strips of paper for the exposed sticks and glue to the top of the tepee. Fit the completed tepee around the door. Secure with filament or duct tape. Construct a totem pole from painted cereal boxes, covered coffee cans, or ice cream cartons. Glue or tape together. Set against the wall beside the tepee door.

A "Real" Tepee

Obtain four empty carpet rolls from a carpet store. Lay the rolls in a stack. Tie a piece of rope or leather strip (or filament tape) around the stack, twelve to fifteen inches from one end. With adult assistance, stand and spread the rolls. Cover the tepee with "Paper Animal Skins" (see Art - Day 1) which have been decorated and stapled together. Be sure to leave a space or cut out a triangle for the door.

Day 1 - Introduction, Dwellings

Concept Information

Introduction - As we have learned, hundreds of years ago an explorer named Christopher Columbus sailed across the Atlantic Ocean and discovered a new land. He thought it was a country called India, so he called the light brown people he found on this land "Indians." However, it was not India that Columbus discovered; it was America. But we still call these people American Indians.

Indians were the first people in America. Later, some people called Pilgrims sailed from England to live in America. They also met the Indians. Most likely, all of the Pilgrims would have died if the Indians hadn't helped them. So, as we will learn next week, the Indians played an important part in our holiday Thanksgiving. This week we will learn about the lives of the American Indians long ago.

Dwellings - Long ago, Indians lived in different places all over America. Some Indians lived in the forest, some around the mountains, and some in the desert. They built their homes with things that they found around them.

When we think of an Indian's home, we usually think of the tepee. The Plains Indians lived in tepees. They tied together three or four poles made from trees and leaned fifteen or twenty poles against these to make the frame. The frame was then covered with twenty or thirty animal skins sewn together. A flap was left in front for a door and a hole in the top for the smoke from the inside fireplace. Since the Plains Indians moved around a lot, the tepee was a perfect home. It could be put up or taken down in just a few minutes.

The Indians who lived in the eastern part of America used the trees from the forests to build wigwams. Wooden poles were set in the ground, bent over, and tied together to form arches. The frame was covered with bark or branches. Like the tepee, the wigwam had a smoke hole and could be quickly put up or taken down. Other Eastern Indians lived in longhouses which looked like our houses except they had rounded roofs, were covered with bark, and were very long. Many families lived in different parts of the longhouse.

Indians of the southeastern part of America lived in towns with dirt streets. Each family had four buildings: one was the winter house and kitchen, one was the summer house, and the other two were for storing food, tools, and hides. The houses were made of wood and straw.

Indians in the Southwest lived in hogans of logs and dried mud and had rounded roofs. The Indians who lived around the Rocky Mountains lived in huts which were shaped like tepees, but were covered with grass or brush.

The Indians who lived on the western coast of America were woodworkers. Their houses were made of wood and shaped similar to our houses except that they were big enough for many families. The Desert Indians did not move around like other Indians. They also lived where it was dry and hot, so their houses were made of dried mud or clay-shaped into bricks. These were called pueblos and looked like large boxes stacked one on top of another. The Indians used ladders to climb up to their pueblos.

Language Arts - Social Studies

Discussions   (Introduction and Dwellings)

Before you begin these discussions, have on hand the following materials: a large globe, a map of the United States, a slab of modeling clay about the size of a piece of paper, a piece of bark, a tree branch with leaves, a handful of straw, dirt in a bowl, a glass of water, a box of large pipe cleaners, and pictures or posters of Indians and dwellings. An animal skin, even that of a squirrel or rabbit, would be a bonus. (Paper "skins" can be substituted.) Duplicate, color, and cut out "Indian Dwellings." Tape lightly on correct areas of the United States map.

Introduction - Define vocabulary words and share the concept information, referring to the globe and Indian pictures.

Dwellings - Define vocabulary words and share concept information. As you relate the material, point out each Indian home on the map; and show pictures. Use the pipe cleaners stuck in the clay to demonstrate construction methods. Show the materials used to cover these dwellings such as: the bark, hay, leaves, and animal skins. To demonstrate construction material of the pueblos, mix the dirt and water; and set in a sunny place to dry. The children can check on this each day.

Poem - "Then and Now"
I wonder how it felt to be,
An Indian child wild and free,
No stores to buy my meat or bread,
Hunting for animals to eat instead,
Deer, buffalo, and grizzly bear,
Skins for my clothes and feathers in my hair.

342

Rivers and streams untouched by man,

Mountains and woods covering the land,

Not one city, street, or park,

Fires, not streetlights, for the dark.

No bicycles, no cars, no color TV,

I like Indians, but I'd rather be me!

Discuss the meaning of the poem. Take the class outside and sit in a circle. Have the children imagine how the area would have looked long ago. Encourage responses.

Book - Three Little Indians by Gene S. Stuart

Read or tell the story and show the pictures. Make three columns on the board; and compare the characteristics, etc., of each tribe in the book.

Film

Show and discuss a film about the American Indian. Construct "The Real Tepee" (see Room Environment and Art - "Paper Animal Skins").

Fingerplay - "Five Little Indians"

Five little Indians in a tepee (right hand flat, palm down, left hand
                                cupped - knuckles make peak for tepee)
Sleeping quietly as can be. (same)

Along comes the Chief, and what do you think? (1 finger of left hand
                                walking toward right hand)
Up jumped the Indians quick as a wink! (right hand up - fingers straight)

Art

Paper Animal Skins - Indian Rugs

Preparation - Collect a large grocery sack for each child. Provide scissors, tempera paint or markers, and a large tub of water. Plan to conduct this activity outside.

Procedure - Cut down one side of the bag and around all four sides of the bottom. Crumple the paper, and dip in water. Shake off excess. Spread the "skins" on a flat surface to dry. Use paints or markers to decorate with Indian symbols or patterns. Fringe two ends.

Variation: Fill empty deodorant bottles with tempera paint, and let the children roll the paint onto the rugs.

For Real Tepee - Cut and wet the paper sacks, and dry flat as above. Punch holes around the edges. Cut lengths of yarn for sewing skins together. Tie to a very blunt, large needle or a bobbie pin. The children sew the skins together to form a large rectangle. Knot the ends of the yarn. (Measure your standing carpet rolls for width and length needed.) Drape around carpet rolls. Staple to secure, leaving opening for door.

Paper Tepee

Preparation - Make cardboard patterns, as shown, for Paper Tepee. Provide kraft paper or paper bag scraps, four toothpicks per child, scissors, glue, Q-tips, and paint.

Procedure - The children trace and cut out the tepee on paper. At the top, glue toothpicks to the back to represent exposed poles. Paint with Q-tips. (Four or five patterns can be shared.)

Stand-Up Tepee

Preparation - Duplicate "Stand-Up Tepee" page on construction paper. (Use "earth colors.") Provide scissors, markers, and stapler.

Procedure - Cut out tepee. Hold up tepee with curve downward. Grasp each corner and overlap to form cone shape. Staple. Decorate.

Indian Puppets

Preparation - Collect toilet tissue rolls, one per child. Provide scraps of construction paper, material, yarn, glue, scissors, and crayons.

Procedure - Glue hair and feathers to the top portion of the roll and Indian clothes to the bottom portion. Use crayons for features. The Indian puppet is placed on three or four fingers to manipulate. Use with "Ten Little Indians" song (see Music - Movement - Games - Day 1), "Five Little Indians" fingerplay (see Language Arts - Social Studies - Day 1), or "The Braves" song (see Music - Movement - Games - Day 3).

Math

Stand-Up Village

Count the dots on each hogan's roof, and write the corresponding numeral on the door as shown in the example. Cut out the hogans in numerical order from left to right. Spread glue on the bottom portions. Glue on the correct lines on the second page of the activity.

Music - Movement - Games

Song - "Ten Little Indians"

Count off ten little Indians. Each stand on cue with the song ending with ten little Indians standing. Starting with the tenth Indian, the process is reversed until there are no little Indian boys. Repeat choosing other children.

Game - "Indian Chief"

One child is chosen as the Chief. The rest of the children join hands in a circle. The Chief runs around the outside of the circle and taps two "braves" on the shoulder. After two braves are tapped, they drop hands and chase the Chief. The Chief can escape capture by entering the spaces left by the braves or by breaking through the other braves' hands and joining the circle. If the Chief is successful, he may choose a new Chief. If he is caught by one of the braves, this brave becomes the new Chief. The Chief must then sit in the middle of the "tepee" (circle).

Story Time

Book - One Little Indian - Emma L. Brock

Book - American Indian Fairy Tales - Margaret Compton

Table Display

Obtain a shallow corrugated box about the size of a large table. (This can be made by cutting an appliance box.) Cover the bottom of the box with an inch of sand. Make an Indian village, using the Stand-Up Tepees (see Art - Day 1), trees, a river, canoes, animals, etc., as shown and explained on the illustration. Allow room for a Pilgrim settlement to be added during the Pilgrim unit.

Day 2 - Language and Communication

Concept Information

When you want something or feel something and wish to tell another person, you use your voice to say words. This is called talking or speaking. In the United States, we speak the English language. So, if you <u>travel</u> across the United States to another state and ask for a glass of milk, they will <u>understand</u> you. But if you go to another <u>country</u>, such as France, and ask for a glass of milk, they will not understand because they do not speak the English language. They speak the French language. Their word for "glass" or for "milk" is something different. The French word for glass is "glasse," and "milk" is "lait" in French. Indians lived in tribes which were <u>groups</u> of people and families that lived together in <u>villages</u>. The tribes had different names such as: the Cheyenne, the Navahoes, and the Pueblos. Each tribe had a different language or different words for the same thing. When two tribes met, they could not understand each other's words. So the Indians of the western <u>Plains</u> made up a gesture or sign language so all tribes could understand each other.

Another way to share what you are thinking is to write. Someone can read your words and understand. The Indians did not write words. To leave messages or "tell" a story, Indians drew pictures in the dirt with sticks, or on stones or trees with the juice of berries or other plants. This is called Indian picture language. Another way Indians made <u>signals</u> was with smoke. Smoke signals were made by waving a blanket over a fire of <u>green</u> wood. This made the smoke <u>puff</u>. A certain number of puffs meant a word or sentence.

Today, I will show you some of the sign language and picture language that the Indians used long ago.

Language Arts - Social Studies

Discussion

Enlarge and display the Indian sign and picture language charts. Define vocabulary words and share the concept information. During the discussion, demonstrate a gesture ("come here" or "goodbye"). Show the charts. Practice some of the sign language and form a sentence. On the board, demonstrate drawing the symbols for words. Allow the children to practice on scratch paper.

Transparency Activity

Set up the overhead projector, and draw picture language sentences (with wipe-off markers) for the children to decode. They may refer to the chart. At Activity Time, use this as a station where the children may practice themselves.

Poem - "Hiawatha's Childhood" by Henry Wadsworth Longfellow
(Childcraft Vol. 2 Storytelling and Other Poems)

Read and explain each verse. Then reread the entire poem. Show the pictures.

Sign Language Game

Practice the sign language. Direct each child to learn one sign. Take the chart down. Call on a child to make a sign. (They may consult the chart and need some last minute coaching from the "sidelines.") The other children volunteer the answer by raising their hands. The first to guess correctly gets the next turn.

<u>Indian Picture Language Rebus Story</u> - "The Lost Indian Boy"

Place the story sheet on the opaque projector. Read it, allowing the children to supply the picture-words.

Art

Picture Messages

Preparation - Supply twelve to fifteen inches of adding machine tape or paper strips for each child and pencils and crayons.

Procedure - The children draw and color picture language symbols on their strips. They may form messages if they have progressed this far. The teacher writes the correct word under each symbol. Post at different angles in the hall or on a classroom wall. Label "Indian Messages."

Tom-Toms

Preparation - Collect an oatmeal box, or coffee, shortening, or Kool-Aid can with tops for each child. Provide precut paper to cover (or direct the children in cutting it to size), markers, scissors, and glue or rubber bands.

Procedure - If necessary, cut the paper to fit the can or box and decorate with Indian symbols or patterns. Glue to can or box or secure with rubber band. Use in movement and math activities.

Egg Carton Totem Poles

Preparation - Show a picture of a totem pole; and explain that Indians carved them from trees, carving animals and faces which were important to them. Collect cardboard egg cartons, one for every two children. Cut the top and bottom sections apart. Cut the cup section in half, and the top in half (cutting away the four sides). Provide different colors of tempera paints and glue. Give each child one (six cup) section and one

349

tempera paints and glue. Give each child one (six cup) section and one (half) top. (This top section will be a long strip.)

Procedure - Paint the cups different colors and add features. Paint the top section. Allow these to dry. Glue the top section behind the second "cup" from the top (to represent the wings).

Note: To place in Table Display (see Day 1), staple bottom cup to a square of cardboard; and anchor in sand.

Math

Tom-Tom Count

Seat the children in a circle with their tom-toms. Hold up a numeral card and, call on a child to provide the correct number with beats on the tom-tom. Repeat, calling on all children.

Variation - Pick a child to choose the number of beats while the class counts to discover the answer.

Music - Movement - Games

Song and Sign Language - "You're My Friend"

Tune - "Jimmy Crack Corn" (chorus)

means you're my friend.

(same as above) means you're my friend.

(same as above) means you're my friend.

Your   heart   is   good   and   true.

On the first three lines, the sign language replaces the first three beats of the tune. It is performed in silence but the words, "means you're my friend," are sung as usual. Sing the complete last line while signing the words.

Game - "Tom-Tom Says"

Holding their tom-toms, the children form a circle. The Chief (teacher) will conduct the movements with his or her tom-tom. Beat the tom-tom slowly and softly. The children join in on their tom-toms, tiptoeing in time to the beat. Increase and decrease speed and volume.

Story Time

Book - Arrow to the Sun - Gerald McDermott

Kindergarten Kitchen

Succotash

1 can corn

1 can lima beans

1/2 teaspoon salt

3 Tablespoons butter

Mix all the ingredients in a pot. Heat until butter and vegetables are warm.

Note: This dish was invented by the American Indians.

Day 3 - Clothing and Food

Concept Information

Most of the Indian's clothing and food came from the animals living around them. Indians hunted animals like bear, beaver, elk, fox, and rabbit; but the most important animal to the Indian was the buffalo. In the woods, the Indians hunted on foot; but they usually used horses to hunt buffalo.

After animals were killed, they were skinned. The skins were soaked in water for two or three days and scraped with a tool to remove the hair. Then they were stretched, softened, and smoked. The skins were used for tepees, boats, war shields, and for clothes.

During warm weather, Indian men usually wore only a breechclout and moccasins. A breechclout was a strip of leather which was placed between the legs and pulled up and over a belt at the waist. In the woods, they wore leggings which were similar to the legs of pants suspended by a leather strip from the belt. In winter, they wore a fur robe and leather boots.

Indian women wore skirts which were wrapped around the waist. They, too, wore moccasins and leggings when needed. In warm weather, the women wore only the skirt; but in colder weather they wore a poncho-like covering. Some women wore a dress made of two skins sewn together at the shoulders and belted at the waist. Until they were ten years old, children wore no clothes except robes and moccasins in cold weather. After age ten, they dressed like adults.

Because it was so difficult to sew through the leather with bone needles, little sewing was done on Indian clothes. They were cut so that they could be easily worn.

As we will learn later, the Indians used every part of the animal for something. They used the skin of animals for clothes, and the meat of the animals for food.

Some of the meat was smoked. This was done to keep it from <u>spoiling</u>. Also, when there was no fresh meat, it could be kept in supply. Fresh meat was cooked over the fire on a stick or boiled in water in a <u>birch bark</u> pot. The pot was hung over the fire from a pole which rested on a <u>forked</u> limb and was held down by a stone. Inside the tepee, a pole was held over the fire by the tepee frame.

<u>Language Arts</u> - <u>Social Studies</u>

<u>Discussion</u>

Define vocabulary words and share the concept information. Use reference books, such as <u>Indians</u> by Edwin Tunis, to show pictures of the animals, Indian clothing, and cooking methods. Cut a paper animal skin to show how skirts and ponchos, etc., were made.

<u>Story Sequence</u> - "The Old Stump"

Read "The Old Stump" to the children. Duplicate the stump on heavy paper, color, and cut out. Put stumps together and punch holes in three sides. Use yarn to lace together. Color and cut out the picture squares. Retell the story while the class puts the correct picture squares into the stump. Let the children take turns telling the story.

"The Old Stump"

Once, deep in the woods, a hungry owl spotted a rabbit hopping through the trees. "Yum, yum!" said the owl, "I will have a fine supper tonight." And off he flew to catch the rabbit. Quickly the rabbit jumped into an old stump to hide. While the owl looked for the rabbit, along came a fox. "Mmm," he said, "a nice juicy owl for supper!" And off he ran to kill the owl. The owl quickly jumped into the old stump. Well, by now the fox was heading for that old stump when along came Moon-Over-the-Water Indian brave. "Uh-huh!" whispered the Moon-Over-the-Water, as he crept up on the fox; and "ROAR!" went the big black bear who was right behind him. Plunk, Plunk!--the Indian jumped into the stump right behind the fox. Feet were stomped, eyes were poked, ears were pinched, and the big black bear circled 'round and 'round outside. Finally, not knowing what else to do, that big black bear plopped himself down right on top of the stump! "Kerbloom!" The stump exploded like a cannon, and the bear was the cannonball! So that night, the old stump made good firewood; and the big black bear turned into bear stew--just enough for four!

Dyed Indian Headbands

Cut a twenty-inch square of unbleached muslin (or an old sheet) for each child. For dye, do as the Indians did. Use two or three of the following: coffee or tea leaves, berries, greens or spinach, dead flowers, onion skins, and beets or cherries. Provide a pot of water (one quart) for each color, two tablespoons of alum per pot, spoons, and a hotplate or stove. Boil the water; add dyeing ingredient; and stir until the color is deep. Add the material (several at a time) and stir. Leave them in the dye until the fabric is darker than the color you desire. Remove and dry. Fold into a triangle and roll, starting from the point. Tie around forehead and knot behind the head.

Cooking Scene

The children create the cooking scene, as shown, using straw and/or pine straw or toothpicks for the sticks and firewood. Use a flat rock for the stone. Glue all in place. Draw the pot and color the fire.

Art

Animal Tracks

Preparation - Draw and cut out different animal footprints on thin sponges. Thick sponges may be cut in half with a knife. Provide newsprint, thinned tempera, and pie tins or trays.

Procedure - To hold the sponge, pinch the top of it with your thumb and index finger. Dip in paint and print on the paper.

Note: Animal tracks can be found in encyclopedias or science books.

Indian Vests

Preparation - Collect one grocery sack per child. Cut out the neck and down the middle, as shown. Cut a fifteen-inch piece of yarn for each child. Provide scissors and paints or markers. Have a stapler and hole puncher available.

Procedure - Cut out the sides on the folds, as shown. From these, cut two 9" x 2" rectangles. Punch two holes at the neck; cut yarn in half; and tie one piece in each hole. Staple rectangles as side "belts." Decorate and fringe all around the bottom.

Math

Smallest - Largest Animals

Use animal cards for this activity. Place on chalkboard ledge. Demonstrate. Choose a child to put the animals in order of size, proceeding from left to right. Call on other children to repeat.

Set of Animals

Direct the children to find and cut out animals from old magazines. Glue on a page labeled "Set of Animals."

Music - Movement - Games

Action Song - "The Braves"

Tune - "The Ants"

The braves go creeping in the woods

To hunt, to hunt.

The braves go creeping in the woods

To hunt, to hunt.

The braves go creeping on quiet feet

To hunt for food so they can eat,

And the arrows go swish-swish, swish-swish, swish-swish, swish-swish!

(The children act out the song as they sing the words.)

Action Story - "Brave Little Indian" - Author Unknown

Once upon a time, there was a brave little Indian. He said to his happy, little Indian friends, "I am going hunting to find a grizzly bear!" So he walked out the gate, and he slammed it. He hadn't walked far until he saw a rabbit; but he didn't see a bear. So he walked on. He came to a bridge, and he walked across. But he hadn't walked far until he saw a deer; but he didn't see a bear. So he walked on. Soon he came to a ditch. He couldn't step across; so he backed up. He said, "I jump ditch!" He started to run . . . faster . . . faster . . . faster! He jum-m-m-m-ped in, and he swam across. Then he jum-m-m-m-ped out, and he walked on. Oh! Oh! Oh! HE SAW THE BEAR. Who-o-o-o-o-o-o-o-o!! He turned around, and he ran down the hill. He jumped into the river, and he swam across. He jumped out, and he ran on. He jumped over the ditch, and he ran on. He saw a rabbit; but he ran on. He ran across the bridge. He saw a deer; but he ran on. When he got home, he slammed the gate. And he said, "I s-s-saw a b-b-bear!!" And the other little Indians said. . . "Ugh." And that's the story of the brave little Indian.

Directions

Everytime we read the word, Indian, you can be an Indian with feathers in your hair.

Whenever the brave little Indian walks, you can make the sound of his walking by slapping your legs with your hands. Left, right, left, right on the knees.

Whenever the brave little Indian slams the gate, you clap your hands, just once.

Whenever the brave little Indian sees something, you can shade your eyes with your hands and look around, too.

Whenever the brave little Indian crosses the bridge, you can hear him walking by pounding your fists on your chest. Left, right, left, right on chest.

Whenever the brave little Indian jumps, you raise your hands above your head as if you were jumping, too.

Whenever the brave little Indian runs, you slap your legs very fast with your hands (like walking, but faster).

Whenever the brave little Indian swims, you can hear him swim by brushing your palms against each other.

Action Game - "Hunter"

One student is designated as the <u>hunter</u>. The <u>hunter</u> will go to the front of the class and say, "Who wants to go hunting with me?" All of the other students will then form a line behind the <u>hunter</u>, and the hunt will begin. Students will follow the <u>hunter</u> until the <u>hunter</u> spots a bird, raises an invisible gun, and shoots. When shooting, the <u>hunter</u> says, "Bang!" At this signal, all students hurry toward their seats. The first student properly placed in his seat becomes the new <u>hunter</u>.

Story Time

Book - <u>Running Owl, the Hunter</u> - Nathaniel Benchley
Book - <u>Cherokee Animal Tales</u> - George Schier

Kindergarten Kitchen

Spoon Bread

2 cups yellow corn meal

2 cups water

2 cups whole milk

4 eggs, separated

2 teaspoons salt

4 Tablespoons baking powder

2 Tablespoons butter

Preheat oven to 450°. Separate eggs. Beat egg yolks and set aside. Beat egg whites until stiff. Mix water and milk in a saucepan. Add corn meal. Cook for five minutes on medium heat, stirring constantly. Add baking powder, salt, butter, egg yolks, and egg whites. Mix well, and pour into greased casserole dish. Bake for 45 minutes. Serves ten to twelve or a "taster's serving" for a class.

Day 4 - Weapons, Tools and Crafts

Concept Information

The American Indians had no stores where they could buy the <u>tools</u> and <u>weapons</u> they needed. They made their weapons and tools from things around them.

To hunt animals, the Indians used bows and arrows, lances, blow guns, and rabbit sticks.

Bows were made of thin pieces of wood tied together by sinew, the cords of animal muscles. Sinew was also used for the string of the bow.

Arrows were also made from wood, usually <u>cane</u> which was <u>smoked</u> and heated over a fire, and <u>polished</u> with stone. The <u>arrowheads</u> were sometimes of stone, but mostly from animal <u>bone</u> or <u>iron</u>. The feathers were tied on the arrow with sinew after they had been glued with <u>animal glue</u>. Most arrows had three split feathers at the end. Each Indian painted his arrows with different colored stripes below the feathers.

Lances or spears were used to kill animals while the Indians rode on horseback. They were <u>similar</u> to arrows, but much larger. Feathers and <u>streamers</u> were hung from the end.

Blow guns were six foot <u>tubes</u> made from <u>hollowed</u> out wooden <u>rods</u>. The sharp wooden <u>dart</u> was about eighteen inches long. The dart was put in the tube and blown out--much like a pea shooter. Blow guns were used to kill birds and small animals.

Rabbit sticks were curved pieces of wood similar to <u>boomerangs</u>. They were used as throwing sticks to kill small animals.

Knives or daggers were used as weapons and as tools to skin animals, cut wood, and so forth. They were made of animal bone or later iron or copper. Cane knives were sharpened pieces of thick cane which were made hard with fire. Shovels and hoes used in farming were made from the large bones of animals tied to wooden poles. Even sewing needles and fishhooks were made of animal bones and wood.

The Indians, especially the women, also used their great skills to make things that were both useful and beautiful. Some of the Indians made beautiful bowls, dippers, and cradleboards of wood. They made ceremonial masks which were carved on a tree and then removed. This was done because the Indians thought the live tree would give the mask life.

Certain Indian tribes wove beautiful baskets from thin pieces of wood which had been soaked in water. Others used plant fiber and grass which were dyed different colors by boiling them with flowers, roots, or minerals. The baskets were of all sizes and shapes and were used to carry or store things. Tar was "painted" inside of some so that they could hold water.

Pottery was another Indian craft. Clay was dug from the ground, dried, pounded, and mixed with sand and water. From this, the potter made bowls, storage jars, cooking pots, and smoking pipes. Once the clay dried, it was decorated with paints made from colored earth and baked.

Some of the Indian tribes were famous weavers of blankets. They grew cotton, spun it into thread, and wove it on a loom. Different colors were made by dyeing the thread before weaving.

After the Spanish settlers showed the Indians what <u>silver</u> was, the Indians made beautiful <u>jewelry</u>. <u>Turquoise</u>, shells, and wooden beads were used with the silver to make necklaces.

The toys of Indian children were also made by the Indian women. Sticks, arrows, and stones were used for games. Dolls were made of animal skins stuffed with moss or grass or vegetables dressed in animal skin clothes.

<u>Language Arts</u> - <u>Social Studies</u> - <u>Science</u>

<u>Discussion</u>

Preparation - Ask to borrow Indian objects from friends and parents. Set up a display of the following items: bow and arrow, lance, a modern shovel and hoe, a wooden pole, animal bones, a metal dipper, baskets, pottery, and such Indian items as turquoise jewelry, blankets, bowls, pictures, etc.

Procedure - Discuss the concept information, defining vocabulary words and showing different items. Construction methods can be drawn on the board. One Indian craft reference book is <u>The Art of the American Indian</u> by Shirley Glubok.

<u>Book</u> - <u>The Girl Who Loved Wild Horses</u> by Paul Goble
Read <u>The Girl Who Loved Wild Horses</u> by Paul Goble. Go through the book again directing the children to point out all of the "Indian details," such as homes, clothing, and symbols.

<u>Experience Chart</u>

Brainstorm for things made and methods used by the Indians. List on the chart. The children may illustrate.

Parent Demonstration

If one of your parents or fellow teachers weaves, makes jewelry, works with wood, or makes pottery, invite him or her to demonstrate. Projects should be simple, such as a wooden dart or arrow, a small pot, a doll blanket, or a simple charm or earring.

Flannel Board Story - "The Sweet Patootie Doll"

Read or tell the story from the book, The Sweet Patootie Doll by Mary Calhoun. At the same time, place the figures (see pattern section) on the flannel board. Then let the children retell the story and display the figures.

Art

Clay Coil or Pinch Pots

Preparation - Provide water-base clay which is pre-wedged (kneaded) and soft and clay tools (or substitute toothpicks, pastry cutters, melon cutters, nails, and so forth). Pass out cardboard squares for working surfaces.

Procedure - For pinch pots, roll the clay into a ball. Push one thumb in the center of the ball and rotate while pressing outward to form the pot. Moisten the rim to smooth. To dry, turn the pots upside down. After several days, paint with tempera and spray with clear lacquer.

For coil pots, roll clay into a long rope. Coil to form the base and sides. Moisten the inside of the pot to "weld together" the coils. Use the same drying and painting procedure as used with the pinch pots.

Note: Clay may be fired, glazed, and refired in a kiln.

Indian Necklaces

Preparation - Cut an eighteen to twenty-four inch piece of yarn for each child. Punch a hole in a small square of paper, and knot one end of the yarn through this. Write the child's name on this square of paper. Wrap tape around the other end of the piece of yarn. In jars, mix food coloring of different colors with water. Add large macaroni, and stir for a _short_ time. Remove and drain on paper towels.

Procedure - The children string the macaroni on the yarn for Indian necklaces. Macaroni can be alternated with pieces of colored straws, shells, and pieces of paper.

Indian Arrows

Preparation - Collect small, straight sticks from the playground. Duplicate the arrowhead and feather sheet on construction paper of various colors. Provide each child with one stick, two arrowheads, two feathers, scissors, and glue.

Procedure - Cut out the arrowheads and feathers. Glue each together with the stick in between. Dry.

Note: A triangular piece of sponge can be cut for the arrowhead. Twist in the end of the stick, remove, add glue, and reinsert.

Math

"Sets Sheet"

Duplicate the Indian Sets Sheet. Count the Indian objects in each box, and circle the correct corresponding number. Color the sheet.

Music - Movement - Games

Game - "Geronimo"

Place two ropes parallel about two feet apart on the floor or ground. Have the children pretend they are Indians being chased by a big bear. The children line up single file and jump "over the river." The ropes are moved farther apart each time, and the procedure is repeated. When a child falls into the river, he or she must yell "Geronimo" and act out swimming to shore. He or she may then rejoin the group. The child who can jump over the river at its "widest" point is the winner.

Game - "Toss the Arrow"

Use a hula hoop or rope to form a three-foot circle. Cut two poster paper strips to divide the circle into four equal sections (⊕). Tape to the hoop or rope. Use Indian arrows (see Art), toy arrows with rubber tips, or arrows made from straws with clay for arrowheads. Use a stick, tape, or a paper strip to mark a line four feet away from the circle. The child stands on his line, and tosses the arrow in the circle. The quarter sections which are nearer to the child count five points; the farther sections count ten points. The child or team with the most points wins.

Story Time

Book - Little Chief - Syd Hoff

Day 5 - War and Ceremonies

Concept Information

When the white man came to America, the American Indians did not seem to mind. But as more and more white settlers took their land and destroyed their hunting grounds, the Indians were forced to move. When the Indians fought the white man, they felt they were fighting for their stolen land.

All Indians did not like to fight, but there were some tribes who enjoyed it. They felt it was good to be brave and cruel. At first, Indians went to war on foot. They would sneak up on their enemies, attack, and then run. Later, Indians rode horses which were brought to America by the Spanish. Indian warriors rode bareback and were taught to fight from childhood. Indians also used canoes made from wood and birch bark for transportation to and from battles.

Indian warriors usually painted their faces with colored earth, wore feather headdresses, and carried shields of buffalo hide. They also carried tomahawks and, as we have learned, lances, daggers, or bows and arrows.

Before a war, the Indians had a ceremony to prepare for the fighting. The Indian braves would do a war dance while the women packed parched corn and maple sugar for them to take as food. Each man also had a "medicine bundle" which contained objects which he felt would protect him in battle.

When Indians killed someone, they cut off his scalp and brought it home to prove how many of the enemy they had killed. Scalps were put on poles in front of the tepees or were hung from the Indians' belts. When enemies were captured, they were sometimes "adopted" as an Indian. Many times they were tortured and killed. The Indians shouted war songs and celebrated.

Besides war ceremonies, the Indians had festivals for planting, for the harvest, and for the new year. At these, the Indians had special dances and activities including games and feasting.

Language Arts - Social Studies

Discussion

Share the concept information and define vocabulary words. Show pictures from reference books or posters. Mention and discuss the validity of the Indian as depicted in western movies, television, and so forth.

Interview

Invite an Indian to visit the class and discuss "Indians Yesterday and Today."

Indian Headdress Color Sheet

Duplicate the sheet. Direct the children to follow the color words in coloring the feathers. If necessary, put a chart on the board with a colored circle beside each color word.

Alphabet Activity

Using flash cards, direct the children to think of an Indian word or object which begins with each letter. Hand out a sheet of paper to each child with an alphabet letter at the top. The children illustrate an Indian object which begins with that letter. Assist when necessary.

Following Directions Review Sheet

Hand out paper. The children fold the paper in half, and in half once again, making four sections. Draw lines on the folds and number the squares. Give directions as follows:

1. In the #1 block, draw an Indian dwelling. Color it brown.

2. In the #2 block, use a black crayon to draw an Indian weapon.

3. In the #3 block, draw an Indian picture word. Color it red.

4. In the #4 block, draw an Indian garment. Color it orange.

Art

Indian Headdresses

Preparation - Collect a large grocery sack for each child. Cut across both layers about ten inches from the top. Discard the bottom. Pull out the sides, flatten, and fold into thirds. Cut out the headband and two feathers, as shown. (You will be cutting through 6 layers of the bag.) Provide scissors and crayons.

Procedure - Direct the children to cut through the headband in one place (so it will not be a circle). Color and fringe feathers. Staple headband to fit. (Two ends will hang down in back.)

Variation: Duplicate "Proud of Our Feather" feather on different colors of construction paper. Children cut and glue on a 2" x 24" strip.

Paper Plate Shields

Preparation - Provide one paper plate for each child, one nine-inch cardboard strip, crepe paper streamers, tissue paper, scissors, glue, and a stapler.

Procedure - The children choose an Indian symbol to draw on the rounded side of the paper plate. The symbol should be about five inches. Cut the tissue paper into two-inch pieces. Crumple and glue to fill in design. Use other colors of tissue squares and glue on background to create a collage effect. Staple the cardboard across the back as a handle. Staple streamers along the bottom.

Ceremony Bustle

Preparation - Make a cardboard feather and circle patterns from the sheet. Provide a paper plate for each child, different colors of construction paper, crepe paper streamers (two 2-foot pieces per child), scissors, glue, a piece of yarn per child (which will reach around their waists), and a hole puncher.

Procedure - The children trace around the feather patterns to make fifteen to twenty feathers, and around each circle pattern once. Glue the feathers around the outside of the plate and the circles in the middle, as shown (on the sheet). Staple the two streamers to the bottom of the plate. Punch two holes in the top of the plate. String the yarn through the holes and tie around the waist. The bustle will be in back.

Math

Feathers for the Indian Braves

Duplicate the sheet. The children draw and color feathers to correspond with the numerals. Color the Indians.

Music -Movement - Games

Game - "Moccasin Guessing Game"

Provide a pair of moccasins and two stones, one marked with an orange or red dot. Divide the class into teams. One member of a team puts a stone under each moccasin. A member of the other team covers his eyes and then guesses which moccasin is covering the stone with the dot. A correct guess earns one point for the team; an incorrect guess earns one point for the other team. Alternate players and "roles" after each turn. The team with the most points wins.

Movement - "Horses"

Pair off the children and form a circle. The "horse" stands in front with arms outstretched to the rear. The "rider" faces the horse's back and holds his hands. Use voice commands and/or a tom-tom or music with changing tempos to signal the horses and riders to trot, canter, gallop, and so forth. The riders and horses then change places, and the procedure is repeated.

Variation: The following poem may be used for this activity with everyone falling at the end:

Five little Indians on a nice fall day

Jumped on their ponies and rode far away.

They galloped in the meadow, and they galloped up a hill,

They galloped so fast that they all took a spill.

Game - "Dance With the Indian"

Materials: broom, paper bag, colored paper for feathers

This game requires a little preparation beforehand. Fit a paper bag over a broom. Draw a face on it, and dab some paint on it so it will look like

Indian war paint. Make a headband with colored feathers, and fit it on the top of the bag. Now you are ready for your game. An uneven number of children have to play this. Have some slips of paper ready which are all blank except one. On this slip, write the word, "Indian." The child who draws this slip has to dance the first dance with the "Indian." All the others choose partners. When the music begins, everyone dances. When the music stops, everyone must change partners. The child with the "Indian" passes it to someone else who, in turn, tries to pass it on. No one can refuse to take the "Indian," but they can try to get rid of it as soon as possible. Whoever is holding the "Indian" when the music begins again has to dance that dance with the "Indian."

Story Time

Book - Indian Two Feet and His Eagle Feather - Margaret Friskey

Field Trip

Visit an Indian museum. Afterwards, review this on an experience chart.

Indian Dress-Up - (Culminating Activity)

Put on war paint (tempera or greasepaint, see Circus Unit - Day 2), headdresses, vests, necklaces, bustles, and carry tom-toms. Visit another class and discuss information learned or perform a war dance.

Concept Evaluation - (See Introduction)

Dear Parents,

On _____, we will begin our unit on Indians. We will learn about the history and customs of the American Indian and their role in the first Thanksgiving. Below are ways you can help.

Things to Send: _____

_____

_____

Ways to Volunteer: _____

_____

_____

Follow-Up: At the end of the unit, ask your child to share the following songs, etc.

_____

_____

_____

Follow-Up Questions to Ask Your Child:

1. Who were the first people in America?

2. Name the different types of Indian homes (tepees, pueblos, longhouses, hogans, wooden houses).

3. Draw some Indian picture language symbols.

4. Where did the Indians get their clothes and food?

Thank you for your help.

Sincerely,

America, Long Ago

Proud Of Our Feathers

Copyright © 1987. Carol Taylor Bond

"Proud Of Our Feathers"

Pattern For Indians

(sample face)

Copyright © 1987. Carol Taylor Bond

Proud Of Our Feathers

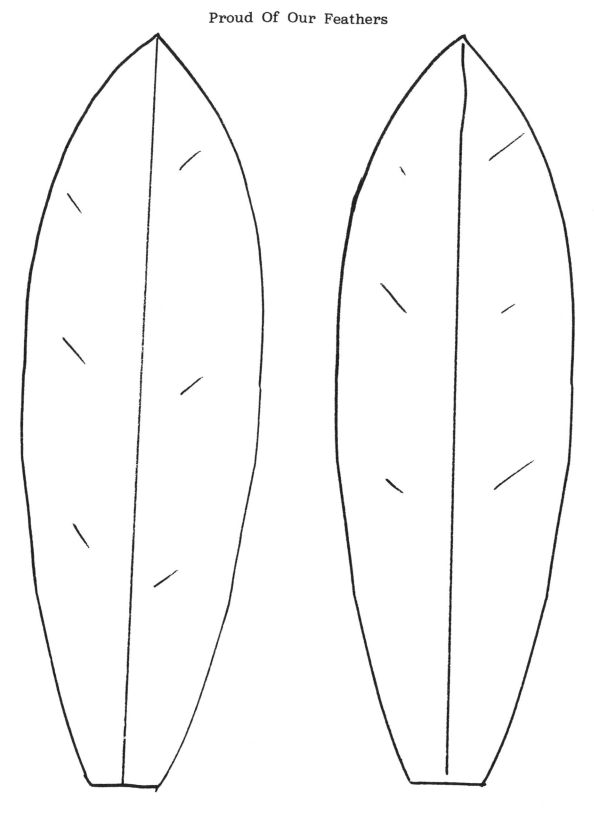

Feather Patterns

Copyright © 1987.   Carol Taylor Bond

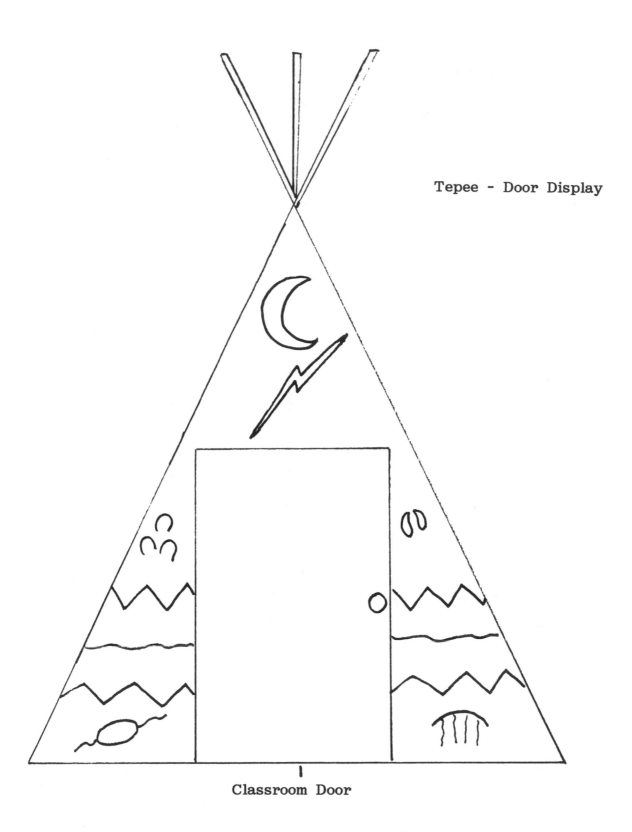

Tepee – Door Display

Classroom Door

Copyright © 1987. Carol Taylor Bond

376

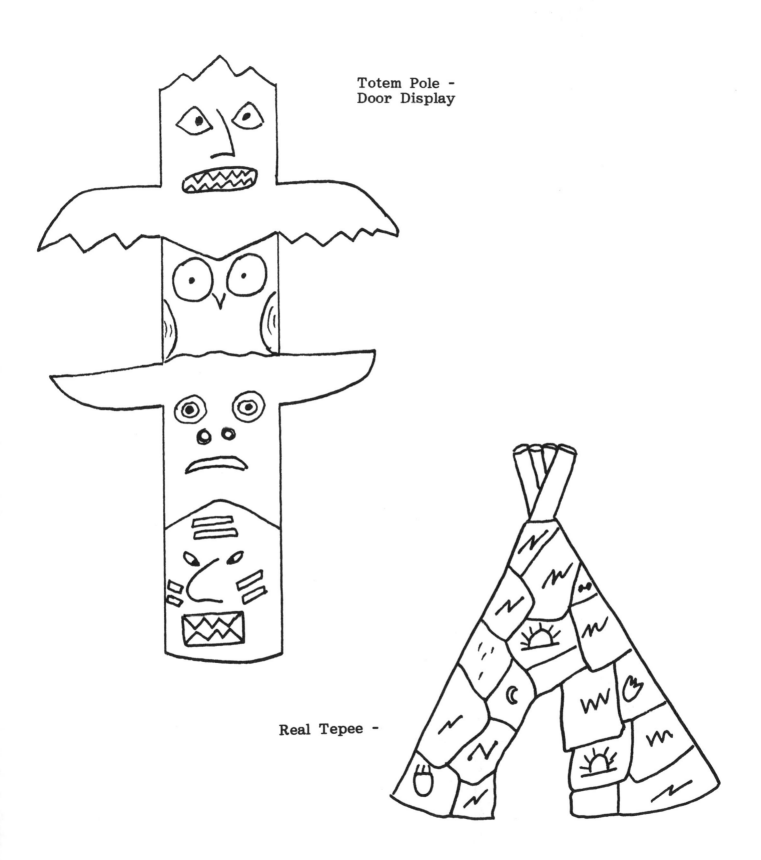

Totem Pole -
Door Display

Real Tepee -

Copyright © 1987.   Carol Taylor Bond

377

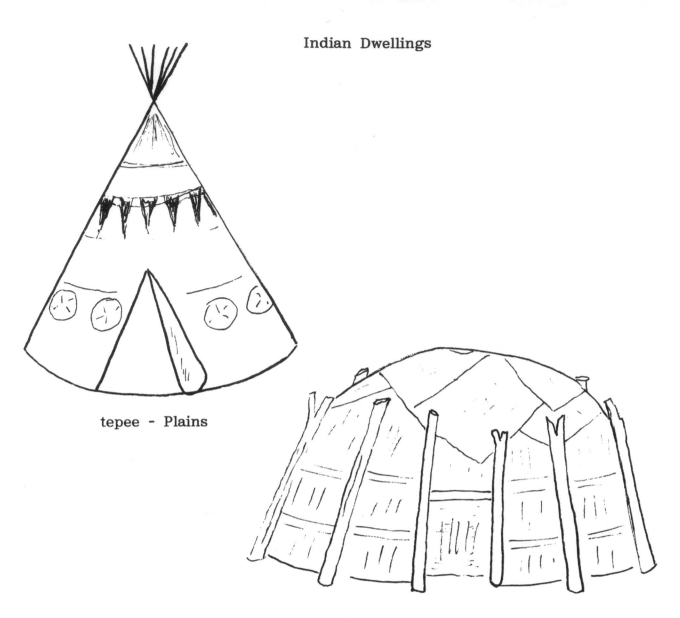

tepee - Plains

wigwams - Eastern

longhouses - Eastern

Copyright © 1987.   Carol Taylor Bond

Indian Dwellings

houses - Southeastern

huts - Rocky Mountains

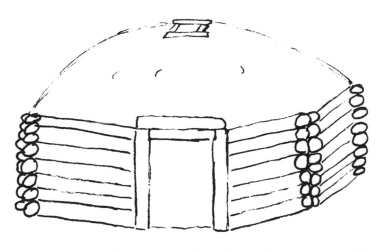

hogans - Southwestern

Copyright © 1987. Carol Taylor Bond

379

houses - Western Coast

pueblos - Desert

Copyright © 1987.   Carol Taylor Bond

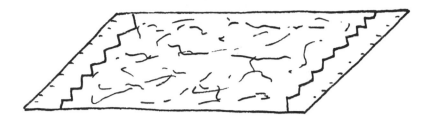

Indian Rug
Example

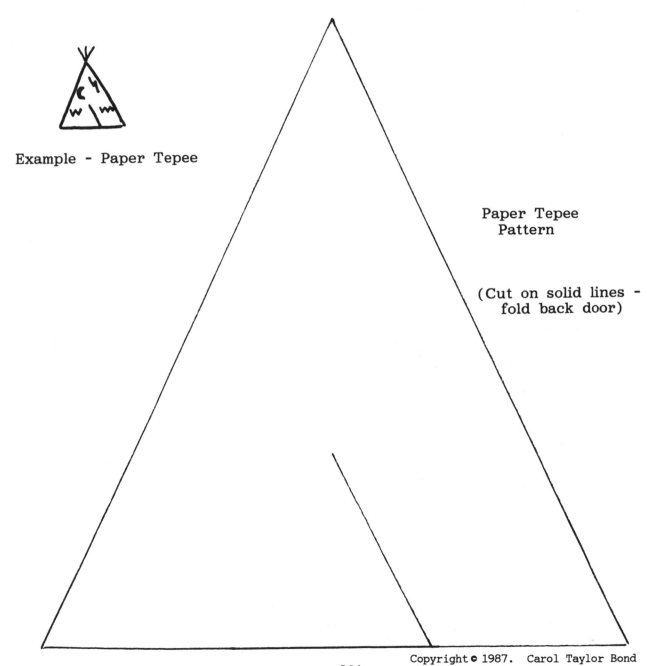

Example - Paper Tepee

Paper Tepee
Pattern

(Cut on solid lines -
fold back door)

Copyright © 1987.   Carol Taylor Bond

Stand-Up Tepee
Pattern -

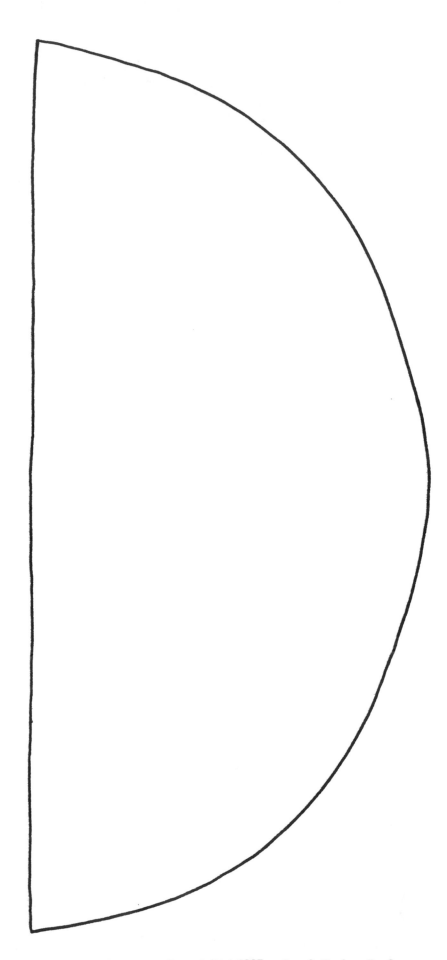

Indian Puppet
Example

Copyright © 1987. Carol Taylor Bond

Stand-Up Village

(Page 1)

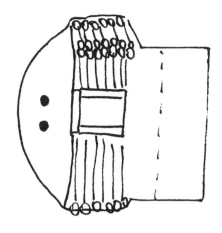

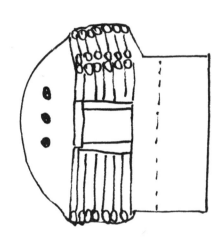

A. Number and Color
Cut Out

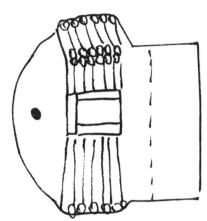

Example:

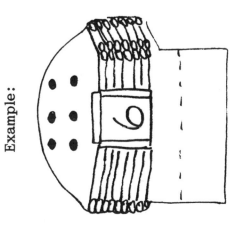

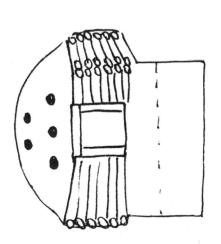

Copyright © 1987. Carol Taylor Bond

Stand-Up Village

(Page 2)

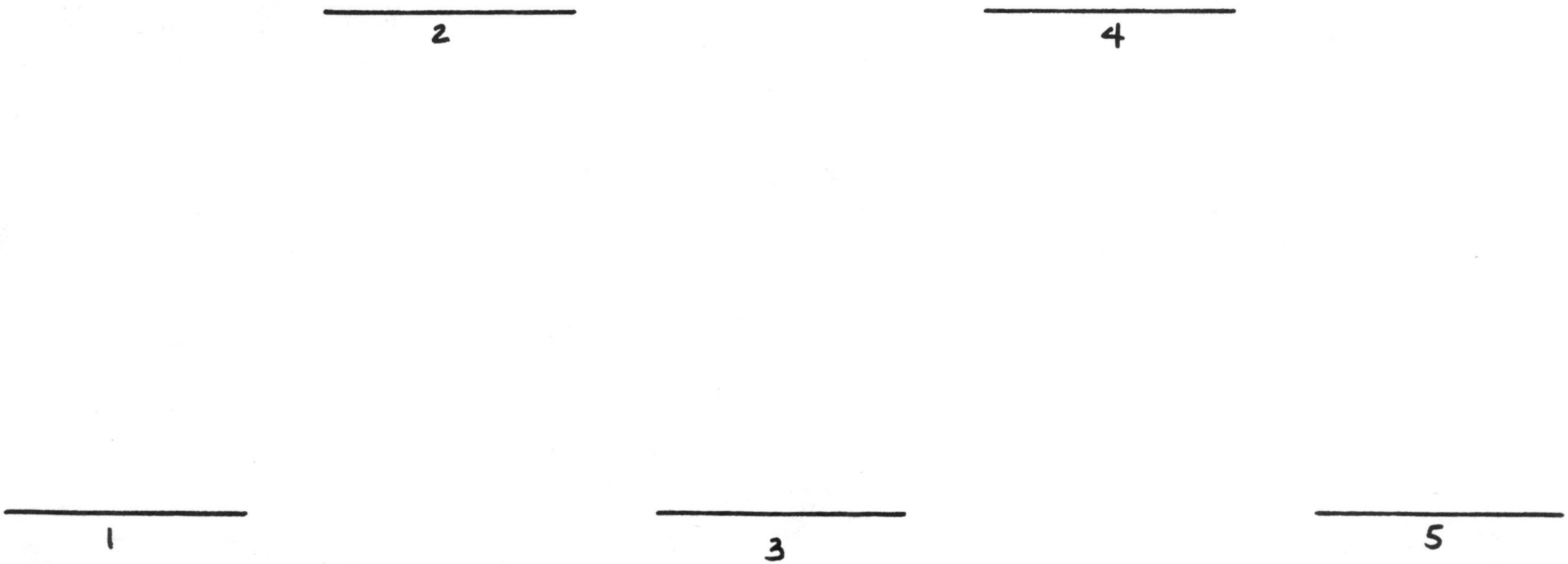

2

4

5

3

1

B. Fold hogans on dotted lines.

C. Glue hogans on the correct lines.

384

Copyright © 1987. Carol Taylor Bond

Table Display

(Objects will be standing upright in the sand.)

Fire   - Toothpick pieces, orange paper

River   - Mix a small amount of water with glue in large bowl. Mix in blue crepe paper. Place it in the sand to form river. Dry.

Tepees   - Stand-Up Tepees (See Art - Day 1.)

Totem Poles - See Art - Day 2.

Canoes   - Fold paper in half. Cut, as shown, ⌐▱⌐-fold and glue each end together.

Animals   - Cotton balls colored with dry tempera. Two half pipe cleaners twisted around cotton ball body for legs. Marker eyes.

Indians   - Pipe cleaner men, paper faces, and feathers

Trees   - Roll pieces of brown paper, glue, and slit top. Cut tree top shape, and insert in slit.

Copyright © 1987. Carol Taylor Bond

INDIAN SIGN LANGUAGE

Water	Sleep	Drink	Eat	Yes	You or Him	I or Me	Listen
Woman	Man	Friend	Talk	Walk	Bring	Come	Go
Tongue	Sunrise	Scout	Mind	Hungry	Moon	Sun	Night
True	Brave	Good	Heart	Day	With	Run	Take

Reprint courtesy of
Boy Scounts of America

386

Indian Picture Language

Reprint courtesy of
Boy Scouts of America

DISCOVERED · THREE DAYS · THREE NIGHTS · PLENTY OF FOOD · COLD & SNOW

BEAVER · CAMPFIRE · RAIN

DEER · LAKE · FEAR · CLEAR WEATHER

BIRD TRACKS · RIVER · HUNGRY · STORMY

GOOD · DEAD · BROTHERS · UNCLE PRIEST · MEDICINE · NORTH-S-E · MAN ON HORSE · EAT

ALIVE · ARROW · EVENING · BOY · SPIRIT

PEACE PIPE · BROKEN CAMP · LIVE TOGETHER · NOON · WOMAN · HEAR

PLENTIFUL · MORNING · MAN · TEPEE

387

The Lost Indian [boy] Boy

One day an Indian [boy] boy walked beside the ~~~ river which was near the △△△ Indian camp. He pretended he was a brave Indian [man] man on a [deer] deer [arrow] hunt. Soon it was evening, and the Indian [boy] boy felt great [fear] fear. He was lost, and he was hungry! The Indian [boy] boy remembered what he had been taught by the [sun] wise man. He [looked] looked at the stars and followed the [tracks] horse tracks back to the △△△ Indian camp. First he saw a △ tepee, then the ✕ campfire, and best of all, [tepee with food] plenty of food!

 Copyright © 1987. Carol Taylor Bond

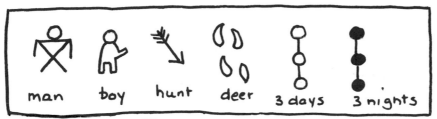

Picture Messages

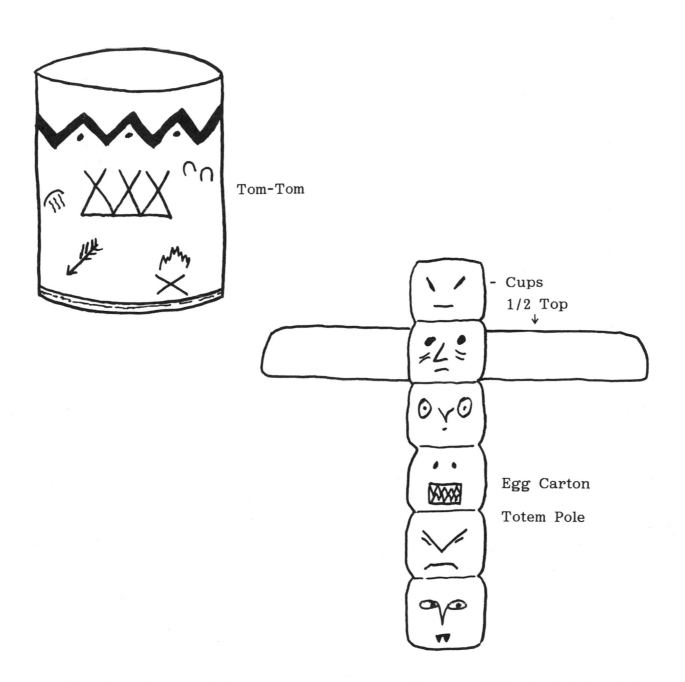

Tom-Tom

- Cups
1/2 Top
↓

Egg Carton

Totem Pole

Copyright © 1987. Carol Taylor Bond

389

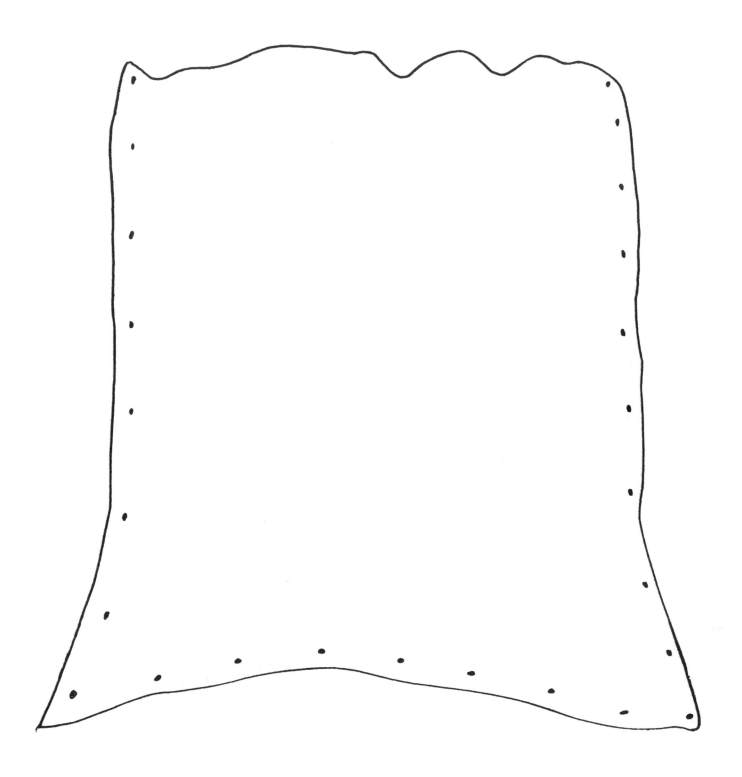

Duplicate two

Copyright © 1987. Carol Taylor Bond

The Old Stump - Pictures

 Copyright © 1987. Carol Taylor Bond

Cooking Scene

Indian Vest

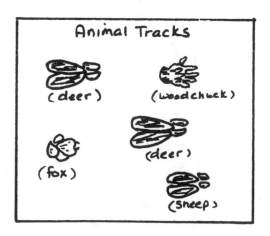

Animal Tracks

(deer)   (woodchuck)

(fox)   (deer)

(sheep)

Copyright ©1987. Carol Taylor Bond

The Sweet Patootie Doll

Copyright © 1987. Carol Taylor Bond

393

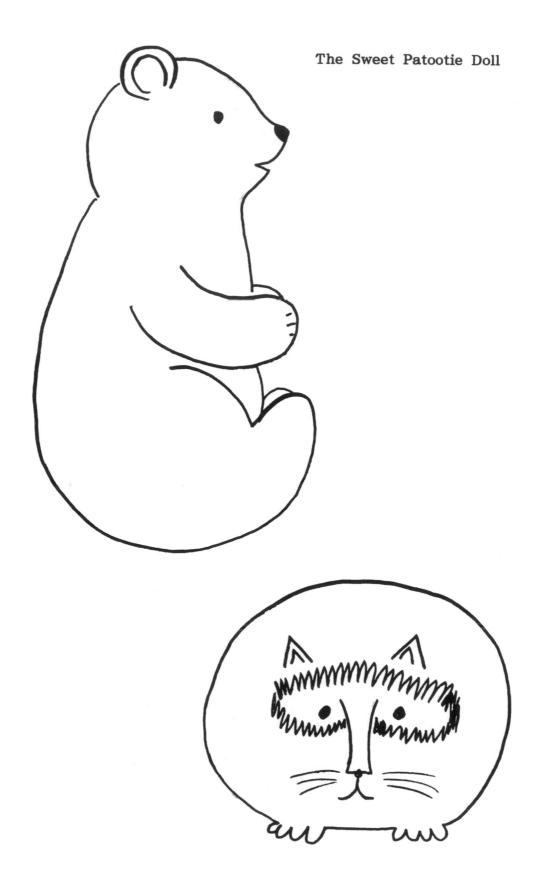

The Sweet Patootie Doll

Copyright © 1987. Carol Taylor Bond

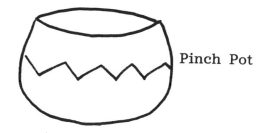

Pinch Pot

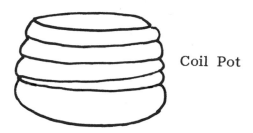

Coil Pot

Art Examples

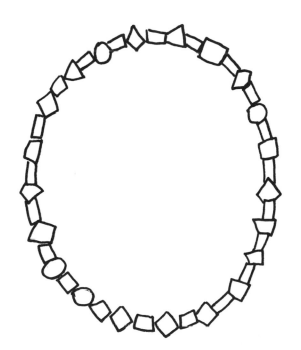

Indian Necklace

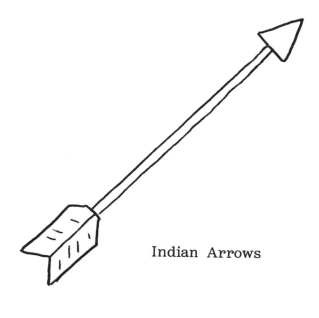

Indian Arrows

Copyright © 1987. Carol Taylor Bond

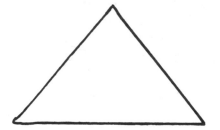

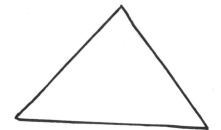

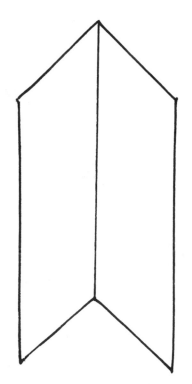

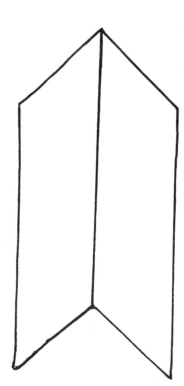

Copyright © 1987.   Carol Taylor Bond

Indian Sets Sheet

Circle the Correct Number

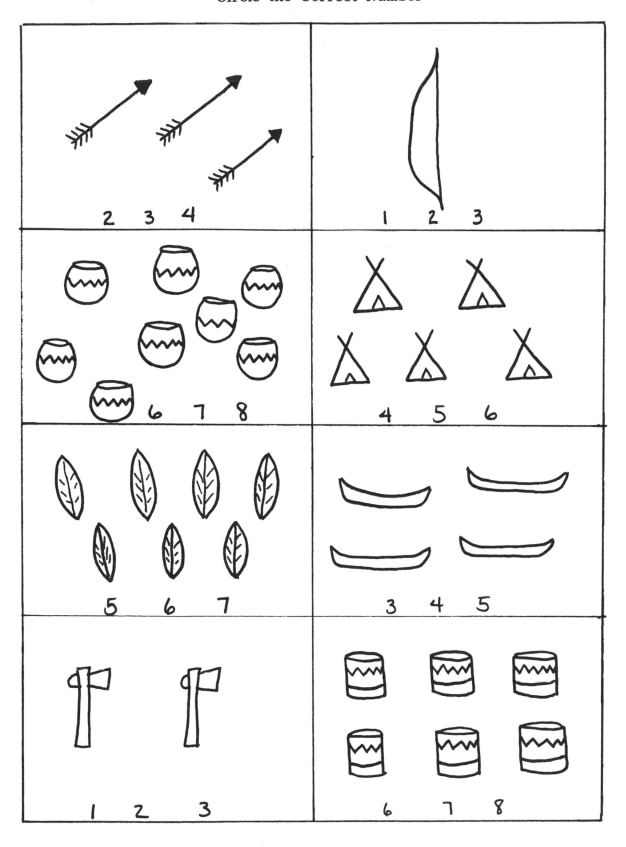

2 3 4

1 2 3

6 7 8

4 5 6

5 6 7

3 4 5

1 2 3

6 7 8

Name - _____

Copyright © 1987. Carol Taylor Bond

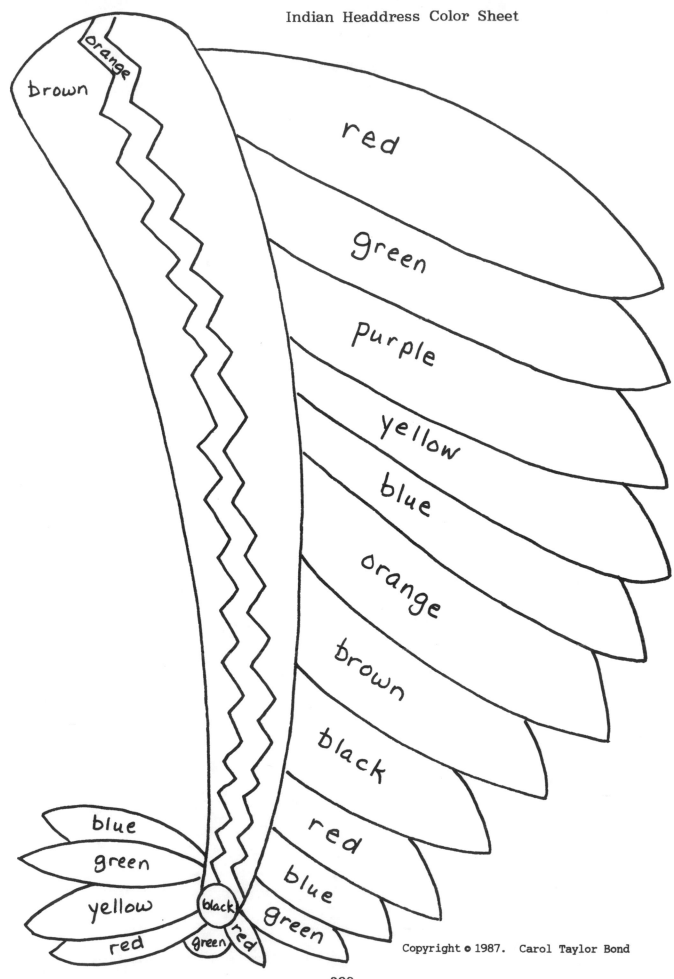

red

green

purple

yellow

blue

orange

brown

black

red

blue

green

brown

orange

blue

green

yellow

red

black

green

red

Copyright © 1987. Carol Taylor Bond

Ceremony Bustle

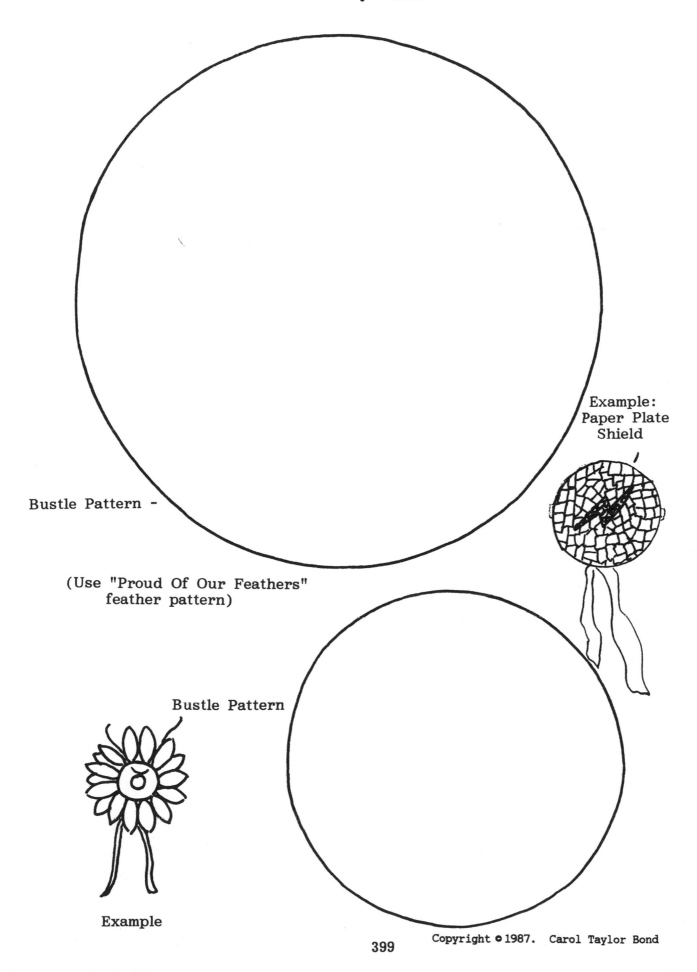

Bustle Pattern -

(Use "Proud Of Our Feathers"
feather pattern)

Example:
Paper Plate
Shield

Bustle Pattern

Example

399

Copyright © 1987. Carol Taylor Bond

Feathers For The Indian Braves

1

2

3

4

 Copyright © 1987. Carol Taylor Bond

Pilgrims

<u>Proposed Time</u>: 5 days

<u>Unit Objectives</u>

To develop understanding of Thanksgiving

To explain our current Thanksgiving customs

To encourage thankfulness in our daily lives

To develop understanding of the Pilgrims

<u>Room Environment</u> - <u>Bulletin Boards</u>

"We're Thankful For. . . ."

Make children's faces from paper circles or paper plates. Add facial features and yarn or curling ribbon for hair. Staple along the bottom of the bulletin board. From white paper, cut "thought bubbles"; and place on the bulletin board, as shown. Direct the children to cut out magazine pictures showing things for which they are thankful. Staple these in the thought bubbles. Discuss each child's contribution.

"America Long Ago"

On poster paper, draw and cut out the Mayflower as shown. Direct some of the children to paint it with black tempera paint. The rest of the children can trace and cut out small circles to represent the Pilgrims. Add facial features and Pilgrim hats, and staple above the side of the boat. Several complete Pilgrims can be made to stand on shore. Add this to the bulletin board "America Long Ago," see Indians, Room Environment.

Room Environment - Wall or Door Displays

"Paper Chain Turkey"

Draw the turkey on brown poster paper. Use tempera paint for features. Have the children make a long paper chain of Thanksgiving colors. Begin gluing the chain to the tagboard in the center of the turkey's body. Wind around and around until the entire body is filled in with the chain. Mount on the classroom door (or on the wall).

"Thankful Turkey"

Draw the "Thankful Turkey" on brown poster paper. Paint features with tempera. Trace turkey feathers on different colors of construction paper. Give each child a feather to cut out. The children should use a black marker to write his or her name on the feather and one thing he or she is thankful for. Glue the feathers on the tail section, working from the outside toward the center as shown. Hang on the classroom door (or wall).

Room Environment - Table Display

(See Indian Unit - Day 1 Table Display.)

Add Pilgrim houses (see Day 1 - Art) and several pipe cleaner Pilgrims to the display. Follow the same procedure in making the pipe cleaner figures, but add small black hats rather than feathers.

Day 1 - Introduction

Concept Information

Today, we are going to talk about why the Pilgrims came to America and their voyage across the ocean.

In 1600, the people of England all had to go to one church, the Church of England. They were also told what to believe. Some of the people disliked this. They wanted freedom to believe what they wished, to study the Bible, and to have a church in which they could worship as they pleased. But in 1600, it was against the law to do this. People were put in jail for trying to leave the Church of England and worship on their own. So a group of people, who were later called the Pilgrims, secretly left England and went to Holland to live. In Holland, they were able to have their own church. But the Pilgrims were not happy in Holland. They could not get good jobs and did not have the money to buy farms. The Pilgrims wanted a place of their own. A company told the Pilgrims that they would send them to America and give them free land. But the Pilgrims would have to work for the company for seven years. Some of the pilgrims decided to go to America.

In September of the year 1620, the Pilgrims and other people who wished to go to America sailed on two ships, the Mayflower and the Speedwell. The Speedwell began to leak so some of the passengers were left behind. The rest went on the Mayflower. The Mayflower was very crowded, and the trip to America took two months. There were storms. Some of the passengers were sick, and some died. When the Mayflower reached America, the Pilgrims gave thanks to God.

<u>Language Arts</u> - <u>Social Studies</u> - <u>Science</u>

<u>Filmstrip</u> - "The First Thanksgiving" (Troll Books)

Show and read the captions of the filmstrip which tells a simplified version of the Pilgrims' voyage, first year, and the first Thanksgiving.

<u>Discussion</u>

Share the concept information and define vocabulary words. Use a reference book, or display pictures of the <u>Mayflower</u> and the Pilgrims. Show the inside structure of the <u>Mayflower</u> with a drawing, or use the picture in <u>Turkeys, Pilgrims and Indian Corn</u> by Edna Barth (drawings by Ursula Arndt). Tape a piece of yarn on a globe or map showing the route of the <u>Mayflower</u> which was straight across the Atlantic Ocean from England to Massachusetts. Ask the children to close their eyes and imagine that they are Pilgrims. They are leaving their friends and possibly some of their families. They sail on a big ship for two months. The ship is crowded. There are storms, and many of the people get sick. The ship is sailing to a strange country. Ask the children, "How do you feel?"

<u>Shadow Play and Choral Reading</u>

"Shadow Stage" - Hang a sheet across a corner of the classroom. Turn a long table on its side and position it behind the sheet. Place a clamp-type light on the back of a chair in the corner. To use an existing puppet stage, put a piece of an old sheet over the stage opening and a light source at the rear of the stage.

"Shadow Play Characters" - Enlarge and make the <u>Mayflower</u> pattern from the "America Long Ago" bulletin board. Also, make and distribute tagboard patterns of the "Shadow Play Characters." Each child should have one character. Direct the children to trace around the pattern , cut out, and glue to tongue depressors or heavy cardboard strips.

Note: Two children may be assigned to the Mayflower figure.

Shadow Play Procedure - Practice the choral reading until the children learn the chorus. (Use a hand signal to indicate when the chorus is recited.) Divide the class into four groups, one for each verse. (One group performs while the others watch.) Characters for each verse are as follows:

Verse 1 - Pilgrims, the Mayflower

Verse 2 - Pilgrims, Plymouth Rock

Verse 3 - Sunshine, Indians, Pilgrims, Houses, Corn

Verse 4 - Turkeys, Pumpkins, Corn, Pilgrims, Indians

Seat the audience in four rows according to appearance in the play. Hold a trial run. Direct the first row to their positions behind the table. Show the children how to manipulate their characters. (Instructions are in parentheses following each line.) Repeat the procedure with each group. Turn on the light and begin the play.

Variation: The play and choral reading can be separate activities. The children can manipulate the characters as you tell the story of Thanksgiving.

Shadow Play and Choral Reading

(The Chorus for each verse will be repeated after each line.)

Verse 1 -

> The Pilgrims sailed on the Mayflower long, long ago.
>
> > (The Mayflower sails with the Pilgrims on deck.)

The ship was crowded, and the voyage was slow.

(The _Mayflower_ sails with the Pilgrims on deck.)

For many weeks, they crossed the sea.

(The _Mayflower_ sails with the Pilgrims on deck.)

To America, where they could be free.

(The Mayflower sails with the Pilgrims on deck.)

CHORUS: And they sailed; and they sailed; and they sailed.

Verse 2

The Pilgrims arrived in the land of the free

(The _Mayflower_ stops; the Pilgrims walk off the ship,

step on Plymouth Rock, and walk forward in a line.)

And named their new home Plymouth Colony.

(Pilgrims stand; the _Mayflower_ remains docked.)

The winter was cold; and the food was low;

(Pilgrims shake.)

But the Pilgrims were brave, as we all know.

(Pilgrims stand in place.)

CHORUS: And they worked; and they worked; and they worked.

Verse 3

Spring finally came, and the weather grew warm.

(Pilgrims standing - sun rises.)

Indian friends helped the Pilgrims farm.

(Indians and Pilgrims planting.)

The houses were built, and the corn grew tall.

(Houses and corn come up.)

And there was food for one and all.

(Pilgrims and Indians pick corn.)

406

CHORUS: They were glad; they were glad; they were glad.

Verse 4

There were turkeys, pumpkins, and corn a-plenty

(Show turkeys, pumpkins, and corn.)

Enough to hold a feast for many.

(Show Pilgrims in a group.)

The Indians joined them to eat and play

(Indians and Pilgrims picking up food and playing.)

On that our First Thanksgiving Day.

(Indians and Pilgrims bow to each other.)

CHORUS: They gave thanks; they gave thanks; they gave thanks.

"Activity on Air"

Preparation - Make a Paper Mayflower (Instructions below). Have available: a fan, a pinwheel, two balloons, two 10-inch pieces of string, a wire clothes hanger, a soft drink bottle, a clear glass bowl two-thirds full of water, and a flat pan two-thirds full of water.

Paper Mayflower (See illustrated steps)

Use the flat side of a black crayon to color both sides of a piece of lightweight white paper.

1. Fold the paper in half lengthwise.
2. With the fold at the top, bring the right top corner down so that it covers half the page and crease. Repeat with the left top corner.
3. Fold up the top layer of the bottom flaps and crease. Turn over and repeat with the remaining bottom flap.
4. You will have a paper hat.

5. Turn upside down, and open so that it resembles a cup. Bring the two points together; place on a flat surface; and crease. (It will now be a square.)

6. On each side, fold down the top points even with the bottom point. (It is now a triangle.) Open cup and fold opposite way so that highest points meet. Flatten. (It is now a diamond.)

7. Grasp the bottom points on both sides and pull out. Turn over and you will have a ship. Fold down the middle point. Cut a square of paper for the sail. Make two slits in the sail, and insert a half straw.

8. Staple the straw to the folded down middle point.

Procedure - Explain that air is all around us, and we must have it to live. We cannot see, touch, smell, or taste it; but we know that it is there. Turn on the fan and discuss what the air is doing (moving things). Turn the soft drink bottle upside down and lower it into the clear glass bowl of water. Observe that no water enters the bottle. (Conclusion: It is filled with air.) Use air to blow up the balloons. Knot the ends. Tie one piece of string to each balloon. Then tie each to either "corner" of the clothes hanger and hang on a nail, or whatever is available. Pop one balloon. Discuss why the balloons no longer balance, i.e., air has weight. Relate that in the days of the Pilgrims, ships had no engines. How did the Mayflower move across the ocean to America? Put the Mayflower in the pan of water and blow on the sail. Use the fan for the same purpose. Then put the pinwheel in front of the fan. Discuss and show pictures of how we use air--to cool us, to vacuum, to sail boats, and to fly kites.

Note: Encourage the children to participate in these activities as much as possible.

Art

Sailing Mayflower

Preparation - Duplicate the "Sailing Mayflower" on white construction
paper, and the "Sea" on light blue or green. Distribute the two sheets to
each child. Provide scissors, crayons, and a paper drinking straw per
child. A stapler will be needed.

Procedure - Cut out the ship and sail. Fold the sail in half, and make a
cut on each dotted line. On the "Sea" sheet, the "path" (dotted line) is
cut by folding the paper and making a small cut on the line. The sheet is
then unfolded, and the scissors are inserted in this cut. Make sure the
children stop at both ends of the dotted line. Color the Mayflower; insert
the straw through the two slits in the sail; and staple the straw to the
ship. Flatten the part of the straw underneath the ship, and push through
the path on the "Sea" sheet. The children move the ship by holding the
paper with one hand while moving the straw underneath the "Sea" with the
other hand.

Pilgrim Paper Bag Puppets

Preparation - Duplicate and hand out the Pilgrim Paper Bag Puppet sheet.
Provide a paper bag and a piece of black construction paper per child.
Distribute scissors, crayons, and glue.

Procedure - Cut out the two pieces of the face. Glue the straight edge of
the larger piece even with the lower edge of the bottom section of the
paper bag. Lift this section, and glue the straight edge of the smaller
piece even with the crease. While this dries, direct the children to use a
yellow or orange crayon to draw a Pilgrim hat and the hat band on the
black construction paper. Cut out. Draw the facial features on the face

pieces of the bag, placing the upper lip at the bottom of the movable section. The lower lip is drawn below it on the smaller piece of the face. Glue on the hat. Note: Use the puppets throughout the week as you sing Thanksgiving songs.

Math

Flannel Board Picture

Preparation - Place pellon over the Flannel Board Picture figures. (Use the Mayflower from the "America Long Ago" bulletin board as a pattern.) Cut out and color with markers, or use colored pellon.

Procedure - Give the following directions:

Put the Mayflower on the flannel board.

Put the sun above the ship.

Place the water under the ship.

Place the cloud below the sun.

Put the whale behind the ship.

Put the Plymouth Rock before the ship.

Music - Movement - Games

Action Song - "This Is the Way"

Tune - "Here We Go 'Round the Mulberry Bush"

This is the way the Pilgrims walk,

The Pilgrims walk, the Pilgrims walk.

This is the way the Pilgrims walk

Thanksgiving Day in the morning.

This is the way the turkey struts,

The turkey struts, the turkey struts.

This is the way the turkey struts

Thanksgiving Day in the morning.

This is the way the Indians dance,

The Indians dance, the Indians dance.

This is the way the Indians dance

Thanksgiving Day in the morning.

This is the way we all give thanks,

We all give thanks, we all give thanks.

This is the way we all give thanks

Thanksgiving Day in the morning.

Chanting Game - "Who"

Group: "Who stole the turkey from the turkey pen?"

Group: "Number one stole the turkey from the turkey pen."

Child One: "Who, me?"

Group: "Yes, you!"

Child One: "Couldn't be!"

Group: "Then, Who?"

Child One: "Number two stole the turkey from the turkey pen!"

Child Two: "Who, me?"

Variations: Who stole the pumpkin from the pumpkin patch?

Who stole the cranberries from the cranberry bog?

Procedure - The children say the chant while clapping one beat with both hands on thighs, and the next with both hands together. See above the words for rhythmic beats.

Story Time

Book - The Thanksgiving Book - Alice Dalgliesh

Day 2 - The First Year

Concept Information

In November, the Pilgrims <u>landed</u> at a place they called Plymouth. It is believed that, when they climbed out of the boat, they stepped on a large <u>boulder</u> which is called Plymouth Rock.

The <u>Mayflower</u> stayed in the harbor throughout the winter while the Pilgrims built houses. The Pilgrims could go there when the weather was bad or when they were sick. Still, many people died of <u>pneumonia</u> and other diseases. Then, they did not have the medicine that we have now.

When springtime came, the <u>Mayflower</u> sailed back to England. By then, the Pilgrims had built the "Common House," which was used as a hospital, and seven houses. The Pilgrims began planting seeds to grow their food.

One day a friendly Indian walked into Plymouth. He name was Samoset. He had learned to speak English from English fishermen. Later, he brought an Indian named Squanto to meet the Pilgrims. He could also speak English.

Squanto decided to live with the Pilgrims at Plymouth. He taught them how to fish and how to plant corn. He showed the Pilgrims how to make little hills, and then plant the corn <u>kernels</u> along with two or three fish in each hill. The fish were like the <u>fertilizer</u> farmers use today. Squanto also taught the Pilgrims about the land and to understand the Indian ways.

Discussion

Display pictures of Plymouth Rock, Plymouth Colony, and Samoset and Squanto as you discuss the concept information. Define vocabulary words. Show the children corn kernels and an ear of corn.

Fingerplay - "Indian Corn"

One little Pilgrim looking at the land (Hold up thumb)

Two little Indians offer a helping hand (Hold up index finger)

Three little Pilgrims planting the seeds (Hold up middle finger)

Four little Indians adding the fish it needs (Hold up ring finger)

Five little Pilgrims early one morn (Hold up little finger)

Out in the fields picking Indian corn. ("Pick and put in basket" motion)

Classification Activity

Make tagboard patterns of the person, coat, and chicken leg (sheet). Give each child a half sheet of yellow, red, and brown construction paper. Distribute the patterns and direct the children to trace the person on the yellow sheet, the coat on the red, and the chicken leg on the brown. Features may be added and the figures cut out. Explain that you are going to read a story. Whenever a person, an article of clothing, or food is mentioned, the children should hold up the appropriate picture.

Jonathan was a Pilgrim boy. Early each morning, his mother woke him to go to work in the corn fields. Jonathan quickly put on his shirt, pants, and boots and went to eat his hot cakes.

His mother was already busy cutting carrots and onions for stew. His sister was peeling potatoes. Jonathan finished eating and put on his cap and <u>coat</u>. His <u>mother</u> gave him some <u>corn bread</u> to take with him. Jonathan put it in his <u>pants</u> pocket and ran to help his <u>father</u>.

Art

Pilgrim Houses

Preparation - Collect one-half pint milk carton for each child, rinse, and dry. For a tall, thin milk carton, cut a 10" x 2-3/4" piece for the walls, and a 5" x 2-3/4" piece for the roof from manilla paper. For a short, fat milk carton, the wall piece will be 12" x 2", and the roof piece will be 6" x 1".

Supply stapler, crayons, glue, and scissors. For the thatched roof, supply pine straw, toothpicks, or pieces of straw cut from an old broom. (Cut off worn ends, wash, and spread on paper towels to dry.)

Procedure - Draw lines for planks on the wall piece. Cut out the wall piece and glue to the milk carton. Fold the roof piece in half. Place over the top of the milk carton and staple. Use crayons to add windows and doors. Glue pine straw, toothpicks, or straw to the roof.

Indian Corn

Preparation - Duplicate ears on white paper and husks on green. Mix yellow tempera paint, and pour thin layers in shallow pans or pie plates. Provide crayons, scissors, and glue. Have a red and black ink pad available. Pass out "Indian Corn" sheets.

Procedure - Cut out the parts of the corn. Dip one finger in the yellow tempera paint, and make fingerprints on the ear of corn to represent kernels. Once this has dried, add red and black fingerprints. Glue husks on either side of the ear.

Note: Pieces of golden brown thread can be glued to the ear to represent corn silk.

Math

Planting Corn

Preparation - Duplicate and distribute the sheet. Provide crayons and glue. Give each child one kernel of (unpopped) popcorn and two fish-shaped crackers per mound on the page.

Procedure - Color each mound brown. Glue one popcorn kernel within each mound. Go back and glue two fish within each mound.

Music - Movement - Games

Song - "Growing"

For words and music, see the sheet in the pattern section.

Procedure - Show pictures and explain how each vegetable grows. Direct the children to use their bodies to "become" each growing vegetable as they sing the song.

Game - "Guarding the Crops"

One child is chosen as the Guard. The guard is given a sponge-type ball or a beach ball. One half of the class is the "crop." They stand about three feet apart in a row. The remaining children are the birds. They try to "eat" the crops by "flying" around and around them. The guard tries to hit the birds with the ball. Once a bird is hit, he or she is sent to a designated area, called the birdcage, and is out of the game. If the guard hits one of the "crop," the guard must take his place in the row. The new guard continues the game. The last bird flying wins.

Note: Before beginning the game, explain to the children that one job of a Pilgrim boy was guarding the crops. If birds tried to eat the corn or beans, etc., the child threw stones at them.

Story Time

Book - The Thanksgiving Feast - Elaine M. Ward

Day 3 - Pilgrim Men and Women

Concept Information

The Pilgrim men and women of the Plymouth Colony had to be very brave and work hard to keep everyone alive. The men had to hunt and fish for food, chop down trees for wood, build houses, farm the land for food, help care for the sick, and protect the colony from wild animals and unfriendly Indians.

The Pilgrim women cooked, sewed, took care of the children, nursed the sick, and helped with the many jobs in the colony. The pictures we see of the Pilgrims show them in black and gray clothes with buckles on their shoes. The men are wearing black hats, and the women are wearing white bonnets. The Pilgrims could have worn these clothes on Sunday, but they also had clothes of bright colors. The men wore shirts of different colors with pants made of wool or leather. Stocking caps were worn on their heads. The women wore long, brightly colored dresses with full skirts and cloaks with hoods.

Language Arts - Social Studies

Discussion

Relate the concept information and define vocabulary words. Make two columns on experience chart paper labeled "Pilgrim Men" and "Pilgrim Women." Ask the children to recall the tasks of each. Discuss each task, encouraging the children's input. Allow the children to illustrate each task on the chart, half of the class at a time.

"Who Am I?"

Assign each child a role to pantomime, such as:

1. A Pilgrim man building a house

2. An Indian hunting a bear

3. A Pilgrim woman cooking stew

4. A Pilgrim or an Indian planting corn

5. A Pilgrim woman sewing

Have the other children guess who they are and what they are doing.

Parent Demonstration

Invite a parent to come to the class and demonstrate a task similar to those of Pilgrim parents. For instance, a mother could cook stew, hash, or corn bread or sew by hand a simple doll garment. A father could construct something simple from wood, chop firewood, or sharpen tools.

Art

Pilgrim Hats

Preparation - Make a cardboard Pilgrim hat, hatband, and buckle part pattern. Trace one hat for each child on black construction paper with a yellow or orange crayon. Cut black construction paper strips two inches wide and approximately twenty-four inches long. Provide scissors, glue, and a stapler. Distribute hats, hatband, and buckle part pattern. Also, give each child half a sheet of white paper, a five-inch square of tin foil, and a four-inch square of black construction paper.

Procedure - Cut out the hat. On the white paper, trace the hatband pattern; and cut out. Trace around the buckle part pattern on the black construction paper square. Cut out. Fold the foil into fourths, and glue the black "buckle part" in the middle of the foil. Glue the hatband to the hat; then glue the buckle in the middle of this. Staple one end of the long (twenty-four-inch) black strip to one side of the hat. Fit on the child's head, remove, and staple the other end of the strip to the other side of the hat.

Pilgrim Bonnet

Preparation - For each bonnet, you will need a 12" x 18" piece of white construction paper. On one 18" side, draw a 7-1/2" diagonal dotted line inward from each corner, as shown. Give each child a sheet, scissors, and two 10" pieces of white yarn. Have several hole punchers and a stapler available.

Procedure - Fold back and crease about 1-1/2 inches of the long edge (opposite the lines). Punch a hole at each end of the fold. Tie one piece of yarn in each hole. Cut on both dotted lines. The teacher should assist in bringing together the two side flaps over the back section. Overlap the flaps and staple.

Math

Number Hats

Preparation - Duplicate the "Number Hats" sheet. Distribute along with a large sheet of construction paper. Provide scissors, glue, and crayons.

Procedure - Direct the children to count the dots on each hat and write the corresponding numeral in the buckle. They then color and cut out the hats, and glue in order (from left to right) on the construction paper.

Music - Movement - Games

Action Song - "Oats, Peas, Beans and Barley Grow"

The children join hands and form a circle. The farmer is in the center. As the children sing the song and dance around him, the farmer pantomimes planting seeds.

Game - "The Pilgrims' Game of Quoits"

Divide the class into two teams. The teacher keeps score. As in "Horseshoes," put two sticks or stakes in the ground about ten feet apart. Use beanbags to replace the stones or "quoits" thrown by the Pilgrims. One member of a team stand by his or her stake and throws beanbags as close as possible to the opposite stake. The procedure is repeated with a member of the opposing team. The closest beanbag to the stake scores one point for that team. Continue the game until everyone has thrown. The team with the most points wins.

Story Time

Book - Gobble, Gobble, Gobble - Mary Jackson Ellis

Kindergarten Kitchen

Apple Turkeys

Preparation - Give each child an apple and approximately ten toothpicks. Supply raisins and olives stuffed with pimentos.

Procedure - "Fill up" each toothpick with raisins, leaving enough space to hold it in the apple. Insert one filled toothpick in the apple to represent the neck, two for the legs, and the remainder for the feathers of the turkey. One or two of the feathers should be placed underneath the apple for balance. Place a pimento on the end of the "neck" toothpick. Pull the pimento out halfway to represent the wattle.

Day 4 - Pilgrim Children

Concept Information

Even when they were very small, Pilgrim children had to work. The youngest children helped in gathering wood for fire, picking berries, and taking care of the babies. Boys helped their fathers farm, build houses, and hunt. Girls helped their mothers cook, sew, make soap, and wash clothes.

The Pilgrim children did not go to school. Some of them were taught to read and write by their parents. All the children were taught to obey the teachings of the Bible and to obey their parents.

The Pilgrim children did not have much time to play. When they did, they played with toys made from wood or dolls made from cornhusks or rags. They enjoyed exploring around the colony and making up games.

Small boys wore dresses called "coats" until they were six years old. Besides this, the Pilgrim children wore clothes just like their parents.

Language Arts - Social Studies

Discussion

Share the concept information and define the vocabulary words. For a different approach, relate the facts of the concept information in the first person as if you are a Pilgrim child. Ask the children, "Who am I?"

Hornbook

Explanation - The Pilgrim children did not have books. They had hornbooks which were flat boards with handles. A piece of paper showing the alphabet was pasted on the hornbook.

Preparation - On manilla construction paper, duplicate two "Hornbook" pages for each child. Distribute these along with a sheet of lined paper which has been cut to fit within the Hornbook. Provide scissors, glue, and pencils.

Procedure - The children cut out the two hornbooks and glue together (for stiffness). While this dries, the children copy the alphabet on the lined paper. Glue this to the hornbook.

Fingerplay - "Five Little Pilgrims"

Five little Pilgrims on Thanksgiving Day. (Hold up 5 fingers)

The first one said, "I'll have cake, if I may." (Hold up thumb only)

The second one said, "I'll have turkey, roasted." (Hold up index finger)

The third one said, "I'll have chestnuts, toasted." (Hold up middle finger)

The fourth one said, "I'll have pumpkin pie." (Hold up ring finger)

The fifth one said, "I'll give all a try!" (Hold up little finger)

But before they ate any turkey or dressing,

All of the Pilgrims said a Thanksgiving blessing. (Hands folded in prayer)

Art

Pilgrim Collars

Preparation - Use a 12" x 18" piece of tagboard to make a pattern, as shown. The corners are rounded, and the neck opening resembles a keyhole. Make several of these patterns. Give each child a 12" x 18" sheet of white construction paper, a pencil, and scissors.

Procedure - Fold the pattern on the white paper. Trace around the inside and outside. Cut on the pencil lines.

Silhouettes

Preparation - Place a lamp on a table near the wall. Have the child stand between the light source and the wall. Tape a piece of white drawing paper on the wall so that it "frames" the shadow of the child's profile. Sketch the profile. Repeat with every child. Provide a sheet of black construction paper, scissors, and glue for each child.

Procedure - Cut out the silhouette. Use glue to mount on black construction paper.

Note: In the time of the Pilgrims, there were no cameras; and having portraits painted was expensive. So instead, the Pilgrims made silhouettes.

Math

Packing for America

Preparation - Duplicate the sheet. Provide crayons. Tell the children that each Pilgrim family could bring only one trunk containing their personal possessions. (Therefore, each family member had the space contained in a small suitcase.)

Procedure - Fold the suitcase on the dotted line. (The inside will be blank.) Open and draw the things you would take on your trip to the New World. (The teacher labels the items.) Count your items, close the suitcase, and put the number on the line provided. Share your suitcase with the class.

Music - Movement - Games

Song - "Thanksgiving Day"
Tune - "Over the River and Through the Wood" by Lydia Marie Child

Over the river and through the wood

To Grandfather's house we go;

The horse knows the way

To carry the sleigh

Through the white and drifted snow.

Over the river and through the wood--

Oh, how the wind does blow!

It stings the toes

And bites the nose,

As over the ground we go.

Over the river and through the wood,

To have a first-rate play.

Hear the bells ring,

Ting-a-ling-ding!

Hurray for Thanksgiving Day!

Over the river and through the wood

Trot fast, my dapple-gray!

Spring over the ground

Like a hunting hound!

For this is Thanksgiving Day.

Over the river and through the wood,

And straight through the barnyard gate.

We seem to go

Extremely slow--

It is so hard to wait!

Over the river and through the wood--

Now Grandmother's cap I spy!

Hurrah for the fun!

Is the pudding done?

Hurrah for pumpkin pie!

Action Story - "Pilgrim Explorers"

Ellen and John jumped up and down and clapped their hands. They were happy to be in America after living on the crowded ship. They began to explore. Ellen followed John into the woods. As they walked, they looked up at the tall trees and down at all the plants. A deer saw them and ran deeper into the woods. Ellen and John ran after it. Soon they came to a brook. They bent down, filled their cupped hands with water and drank. Then they took off their shoes and stockings and dipped their feet in the water. They smiled and closed their eyes. But it was getting dark in the woods, and they began to get scared. They quickly shook their feet, put on their stockings and shoes, and ran back through the woods. As they ran, they looked from side to side. They were lost. When they heard a rustling sound, they scrambled under a bush. They heard laughing. Father had found them. Ellen and John jumped up and hugged Father. Then they skipped home behind him.

Procedure - The children act out the story by walking, running (in place), etc., as directed.

Story Time

Book - Little Bear's Thanksgiving - Janice

Day 5 - The First Thanksgiving

Concept Information

For many years, people have had <u>celebrations</u> at <u>harvest</u> time. But the First Thanksgiving was a very special harvest celebration. The Pilgrims had been in America a year. Many of them had died. But that fall the <u>crops</u> had been <u>gathered</u> and <u>stored</u> for the winter.

The Pilgrims decided to have a party to give <u>thanks</u> to God for their <u>blessings</u>. The men went hunting and brought back wild turkeys, ducks, and geese. The Indians who were invited to share the <u>feast</u> brought five deer. These were roasted over the fires. There was also stewed pumpkin, green beans, cranberries, corn cakes, and goat's milk. Since there were few tables or chairs, the people sat on the ground to eat. For fun, there were races, games, dancing, and singing.

Since then, Pilgrims, the <u>Mayflower</u>, turkeys, corn, pumpkins, and cranberries have become <u>symbols</u> which make us think of the first Thanksgiving. Now every year we celebrate Thanksgiving to remember the brave Pilgrims and to give thanks for all of our blessings.

Language Arts - Social Studies

Discussion

Place fresh corn, green beans, a small pumpkin, cranberries, and pictures of a turkey, duck, goose, and deer which have been mounted on construction paper in a large brown paper bag. Include a picture of the first Thanksgiving. As you share the concept information and define vocabulary words, take the "examples" out of the bag.

Flannel Board Review (from Story Telling With the Flannel Board by Paul S. Anderson)

Make "The Story of Thanksgiving" flannel board figures (found in the book above). Place these on the flannel board. Ask the children to identify the figures. Take these down. Choose a child to tell the story of the Pilgrims and Thanksgiving using the flannel board figures. Repeat with other children. Children who do not participate may do so at Activity Time.

Acrostic Activity - "Thanks"

Preparation - Mentally divide the class into groups of six. The six children in the groups will each hold one of the letters of the word "thanks." On construction paper of Thanksgiving colors, duplicate the letter sheets accordingly. Provide a letter, a paper plate, scissors, and glue for each child. Form the groups, and teach the "t's" their line, the "h's" their line, and so forth. The whole class learns the last two lines to recite together.

Procedure - Cut out the letters and glue each to a paper plate. Stand in order in line with groups separated. On cue, the letters are held up and the lines recited.

T is for Turkey, H is for Harvest, A is for Autumn,

N is for November, K is for Kitchen, S is for Smells,

Put them together and they spell THANKS,

Which we give at this special time of the year.

"Look Again" Activity

Use the fresh vegetables, pictures, and brown bag from the discussion. Lay these on a table and cover with a towel. Have the children stand around the table. Explain the procedure. Lift the towel and let the children look around for about ten seconds. Cover again; and ask the children to turn their backs to the table; and cover their eyes. Remove one object and place it in the paper bag on the floor. Tell the children to uncover their eyes and turn around. Uncover and ask, "What is missing?" When a child guesses correctly, return the object and repeat the game.

"All On the Table Before You" (from Learning Basic Skills Through Music-Vocabulary by Hap Palmer)

The children learn the names of the items by following the directions of the song. Each child needs a plate, glass, knife, fork, spoon, napkin, cup, bowl, and saucer--so you may wish to have a small group at a time participate.

Fingerplay - "Five Fat Turkeys"

Five fat turkeys were sitting on a fence. (One hand up)

The first one said, "I'm so immense." (Point to thumb)

The second one said, "I can gobble at you." (Pointer finger)

The third one said, "I can gobble, too." (Middle finger)

The fourth one said, "I can spread my tail." (Ring finger)

The fifth one said, "Don't catch it on a nail." (Little finger)

A farmer came along and stopped to say (Pointer of other hand)

"Turkeys look best on Thanksgiving Day."

Art

Paper Bag Turkey

Preparation - Make patterns of the "Paper Bag Turkey" head. Supply each child with a paper bag, a half sheet of brown construction paper, old newspapers for stuffing, a rubber band, crayons, and scissors.

Procedure - Stuff the paper bag with the newspaper, leaving about five inches for the tail section. Use a rubber band to secure or close tightly against the stuffing. Cut the tail section into two-inch strips, and color to represent feathers. Fold the neck of the turkey head on the dotted line. Put glue on this flap, and mount on the front of the paper bag turkey. Feathers may be colored on each side.

Hand Turkey

Preparation - Supply each child with a piece of white paper and crayons.

Procedure - Trace around one hand. Enclose the space left by the wrist and add legs. Draw wattle, beak, and eye on the thumb (head). Color the feathers (fingers). If you wish to cut these out, cut around the legs as one piece.

Paper Plate Turkey

Preparation - Duplicate the turkey head used in "Paper Bag Turkey." Give each child a turkey head, two paper plates, and four half-sheets of different colored construction paper. Pass out glue, scissors, and crayons.

Procedure - Cut out the head, and glue the end on the inside edge of one of the paper plates. Tear each construction paper sheet into three strips for feathers. Glue the ends of eight strips in a fan effect on the side of the paper plate opposite the head. Put a generous amount of glue all around the inside edge of the other paper plate. Place this on top of the other plate so that the edges meet. Press the edges together in different places until the glue bonds. On each side, glue two "side feathers."

Note: This can be hung from the ceiling or light fixtures by attaching a string tied to a paper clip.

Math

"Fill Your Plate"

Write different numerals in the middle of paper plates. Provide one for each child. Direct the children to look in old magazines for foods they would like to eat on Thanksgiving. They need to cut out as many as the numeral indicates, and glue around the numeral. Share with the class.

<u>Music</u> - <u>Movement</u> - <u>Games</u>

<u>Song</u> - "The Pumpkin Ran Away"

Tune - "The Farmer In the Dell"

The pumpkin ran away

Before Thanksgiving Day.

Said he, "They'll make a pie of me

If I decide to stay!"

    The cranberry ran away

    Before Thanksgiving Day

    Said he, "They'll make a sauce of me

    If I decide to stay!"

The turkey ran away

Before Thanksgiving Day.

Said he, "They'll make a roast of me

If I decide to stay!

Pilgrim Game - Stick Pull

Two people sit on the ground with legs outstretched. Their feet should meet. Using both hands, the players hold a stick horizontally between them. They both pull the stick. The winner is the player who pulls the other off the ground.

Story Time

Book - <u>Cranberry Thanksgiving</u> - Wende and Harry Devlin

Kindergarten Kitchen

"Grandmother's Famous Cranberry Bread" from the book <u>Cranberry Thanksgiving</u> (See Story Time)

The recipe for the cranberry bread is found at the end of the book.

Culminating Activity - White Collar Contest

Have the children wear their Pilgrim hats or bonnets and collars to the Thanksgiving lunch. (If you do not eat together, you may wish to enlist the parents' help in preparing a Thanksgiving meal.) Explain that after the meal, the Pilgrim (or Pilgrims) with the whitest collar will win a prize. Prizes may be a Thanksgiving sticker to stick on the collars, inexpensive toy ships, and so forth.

Concept Evaluation - (See Introduction)

Dear Parents,

We will begin our unit on Pilgrims on _____. We will learn about the Pilgrims' lives and their voyage to America, the first Thanksgiving, and our current Thanksgiving customs. Please read below to see how you can help.

Things to Send: _____

_____

_____

Volunteers Needed To: _____

_____

_____

Follow-Up: At the end of the unit, ask your child to share stories, songs, fingerplays, etc.

_____

_____

_____

Follow-Up Questions:

1. Who were the Pilgrims?

2. Why did they sail to America?

3. Who helped the Pilgrims learn to plant corn, hunt, etc.?

4. Why did the Pilgrims have the first Thanksgiving feast?

Thank you for your cooperation.

Sincerely,

Copyright ©1987. Carol Taylor Bond

433

Mayflower

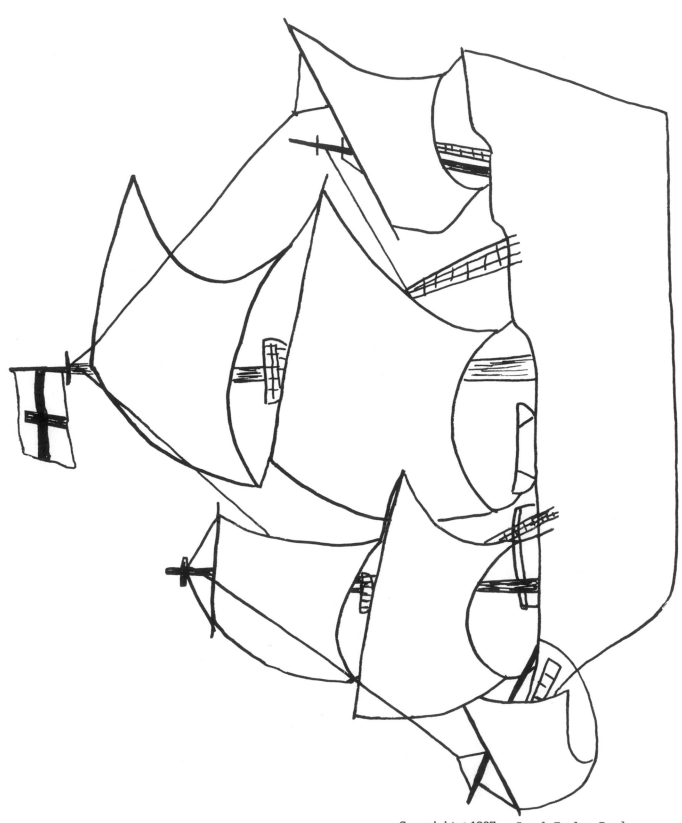

Copyright © 1987. Carol Taylor Bond

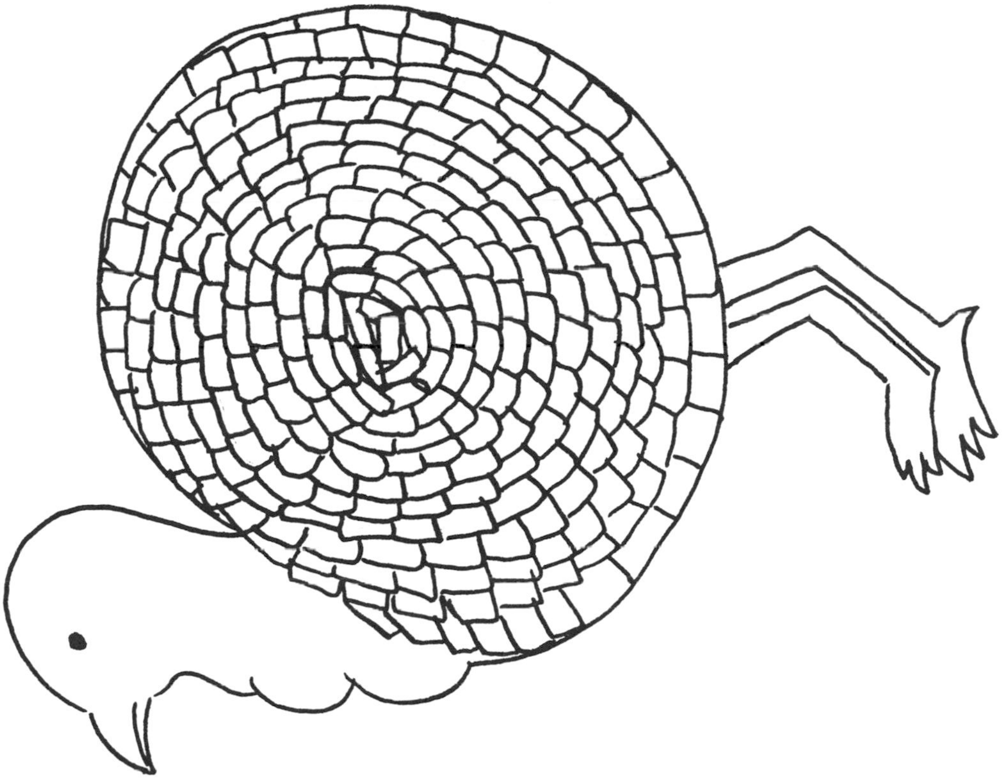

Paper Chain Turkey

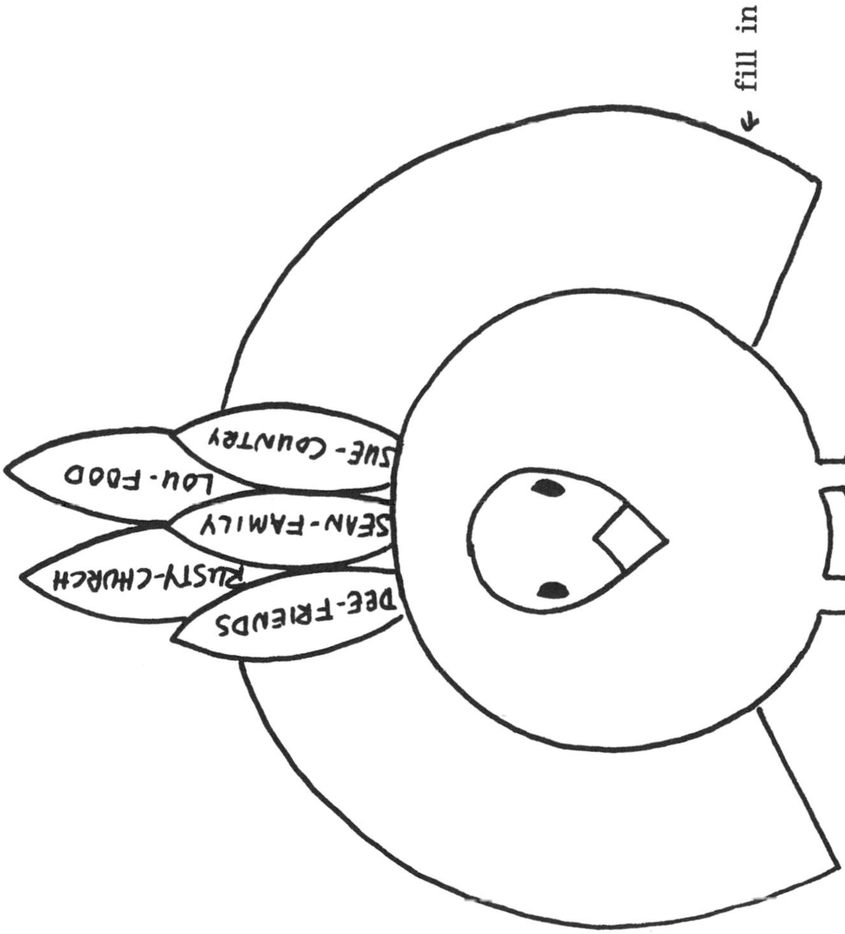

fill in

Thankful Turkey

SUE-COUNTRY
LOU-FOOD
SEAN-FAMILY
RUSTY-CHURCH
DEE-FRIENDS

Wall or Door Displays

Copyright © 1987.   Carol Taylor Bond

435

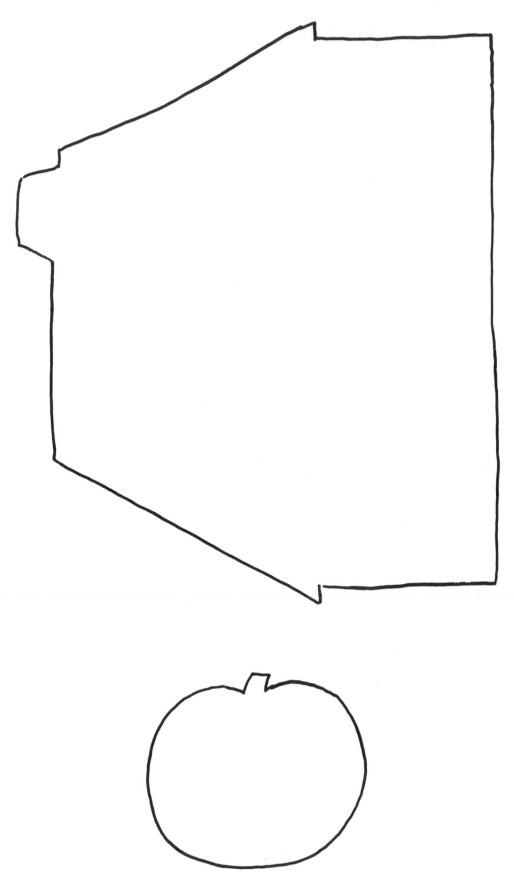

Copyright ©1987. Carol Taylor Bond

436

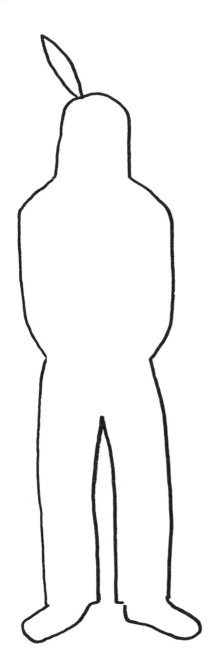

Copyright © 1987. Carol Taylor Bond

437

Copyright ©1987. Carol Taylor Bond

Paper Mayflower

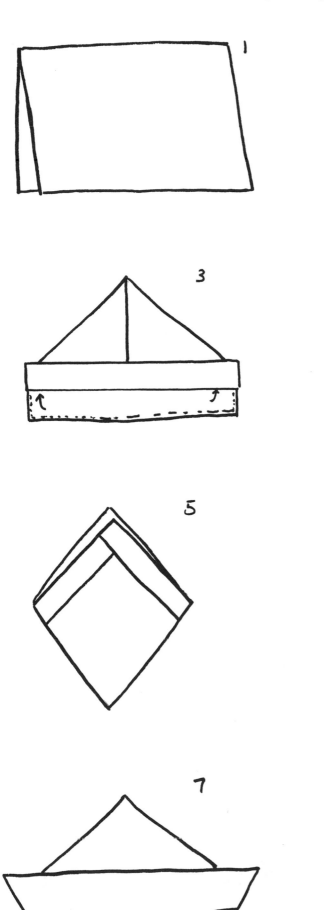

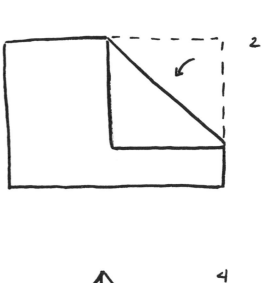

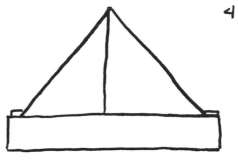

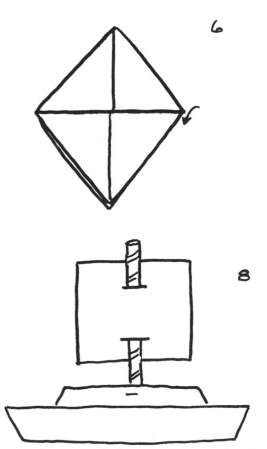

Copyright © 1987. Carol Taylor Bond

439

Sailing Mayflower Sea

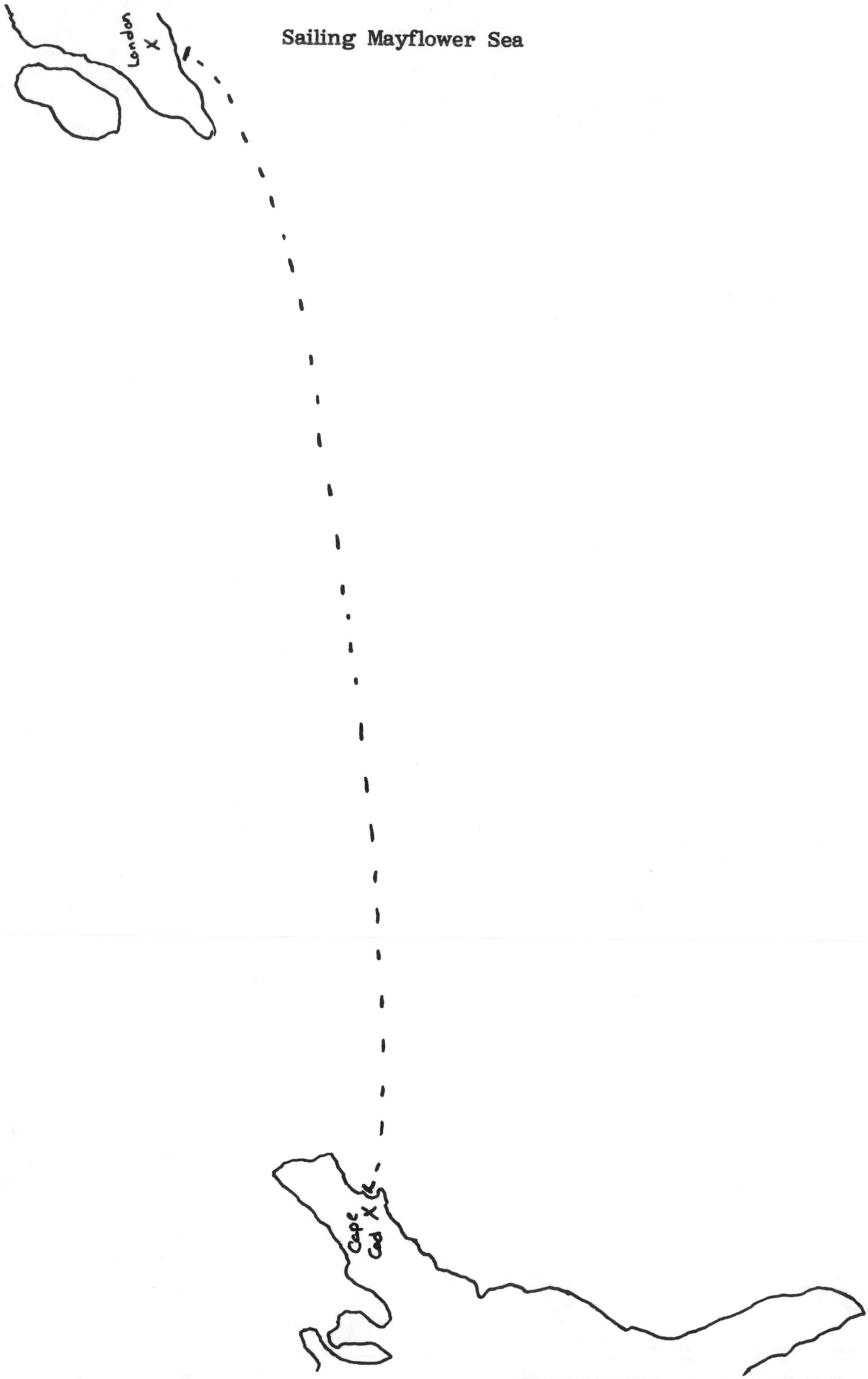

London
X

Cape
Cod X

Copyright © 1987.   Carol Taylor Bond

Sailing Mayflower

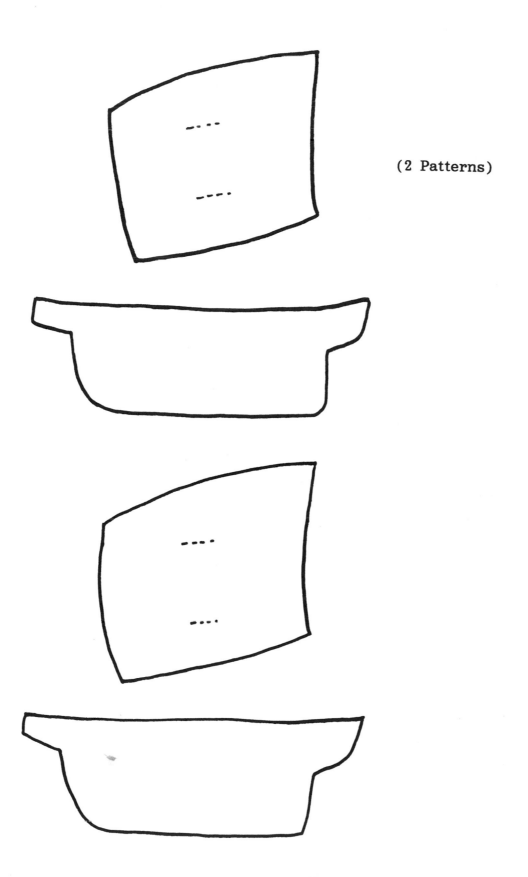

(2 Patterns)

Copyright © 1987.   Carol Taylor Bond

441

Pilgrim Paper Bag Puppet

Copyright ©1987. Carol Taylor Bond

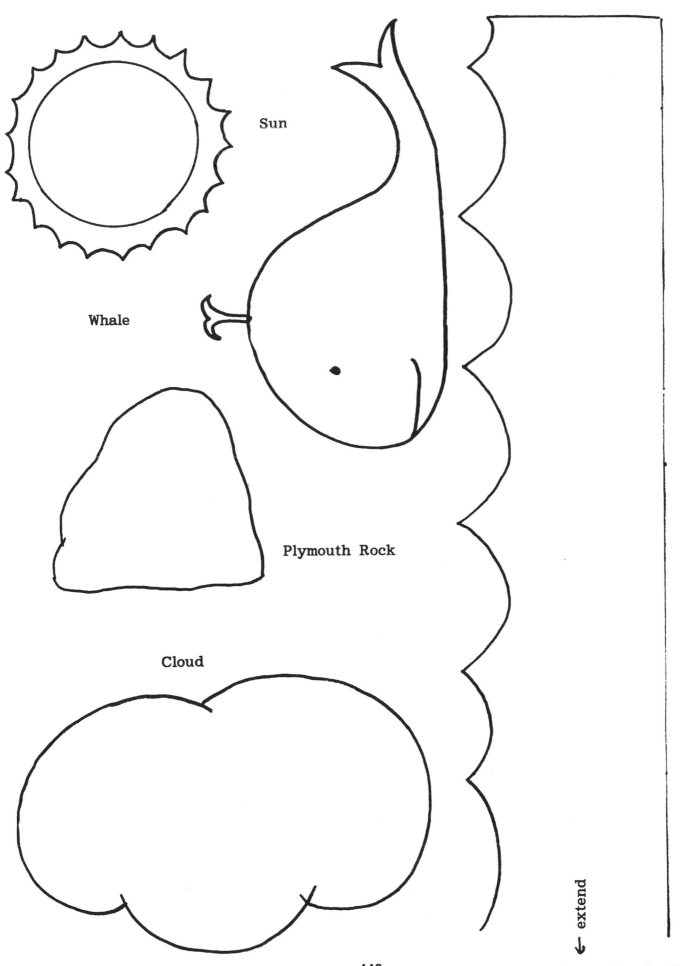

Sun

Whale

Plymouth Rock

Cloud

extend

443

Copyright © 1987. Carol Taylor Bond

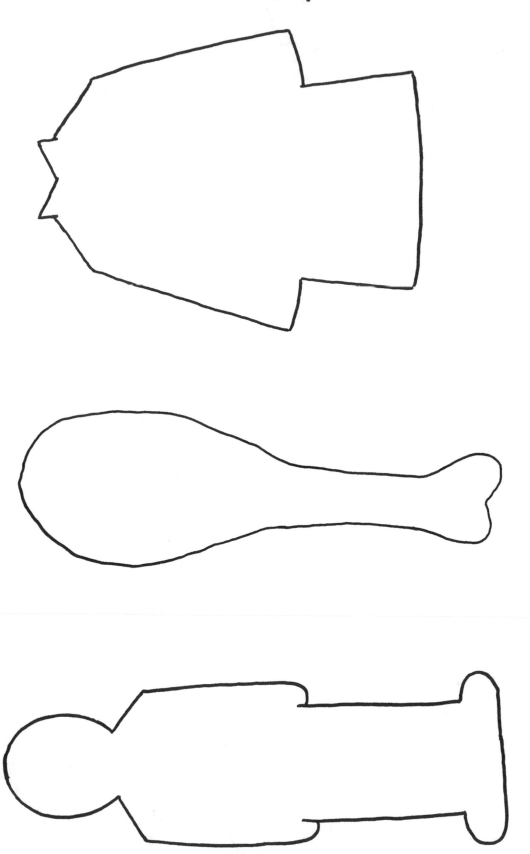

Copyright © 1987. Carol Taylor Bond

Copyright © 1987.   Carol Taylor Bond

Indian Corn - Ear

Example

Copyright © 1987. Carol Taylor Bond

446

Indian Corn - Husks

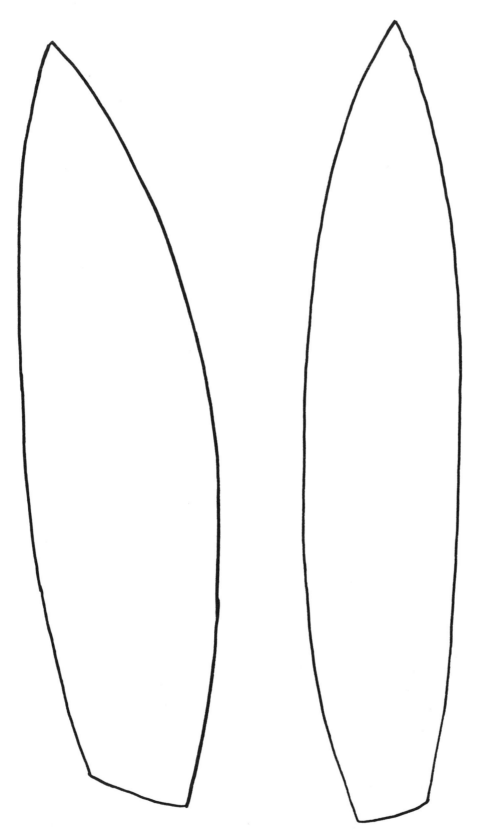

Copyright © 1987. Carol Taylor Bond

447

Name _____

Planting Corn

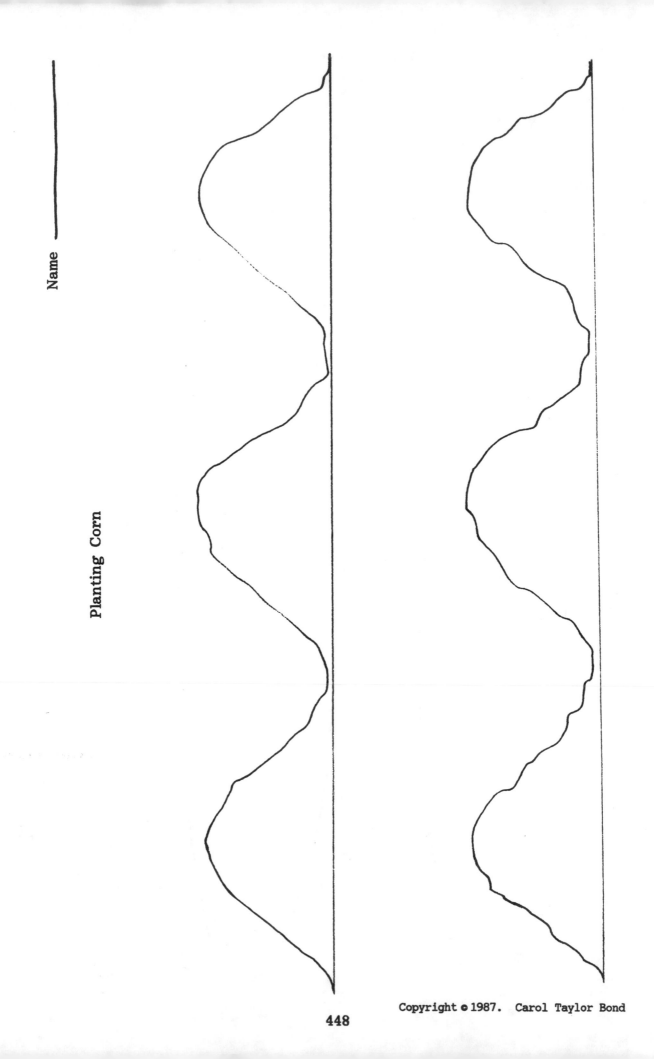

Copyright © 1987. Carol Taylor Bond

GROWING

The corn is grow - ing grow - ing, grow - ing

The corn is grow - ing up, up to the sky.

2. The beans are growing, growing, growing.

   The beans are growing, twining 'round and 'round.

3. The pumpkins are growing, growing, growing.

   The pumpkins are growing, big and fat and round.

4. The carrots are growing, growing, growing.

   The carrots are growing, down, down in the ground.

Copyright © 1987. Carol Taylor Bond

449

Pilgrim Hat

Example

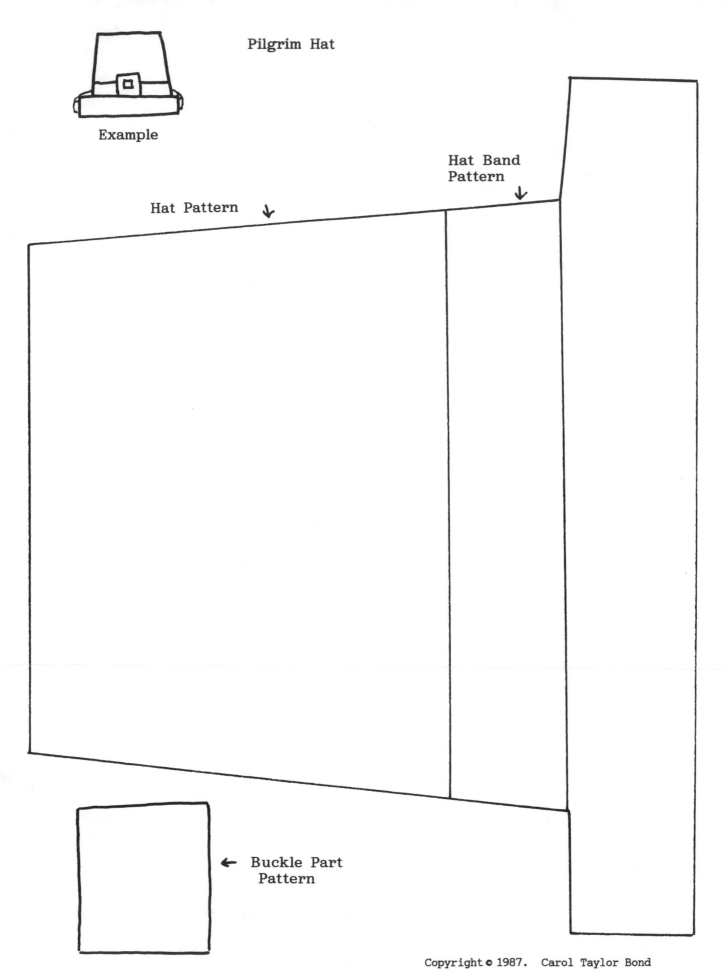

Hat Band
Pattern
↓

Hat Pattern ↓

← Buckle Part
Pattern

Copyright © 1987.   Carol Taylor Bond

Pilgrim Bonnet

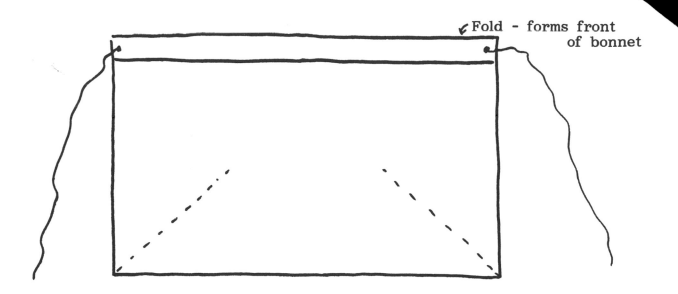

Fold - forms front
of bonnet

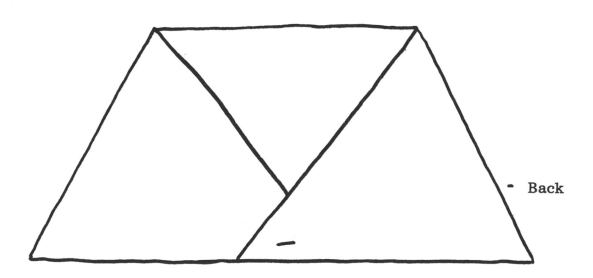

- Back

Copyright © 1987. Carol Taylor Bond

451

Number Hats

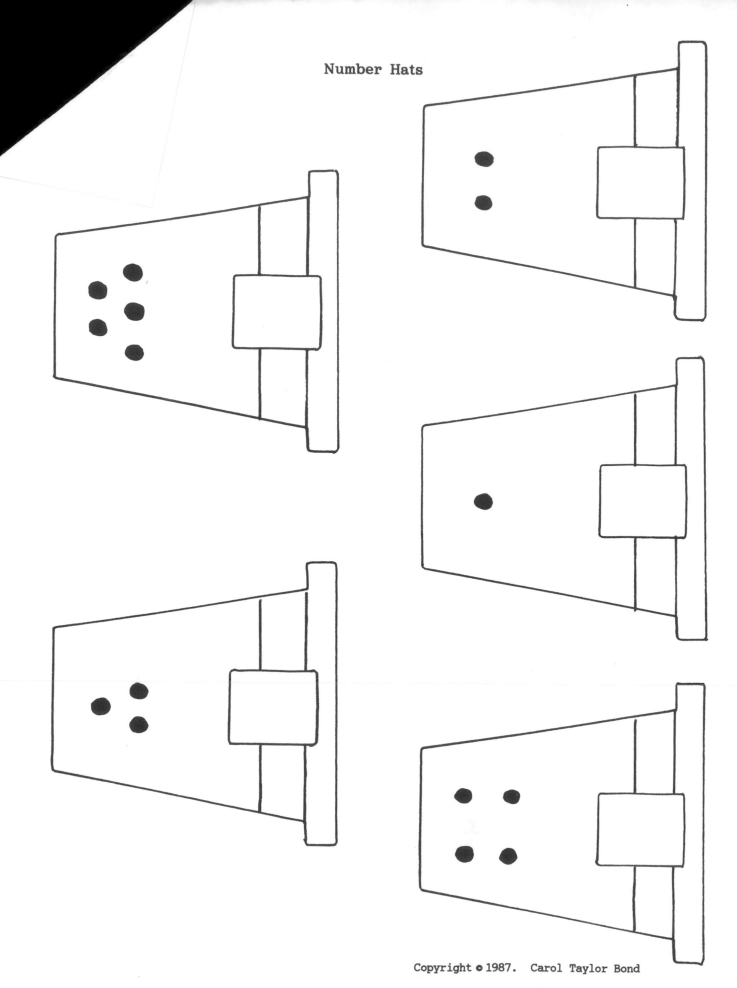

Copyright © 1987.   Carol Taylor Bond

452

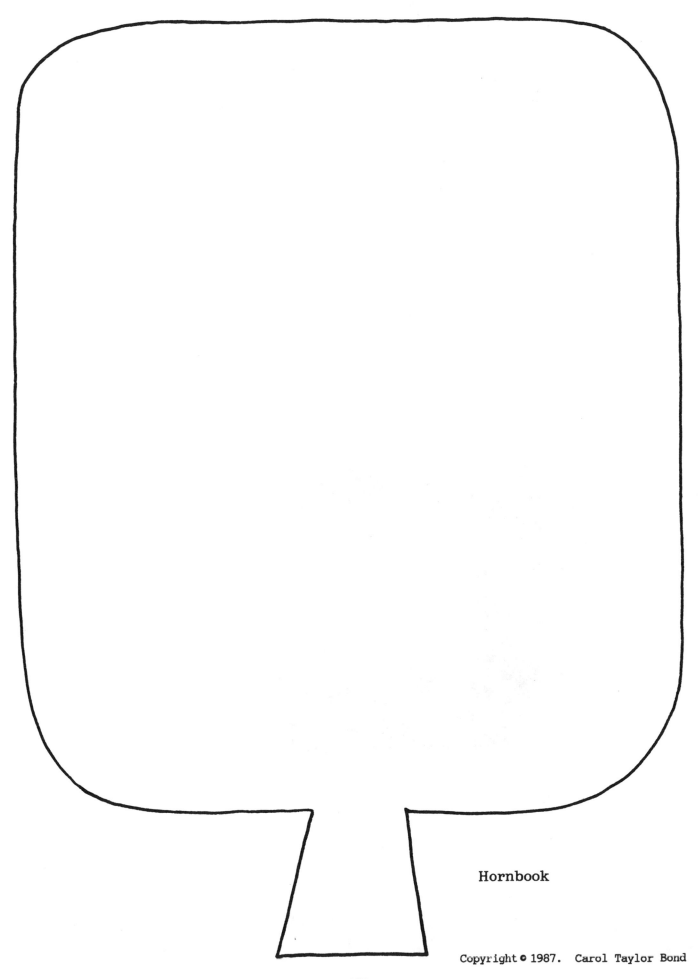

Hornbook

Copyright © 1987.   Carol Taylor Bond

Pilgrim Collar

Cut Away
Black Areas
←

Silhouette

Copyright © 1987. Carol Taylor Bond

Packing For America

Copyright © 1987. Carol Taylor Bond

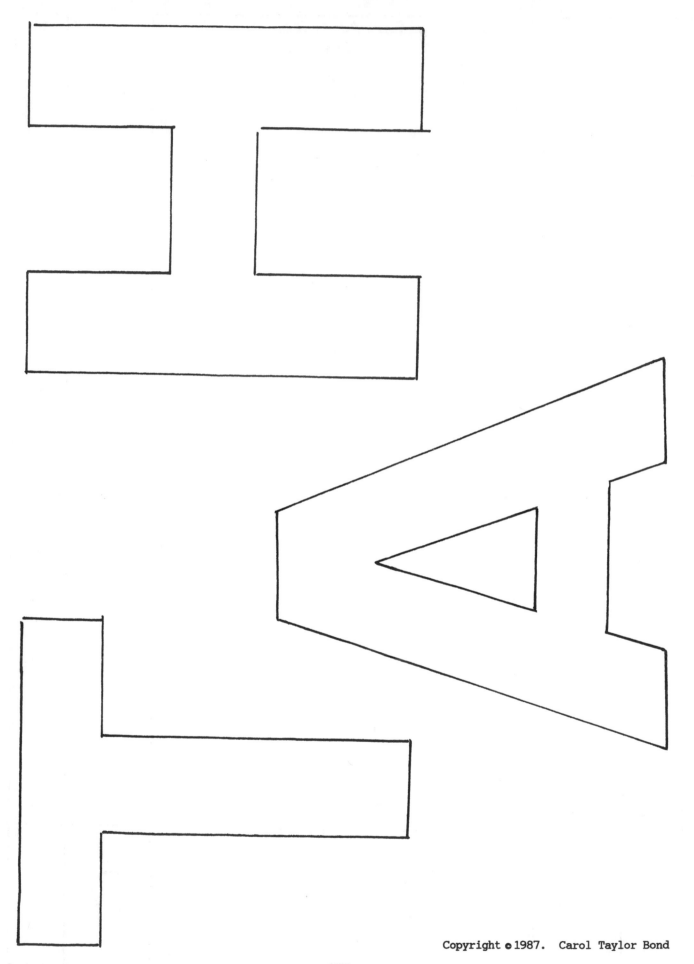

Copyright © 1987. Carol Taylor Bond

Copyright © 1987. Carol Taylor Bond

Copyright ©1987. Carol Taylor Bond

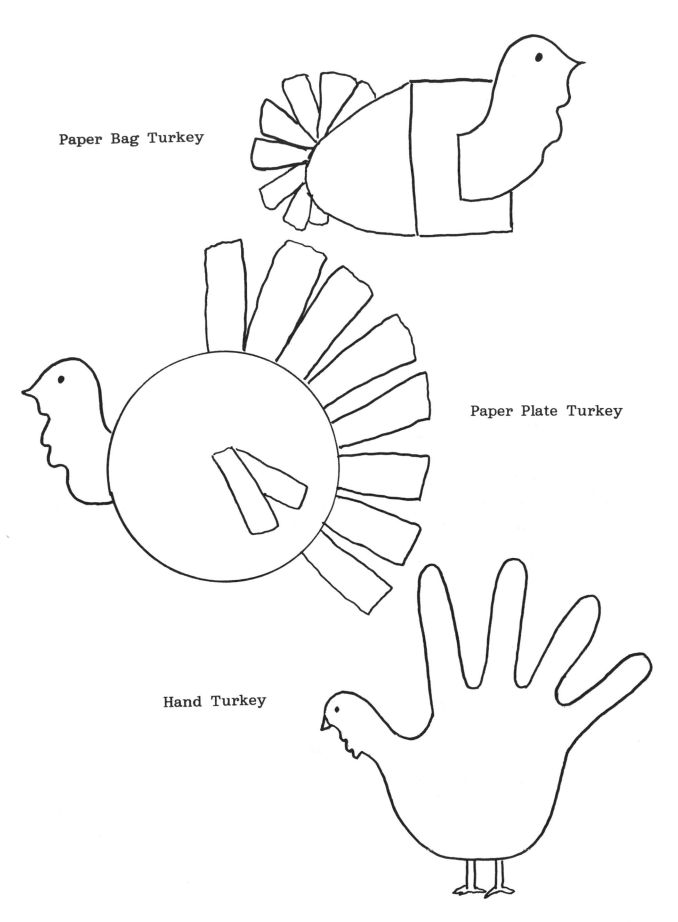

Paper Bag Turkey

Paper Plate Turkey

Hand Turkey

Copyright © 1987. Carol Taylor Bond

459

BIBLIOGRAPHY

"Animals". Childcraft, Volume 7 "Exploring the World Around Us." Field Enterprises Educational Corporation, 1961.

Barth, Edna. Turkeys, Pilgrims and Indian Corn. Illustrated by Ursula Arndt. New York: The Seabury Press, 1975.

Barth, Edna. Witches, Pumpkins and Grinning Ghosts. New York: The Seabury Press, 1975.

Burnett, Bernice. First Book of Holidays. New York: Franklin-Watts, Inc., 1955.

"Circus". World Book Encyclopedia, Volume 3 (C). Chicago: Field Enterprises Educational Corporation, 1969.

d'Aulaire, Ingri and Edgar Parin. Columbus. Garden City, New York: Doubleday and Company, Inc., 1955.

"Owl". World Book Encyclopedia, Volume 12 (O). Chicago: Field Enterprises Educational Corporation, 1969.

Perl, Lila. Slumps, Grunts and Snickerdoodles--What Colonial America Ate and Why. New York: The Seabury Press, 1975.

Sterling, Dorothy. Fall Is Here. Garden City, New York: The Natural History Press, 1966.

Syme, Ronald. Columbus, Finder of the New World. New York: William Morrow and Company, 1952.

Thompson, T. A. Red Indians. Illustrated by T. H. Stubley. Basil Blackwell: Blackwells Learning Library, 1965.

Tunis, Edwin. Indians. The World Publishing Company, 1959.

Zappler, George and Lisbeth. Science In Summer and Fall. Garden City, New York: Doubleday and Company, Inc., 1974.

Zim, Herbert S. Our Senses and How They Work. New York: William Morris and Company, 1956.

Index